Archaeology of Northern Florida, A.D. 200–900

Archaeology of Northern Florida, A.D. 200–900

The McKeithen Weeden Island Culture

Jerald T. Milanich

Ann S. Cordell

Vernon J. Knight, Jr.

Timothy A. Kohler

Brenda J. Sigler-Lavelle

University Press of Florida

Gainesville Tallahassee Tampa Boca Raton
Pensacola Orlando Miami Jacksonville

First published in 1984 by Academic Press, Inc.

02   01   00   99   98   97   6   5   4   3   2   1

Library of Congress Cataloging-in-Publication Data
McKeithen Weeden Island.
Archaeology of northern Florida, A.D. 200–900: the McKeithen
Weeden Island culture / Jerald T. Milanich . . . [et al.].
p. cm.
Originally published: McKeithen Weeden Island. New York:
Academic Press, 1984. With new pref.
Includes bibliographical references and index.
ISBN 0-8130-1538-3 (pbk.: alk. paper)
1. McKeithen Site (Fla.) 2. Weeden Island culture.
3. Florida—Antiquities. I. Milanich, Jerald T. II. Title.
E99.W48M37 1997 97-12249
975.9'01—dc21

The University Press of Florida is the scholarly publishing
agency for the State University System of Florida, comprised
of Florida A & M University, Florida Atlantic University,
Florida International University, Florida State University,
University of Central Florida, University of Florida, University
of North Florida, University of South Florida, and University
of West Florida.

University Press of Florida
15 Northwest 15th Street
Gainesville, FL 32611

Dedicated to William H. Sears

Contents

List of Figures

Figure

List of Tables

Preface

The information collected from the McKeithen site continues to be important to our understanding of the pre-Mississippian period cultures of the southeastern United States. Recent syntheses, such as Judith Bense's *Archaeology of the Southeastern United States,* Brian Fagan's *Ancient North America,* and my own *Archaeology of Precolumbian Florida,* use our interpretations of the Weeden Island culture as examples of the nature of pre-Columbian political and social organization prior to the appearance of complex, chiefdom societies. Many of us believe that the patterns described for the McKeithen Weeden Island can be used to model the social and political organization of contemporary cultures throughout much of Florida and the Southeast.

The excavations and surveys carried out in North Florida have stimulated new research into Weeden Island cultures and the reinterpretation of data collected in the past. Some of the publications resulting from these studies are cited below. Notable is William Sears' article *Mea Culpa,* in which he reinterprets the chronology of the famous Kolomoki site. The Weeden Island chronology for that site now fits much better with the McKeithen radiocarbon dates.

Especially gratifying is the large amount of research done on the post-McKeithen Weeden Island, Suwannee Valley culture of North Florida, present in that region after ca. A.D. 800. Almost totally unrecognized at the time of our research, the Suwannee Valley culture's settlement system appears to be very similar to those of the contemporary late Weeden Island culture found west of the Aucilla River.

That observation raises a question that as yet cannot be completely answered. If the cultural systems of North and Northwest Florida are so similar, why, then, did the Mississippian-related Fort Walton culture (post-A.D. 1000) develop in Northwest Florida, while in North Florida the non-Mississippian Suwannee Valley culture lasted into the colonial period? Why were the colonial period descendants of the Fort Walton population speakers of Apalachee while the Suwannee Valley descendants spoke Timucua, a very different and unrelated language? Our present answers center on greater soil fertility in Northwest Florida and its closer geographical proximity to other Mississippian cultures in Georgia and Alabama. But there must be other factors as well, factors that reach to the heart of the discussion of the evolution and spread of the Mississippian way of life.

Looking back at the report of our excavations at the McKeithen site, one correction is in order. The Big Man interment in Mound B who is described in the text as a "gracile male" is more likely a woman. Analysis of the osteological remains curated at the Florida Museum of Natural History has suggested to several bioarchaeologists that the original interpretation was probably wrong. There is no one to blame for this error but myself. In checking William Maples' original field notes made at the time he examined the individual, I found he noted that it most likely was a female.

There may still be more to learn about the Mound B Big Man. Bruce Smith of the Smithsonian Institution's Department of Anthropology, National Museum of Natural History, was kind enough to have carbon isotope analyses done on osteological samples drawn from the McKeithen site population. As suspected, the results suggested that the people living there were not maize (corn) eaters. All, that is, except the individual in Mound B. Who was that person and where did she or he come from?

Jerald T. Milanich
Florida Museum of Natural History

References

Bense, Judith A.
  1994 *Archaeology of the southeastern United States, Paleoindian to World War I.* Academic Press, Orlando.
Fagan, Brian M.
  1991 *Ancient North America: The archaeology of a continent.* Thames and Hudson, New York.
Johnson, G. Michael
  1985 *Lithic technology and social complexity at a north Florida Weeden Island period site.* Unpublished M.A. thesis, Department of Anthropology, Washington State University.
Johnson, G. Michael, and Timothy A. Kohler
  1987 Toward a better understanding of north peninsular Gulf coast Florida prehistory: archaeological reconnaissance in Dixie County. *Florida Anthropologist* 40:275–286.
Johnson, Kenneth W., and Bruce C. Nelson
  1990 The Utina: seriations and chronology. *Florida Anthropologist* 43:48–62.
  1992 *High plain swamps and flatwoods: archaeological survey of portions of Baker, Columbia, and Union counties in north Florida.* Miscellaneous Project Report 49. Department of Anthropology, Florida Museum of Natural History, Gainesville.

Kohler, Tim A.
  1991 The demise of Weeden Island, and post-Weeden Island cultural stability in non-Mississippianized northern Florida. In *Stability, transformation, and variations: the late woodland Southeast,* edited by Michael S. Nassaney and Charles R. Cobb, pp. 91–110. Plenum, New York.
Milanich, Jerald T.
  1994 *Archaeology of precolumbian Florida.* University Press of Florida, Gainesville.
Scars, William H.
  1992 *Mea culpa. Southeastern Archaeology* 11:66–71.
Worth, John E.
  1992 Revised aboriginal ceramic typology for the Timucua mission province. In *Excavations of the Franciscan frontier, archaeology of the Fig Springs mission,* by Brent R. Weisman, pp. 188–205. University Press of Florida, Gainesville.

Acknowledgments

Without the enthusiastic field assistance of a number of students and other people, the six seasons of fieldwork at the McKeithen site and the surveys and testing program in North Florida could never have been as rewarding as they were. We gratefully acknowledge the contributions of Marigene Arnold, Steve Atkins, George Buffkin, Roseanna Cella, Thomas Chase, Tom Des Jean, Ricardo Diaz, Martin Dickinson, Diane Dugan, Carol Edeburn, Fergy "Jackson" Ferguson, Jon Gittler, Helen Gonzalez, Miguel Gonzalez, Bennett Gross, Virginia Hanson, Jackie Hogan, Mark Iverson, William Jayne, Kathie Johnson, William "Woody" Johnson, Becky Laman, Susan Lansman, Joan Ling, Jere Moore, Wendy Obermeyer, Bruce Piatek, Glenn Rayfield, Michael Russo, Mimi Saffer, Shelly Senfeld, Benjamin Simpson, Malinda Stafford, Donald Stewart, Rick Stokell, Vickie Weglowski, Robin Wright, and Drew Yaros. This list includes students from the University of Florida, Florida Atlantic University, and Florida International University, and a faculty member from Kalamazoo College.

Florida Atlantic University's Anthropology Department lent us their mobile field laboratory and bulldozer for use on the project. William H. Sears instigated the initial loan on our behalf. Our project field camp was situated at the McKeithen site, named for the McKeithen family of Live Oak who owned the property containing the site. The McKeithens gave us complete freedom to work on their land and provided other niceties. Lex McKeithen, perhaps more than any other individual, provided the initial impetus for the excavations at the site, and he continued to be a supporter, source of information, and friend throughout the fieldwork. We all express our sincere thanks to Lex and his family.

The Osaki family of Lake City, landlords for Timothy Kohler and his field crew one season, aided us in many ways and showed informed interest in the progress of our work, frequently visiting the excavations. The Carters, another local family, were an excellent source of information on site locations and facilitated the fieldwork on their properties in northern Columbia County.

Many of our colleagues contributed to the project. William R. Maples lent his expertise in physical anthropology. At one point, while he was recovering from back surgery, Bill practically crawled up Mound B so that he could examine the burial in that mound *in situ*. Bill, then chairman of the Florida State Museum

Anthropology Department, and J. C. Dickinson, Jr., then director of the museum, both facilitated our work in the field and the laboratory.

Arlene Fradkin provided zooarchaeological analyses for the mound excavations. Her interpretations and Kohler's zooarchaeological analyses were carried out under the supervision of Elizabeth S. Wing at the museum. Pru Rice contributed her skills in ceramic technology and supervised much of Ann Cordell's ceramic analysis, also at the museum.

Christopher Peebles, Don S. Rice, and David Brose all contributed to the formation of our original grant proposals. Dave and Chris, along with other Southeast colleagues, offered constructive criticisms of our research as it progressed. George Percy and S. Jeffrey K. Wilkerson visited the site, as did Bill Sears. Vincas Steponaitis and James B. Griffin read a draft of the manuscript and provided us with their comments, as did G. Mike Johnson. Jerry Stipp of Beta Analytic, Inc., supplied us with his usual competent radiocarbon analysis, interpretations, and suggestions. We thank all of these people.

We are also grateful to the National Science Foundation for providing funding for the fieldwork and subsequent analysis. Much of the financial burden of the project was borne by that agency and the University of Florida. We particularly wish to thank the Wentworth Foundation, founded by the late A. Fillmore Wentworth, and its president William M. Goza, for their financial support and their continued interest in this project. Grants from the foundation provided the initial seed money that got us started, and a grant from that same foundation was used for the preparation of the graphics for this book. Bill and Sue Goza not only visited the site on several occasions, but they kindly hosted field crews at their lovely home in Madison, Florida, a welcomed respite from life in the pits.

The expertise of several individuals was combined in the production of the manuscript for this book and for nearly all the graphics that appear in it. Louis Ortega, Laurey Getford, and Jimmy Franco handled the photography and Franco prepared all the final graphics. Cindy Cart, Susan Fabrick, and Annette Fanus all typed parts of the manuscript. Donna Ruhl put in a number of long hours reading, editing, and helping with many other editorial chores, as did Deborah Harding. Merald Clark, a University of Florida student, designed our book cover.

Figures 8.3, 8.6, 8.7, and 8.9 appear courtesy of the Museum of the American Indian, Heye Foundation. The photograph that appears as Figure 4.12 was made available by G. Mike Johnson of Washington State University. David Hally and the Anthropology Department at the University of Georgia lent us the negatives for Figures 8.1, 8.2, 8.4, 8.5, 8.8, and 8.10.

We are grateful to the editorial staff of Academic Press, who, along with James B. Griffin, helped to initiate this book and saw it through to completion.

Last, but certainly not least, we acknowledge the intellectual stimulus provided by William H. Sears, Professor Emeritus at Florida Atlantic University. Dedicating this book to Bill is only a small token of respect and appreciation we and other Southeast archaeologists have for him and his many contributions to archaeology.

Behind the Scenes

It was during the early part of a hot Florida summer in 1975 when Leon A. "Lex" McKeithen, Jr., of Live Oak, Florida, came to the Florida State Museum to talk with someone about the three Indian mounds and adjacent village site on his family's property in western Columbia County. At the time, Milanich was a novitiate curator at the museum and was considering a long-term archaeological project studying the development of the stratified society of the Calusa aborigines of the southwestern Florida coast. McKeithen first talked with D. Gerald Evans, a museum employee who had visited the mounds several years before. Evans, in turn, brought McKeithen to see Milanich and they extracted a promise to look at the mounds and the pottery recovered from one of them.

Checking the files at the museum, Milanich found that in 1966, David S. Phelps, then at Florida State University, had initially recorded the site as 8-Co-17, the McKeithen site. He corresponded with Phelps, who graciously sent copies of a preliminary site map and the information gathered from several test excavations he had made in the 1960s.

Several weeks after McKeithen's visit, Evans and Milanich went for a field visit. There is nothing like a few Weeden Island pots to turn the head of a young archaeologist who has spent several years excavating coastal shell middens and is planning several more years of the same. We wonder if many archaeological projects of note also begin in similar serendipitous fashion.

We were quickly to learn that McKeithen probably knew more about the archaeology of Columbia and Suwannee counties than anyone else alive. He was extremely well read and had applied his knowledge of other regions in Florida to interpret the little-known North Florida area that had previously received almost no notice from professional archaeologists. Prior to our work, the only projects undertaken were Phelps' 1966 testing at McKeithen; some surveys of Spanish–Native American mission locations; the testing of one mission by Calvin Jones of the State of Florida Bureau of Historic Sites and Properties carried out in the early 1970s; and two projects by John Goggin, one in 1949 at an early lithic site on the Suwannee River (1950) and one at a mission dump on the Ichetucknee River, which Goggin investigated from 1949 to 1952 (Deagan 1972).

Throughout the project McKeithen remained an advisor, observer, and sometime participant. His interest in preserving archaeological sites in North Florida and in having his own site investigated in proper fashion before it was destroyed had led to his initial visit to the museum. And his interest and our activities have combined to make the residents of Columbia and Suwannee counties much more aware of their cultural resources.

During the course of the project, and continuing to the present, we were very open about our activities at the McKeithen site, at times providing information for the local press, giving presentations to local civic and church groups, and even conducting tours of the site. As a result, the local people looked after us and provided many services and much hospitality. We had only one incident of vandalism: A hole was dug in a low mound formed as the result of a tree fall. We later used it to bury garbage. No equipment was lost except one camera that had been left on Mound A. A hound that frequently ranged through the site chasing rabbits picked it up. We tracked him for a short way and found the case strap, which had been gnawed off; but we never recovered the camera or the rest of the case. Try explaining that to a university property officer.

During fall 1975 Milanich put together a grant proposal entitled "Archaeological Investigations at the McKeithen Site: Kolomoki–Weeden Island Village Life and Ceremonialism in North Florida" and submitted it to the Anthropology Program of the National Science Foundation (NSF). It was rejected. In order to begin work at the site in the summer of 1976, a grant proposal was submitted to the Wentworth Foundation, founded by the late A. Fillmore Wentworth. It was funded and work began. This grant was later renewed and allowed fieldwork to continue during winter 1977.

The NSF proposal was revised, refurbished, and resubmitted in late 1976 under the title "Weeden Island in North Florida: Archaeological Investigation of a Possible Complex Society" (later shortened by NSF to "Archaeological Research in North Florida"). That simple change proved to be prophetic, given our conclusions relative to our initial hypotheses concerning the Weeden Island culture in North Florida.

The proposal was funded and allowed us to

Figure 1.1 The northerners among our readers who laugh at the rigors of a Florida winter have never stood atop a North Florida mound in 20° weather shortly after sunrise when the upper 2 cm of soil are still frozen.

work at the site for four additional 10-week field seasons (summer and fall 1977; spring 1978; and winter 1979). The northerners among our readers who laugh at the rigors of a Florida winter have never stood atop a North Florida mound in 20° weather shortly after sunrise when the upper 2 cm of soil are still frozen (Figure 1.1). Our general goals and research hypotheses as outlined in that second proposal are explored (and, in most cases, exploded) in Chapter 3.

The same NSF funds also were used for a 9-month program of survey and testing at sites other than McKeithen that was carried out from January to August 1978. This survey was an extremely important part of the overall project and produced comparative data as well as an understanding of the settlement system. The NSF funds were stretched even further to provide support for subsequent analysis of data collected during the entire 1976–1979 period of field activities.

It is appropriate here to single out another individual who contributed a great deal to the project, including much of the initial impetus. William H. Sears, himself no stranger to the archaeology of Weeden Island sites, came to Gainesville in fall 1975 and traveled north with Milanich and Evans to look at the McKeithen site and Lex McKeithen's ceramic collections (now curated at the Florida State Museum with the subsequently excavated materials and data). Sears offered his expertise and ideas on how to approach the field portion of the project as well as the problems surrounding Weeden Island. And he offered the long-term loan of his mobile archaeological field camp, which was used throughout the latter two thirds of the project.

That field camp, along with a bulldozer Sears also loaned the project, enabled us to eliminate most of those logistic hassles that accompany many field projects. The camp consisted of three specially constructed house trailers: a kitchen–laboratory, a two-room dorm trailer with six bunks and bathroom facilities in each room, and an office–bedroom–bathroom–storage trailer. To these we added a surplus Fruehauf semi-trailer, which we refurbished into a bedroom with six bunks and a living room. We added a fourth bathroom (Figure 1.2), put in septic tanks, dug a well, cleared a power line right-of-way, and had electricity supplied to the compound, which was located on the northwest side of the site in a charming oak and hickory hammock.

The result of all of this was a field laboratory; sleeping, eating, and bathroom facilities for 19 people (although an occasional hardy or introverted soul preferred a pup tent, camper trailer, or shanty); and a tremendous saving in time and effort. We could eat, sleep, and work at the site without the worry of fixing lunch to take to the field, driving long distances to the site, or having to haul equipment in and out everyday. Our hotel in the woods, complete with heating, air conditioning, and ice cubes, was in place for the last three field seasons (when, not coincidentally, Milanich worked at the site). It also served as a center for the project's survey crews.

Sears' bulldozer, which the students quickly

Figure 1.2 The fourth bathroom at the McKeithen site field camp.

named Gordon, after another pioneer in Weeden Island research, was the most valuable individual that we have ever had the fortune to take on an excavation (Figure 1.3). After an initial expense of several thousand dollars to put it into almost new condition, its upkeep was minimal and it was worth at least a dozen laborers for moving back dirt, backfilling, digging trenches for profiling, and even removing (very cleanly) mound caps.

The bulldozer, actually a small International Harvester tractor 3040 (with treads and a 4-in-1 bucket), was first used by Sears at the Fort Center site on the west side of Lake Okeechobee in southern Florida. Both the three trailers, constituting the mobile lab–camp, and the tractor had originally been purchased in the 1960s with NSF funds awarded to Sears and Florida Atlantic University. It is doubtful if any other equipment purchased with anthropology grant funds has ever received more use. While at Fort Center, Sears calculated that the weight of the machine per square inch of on-the-ground tread was less than the weight per square inch of an average excavator. Consequently, fears of crushing artifacts in mounds were indeed unfounded.

At this point we could regale the reader with

Figure 1.3 Gordon, the project's bulldozer, was the most valuable individual on the excavation team.

colorful stories of life at the camp—sing-alongs around the fire, toasting s'mores (a Girl Scout concoction of graham crackers, Hershey bars, and marshmallows) over oak coals, and sipping lemonade on hot evenings—but it will suffice to mention simply that we worked hard and relaxed after work. Each week two individuals were designated mom and pop, and they did the shopping and cooking. This resulted in some pretty strange food combinations; the one that still stands out in Milanich's mind is kosher tofu. Our charge account at a supermarket in nearby Lake City worked quite well, except for the initial hassle of convincing university accounting officials that the grant indeed did allow funds for food and other living necessities. Our first submittal of receipts for 6 weeks of field expenditures (at an average of $225 per week and a total of about 6 m of cash register tapes) brought a letter from accounting stating that every item had to be listed—for example, 6 cans of mushroom soup, 12 rolls of yellow toilet paper, 32 bags of junk food. Frantic calls around the state finally located an individual in the state auditor's office in Tallahassee willing to overrule university officials and exempt us from that provision.

The schedule of field investigations and the

resulting preliminary papers, talks at professional meetings, and theses and dissertations that have resulted from the project prior to this final report are listed here. Specific methodologies and sampling strategies pertinent to the field investigations are discussed in the appropriate sections of the following chapters.

As already mentioned, the initial field season at the McKeithen site was summer 1976. Kohler, then a doctoral student at the University of Florida, served as the field supervisor for that season and the two that followed. During the first season, Kohler and a crew of four established a grid system over the site, prepared a detailed topographic map, devised and carried out a surface collecting strategy, and began excavating a stratified random sample of the nonmound areas of the site using 2- by 2-m square excavation units. Kohler and his crew offset the hot summer days in the field with evening swims in the pool of the apartment complex in Lake City, where they lived. This first field season was summarized in a paper by Kohler (1977b) which was distributed in mimeograph form in January 1977.

During winter 1977, Kohler returned to McKeithen with a crew of four to continue his sampling of the nonmound areas. Preliminary conclusions resulting from his statistical machinations were presented in a paper (1977a) delivered at the Society for American Archaeology annual meeting in New Orleans in April of that year and further disseminated in a second mimeograph distributed in June (1977c). Prudence Rice, of the University of Florida, and Kohler jointly presented a paper (1977), which focused on the distribution of ceramics in the village, at the Florida Academy of Sciences meeting in Gainesville toward the end of the second field season.

Kohler returned to the field for a third 10-week session in summer 1977 to complete his sample and to expand excavations in selected village midden areas. His 30 weeks of investigations provided important data and understanding of the areal distribution and sequence of village occupations and demonstrated that non-random patterning of artifacts existed in both time and space. Explanations for these patterns, along with the data, are presented in his doctoral dissertation (1978b), revised sections of which appear in this volume.

During late summer 1977, the mobile field camp was installed at the McKeithen site, and we first occupied it for 10 weeks during that fall. A crew of 11 people and 1 bulldozer began excavation of Mound B, the westernmost and smallest of the three mounds at the site. In good archaeological fashion we started up the east side, expecting to intersect a pottery cache like that which apparently had been present in Mound C (some of the pottery that McKeithen had collected). There was no pottery cache, and Mound B proved to be quite a different type of Weeden Island mound.

During the fall, we received the results of radiocarbon dating of 15 samples collected by Kohler from the village midden. Ignoring two very early dates (30 and 80 B.C.) and three dates from one feature that Kohler felt was probably a stump (and that averaged A.D. 1395), we were left with 10 dates ranging from A.D. 145 to 785. Those dates certainly destroyed any ideas that Milanich was erroneously entertaining about the McKeithen site overlapping in time with early Mississippian occupations elsewhere in the Southeast. Milanich also began to believe the dates (ca. A.D. 1000) David Brose had obtained from early Fort Walton occupations on the Apalachicola River. The dates from Mound B, received shortly after the field season was over, confirmed Kohler's village temporal placement, and Milanich was forced to begin to rethink his ideas regarding the temporal placement of the site and the nature of Weeden Island. It might be pointed out that Kohler and many of his colleagues in the Southeast had already told Milanich those ideas needed rethinking.

During that fall we were able to complete the excavation of Mound B and move our field oper-

ation to Mound C—the northernmost mound and the one that had produced a number of Weeden Island ceramic vessels, some of which were very similar to vessels from the Kolomoki site in Georgia. Our initial explorations in the badly disturbed (by pothunting) east side of Mound C indicated that portions were still intact and that human burials were present.

A research report summarizing the work in Mound B and the initial excavations in Mound C was written by Milanich, Kohler, and Loucks (1978). That same information was also provided to *American Antiquity* and the *Newsletter* of the Southeastern Archaeological Conference for their current research sections.

Spring 1978 saw us returning to the field to complete investigation of Mound C and to begin Mound A. With a crew of 12 and our faithful bulldozer, Gordon, we were able to make sense of the badly disturbed Mound C and to determine that, like Mound B, both A and C initially were low platform mounds that had later been capped, effectively ending the aboriginal use of the mounds. The field crew, composed of University of Florida and Florida International University students, threw their own mound-closing ceremony when excavation of Mound C was completed. That party may someday be viewed as a high point (or low, depending on one's perspective) in archaeological revelry.

At the beginning of 1978, Sigler-Lavelle, then a graduate student at the New School for Social Research, began a program of surveying, locating, and sampling Weeden Island sites in Suwannee and Columbia counties. The results of this important work, presented in her Ph.D. dissertation (1980a), provided a theoretical and pivotal point in our understanding of McKeithen Weeden Island, as we eventually named the North Florida Weeden Island culture. Parts of Sigler-Lavelle's study are included in this volume.

At the annual meeting of the Florida Anthropological Society, shortly after the spring field season had begun, Kohler (1978c) and

Milanich (1978a) gave papers presenting new data important to our understanding of the nature of Weeden Island.

Sigler-Lavelle completed her fieldwork in August 1978, having at that point braved 12 straight months living at the camp (she had participated in the fall 1977 field session at McKeithen). Her data (1980a,b) indicated that the McKeithen site, with its large, horseshoe-shaped village midden and multiple mounds, was the exception rather than the rule in North Florida where sites with well-defined middens were rare.

We organized a symposium for the Southeastern Archaeological Conference (SEAC) held in Knoxville in early November 1978. That session, "Evolution of Weeden Island and Mississippian Non-Egalitarian Societies in the Southeast: New Data, New Interpretations, and Some Speculations from Northern Florida and the Georgia Atlantic Coast," contained papers on our Weeden Island work as well as papers on the Fort Walton and coastal Georgia Mississippian period cultures.

The papers at the SEAC, later published in revised form in *Southeastern Archaeological Conference Bulletin* 22, included summaries by Kohler (1980) and Sigler-Lavelle (1980b). A paper by Rice (1980), who lent her expertise in ceramic technology to the project, was also included in the publication, as well as one by Cordell (1980), then a graduate student working under Rice's supervision. Cordell's data, greatly expanded, formed the basis for her master's thesis (1983); her data are also included in this volume (Chapters 6 and 7).

Milanich's presentation at the SEAC symposium (1978b) was so revised that it appeared as a totally new paper (1980b; one of the benefits of being an editor). The SEAC meeting and subsequent bulletin served to put our data on the table and to open our interpretations to the criticisms of our colleagues, many of whom jumped at the chance and others of whom of-

fered helpful suggestions and ideas. A final current research report was circulated at the close of the field work (Cordell *et al.* 1979).

Several archaeologists should be cited for their respective intellectual contributions to the project during the 1977–1979 period. David S. Brose, in several conversations, offered important perspectives on Weeden Island. Stephen Williams and Christopher Peebles listened and commented on our work several times over the course of the project. Williams, in a 1979 draft of a paper on painted pottery horizons coauthored with John Belmont (later published [1981] by Lousiana State University in a collection of papers in honor of Bill Haag), provided some interesting chronological correlations that reinforced our own findings.

A major eye-opener for our interpretations of the mounds at the McKeithen site was offered by Dan Morse, who questioned some of the preliminary ideas that Milanich presented at the Knoxville symposium; Morse's suggestions were in part responsible for Milanich's subsequent drastic revisions of the paper. The conclusions that Sigler-Lavelle was deriving from her data and Morse's comments regarding Milanich's contention that Mound A was the tomb of a chief, in which retainer sacrifices had been deposited, set us to thinking that, indeed, McKeithen did not possess a constellation of archaeological traits reflecting a chiefdom. Rather, the site represented a point along a continuum in the evolution of Southeast peoples *toward* Mississippian societies. The subsequent excavation of Mound A eventually provided a major piece in the reconsideration of the McKeithen puzzle.

In our final field season at McKeithen, during winter 1979, we completed our excavation of Mound A. After exiting the field, we prepared a current research report which was published in *American Antiquity*. A current research note that appeared in the *Southeastern Archaeological Conference Newsletter* focused on

Kohler's dissertation. Kohler also published an article based on his dissertation attempts to estimate the McKeithen site population (1978a).

At the Florida Anthropological Society meeting in Miami in late winter 1979, Milanich presented an overview of the McKeithen mounds and a fourth mound. The latter was located several kilometers north of the McKeithen site and had been tested during a freezing week in winter 1978. Milanich provided another overview of the projects findings in his paper (1980a) given at the Society for American Archaeology meeting in Philadelphia in spring 1980.

During the remainder of 1979 and into 1980 we concentrated on analysis; Sigler-Lavelle's dissertation was completed, and she accepted a position as assistant curator at the Florida State Museum. Kohler had already completed his doctoral degree and had moved west in fall 1978 to accept an assistant professorship at Washington State University, leaving behind his dissertation—the first real synthesized data from McKeithen—for us to take potshots at as our understanding increased. Cordell was hired by the Florida State Museum and continued work on her thesis (an ever-expanding task that somehow consumed $3\frac{1}{2}$ years and was finally completed in 1983, to everyone's joy).

During analysis, two quantum jumps in interpretation occurred. The first took place in summer 1979. George Luer, a sometime college student whose home is in Sarasota, Florida, was in the museum talking about the Florida central gulf coast, where he had been doing archaeological research with Marion Almy for several years. Always a clear thinker with a questioning mind, Luer was glancing over Milanich's shoulder at Kohler's topographic map of the McKeithen site when he asked why the three mounds apparently formed an isosceles triangle and why there was a funny, low ridge extending from the center of the base of that triangle toward the rising sun at the summer solstice. These features, which we had completely overlooked, certainly raised some interesting questions, which are examined in Chapter 5.

The second event took place in spring 1980 when Milanich had to move all of the furniture out of his office while it was being carpeted. Among his furniture and other paraphernalia was a cast of the often illustrated, pedestaled ceramic duck that Sears had excavated from Mound D at Kolomoki. When Milanich's office clutter was carried into the museum range for temporary storage, by happenstance the duck was set down next to some McKeithen Mound C ceramic vessels that Cordell was reconstructing and studying. The upper portion of one of the McKeithen pedestaled effigy vessels had defied our efforts of assembly. An owl's(?) head, which had the same paste and which should have fit, did not have the connecting pieces to be attached. But what was obvious was that the body shapes of the Kolomoki duck and the McKeithen "owl" were nearly identical. This aroused considerable discussion between all of us, and we bantered about the differences between ducks, owls, and other birds. (At one point the McKeithen owl was dubbed Rosetta Duck because it appeared we might be able to use it to help interpret incised motifs on the other bird effigies.)

Although our wonderment was short lived (and we are sure some of you are wondering how on earth this could be construed as an advance in knowledge), our vocalizations brought Vernon J. Knight, Jr., then a graduate assistant who was writing a dissertation on Mississippian ritual, to the range to see if someone had brought in donuts. Knight's curiosity was aroused and he began to investigate the symbolism present in the Weeden Island effigy vessels; why some animals were portrayed and not others. In several weeks he had put together the paper that appears in our volume as Chapter 8.

Our tangled tale leads us to some comments on how this book was written. This chapter was prepared by Milanich, who hogged the word processor as a reward for devoting portions of several years to the project, and who needed some purging, especially because he originally advanced the hypotheses that proved to be invalid (admittedly, the enjoyment of looking back over the project at its completion was another reason). Milanich was also primarily responsible for Chapter 2. Portions of Sigler-Lavelle's dissertation have been used in Chapter 3; other of her data have been included in various places. Kohler rethought and reworked his dissertation data for inclusion as Chapter 4. In Chapter 6, Cordell presents sections of her thesis, which focused on Weeden Island ceramic technology. Chapter 7, also by Cordell, describes the ceramic vessels from the McKeithen mounds. Knight's study (Chapter 8) of effigy symbolism has been included almost exactly as he originally wrote it. Milanich wrote chapters 5 and 9 and the Appendix and assembled the manuscript, weaving together the various sections, while often relying on information provided by the other authors, all of whom should be considered equal contributors. The completed manuscript was then circulated among everyone for comments, revisions, and so forth. We hope that the result is less of a committee report than it sounds.

As part of these "behind the scenes" remarks, a disclaimer is in order. Our study in North Florida was necessarily limited in scope. All of our fieldwork took place in Columbia and Suwannee counties, mainly in the former, and focused on one major site and on surveys and testing of other sites and locales. There are many sites yet to be investigated and much to learn about their temporal placement and geographic distributions. Likewise, the sites we investigated produced only small quantities of ecofacts (such as the bones of the animals eaten by the Weeden Island villagers), because the soils are too acidic for good preservation and because depositional patterns at the sites did not favor preservation. Consequently, our story is incomplete; much information about the North Florida Weeden Island peoples is still in the ground. And, although we can and do apply our conclusions in the interpretation of other Weeden Island cultures, further research is needed to confirm our conclusions that those other cultures were indeed systematically structured like the McKeithen Weeden Island culture.

These preliminaries out of the way, we can turn to the task at hand—outlining the McKeithen project, telling how and why we collected the data, presenting the data, and interpreting the data. We also compare our ideas with information previously gathered by other Weeden Island researchers and examine the utility of Weeden Island for understanding the evolution of Southeast aboriginal cultures.

2

The Concept of Weeden Island

Like many other Southeastern archaeological cultures, Weeden Island underwent a period of conceptualization a half-century in length. During this period, from the late 1880s to the 1930s, C.B. Moore, Jesse Fewkes, and others excavated at a number of Weeden Island sites. It was Gordon R. Willey, however, who was finally responsible for the formal birth of Weeden Island. Later, in the 1950s William H. Sears reared the concept of Weeden Island to adolescence utilizing data from his work at Kolomoki in southwestern Georgia.

For more than a decade since that time, Weeden Island has remained something of a delinquent child who was argued about and fought over. In the last several years Southeastern archaeologists have completed this assessment of Weeden Island and are now engaged in a variety of new research projects intended to finish the Weeden Island culture history studies begun in the 1940s and before. We are also beginning to use these new research opportunities to examine questions of broader anthropological interest.

Building on the research of Willey and Sears, and on their own work of only several years ago, anthropologists have grasped the concept of Weeden Island by the neck and tossed it out of the closet, where the length and breadth of its development can be examined. The future can only bring greater and more significant understanding of Weeden Island, its place in the context of Southeastern prehistory, and its significance for anthropological interpretation of that prehistory. (Milanich 1980b:11–12, 17)

At the time those words were written in fall 1978, the McKeithen project was underway in northern Florida. As indicated in Chapter 1, our research was to focus both on answering questions of Weeden Island culture history and on providing interpretations that would help in the understanding of the evolution of Southeast aboriginal cultures. We were especially interested in learning whether evidence existed for the presence of complex social systems among Weeden Island societies, specifically the type of stratified grouping present among later (post-A.D. 900) Mississippian peoples elsewhere in the eastern United States, including portions of Florida.

The archaeological data we gathered from North Florida strongly suggest that such social systems were not present among Weeden Island cultures, although some ranking of social statuses certainly was present. Our work also produced unquestionable dating for Weeden Island developments that in the past had been debated. The purpose in writing this book is to present these and other data collected from our project and to use them to test a model of Weeden Island social organization that we developed early on in our research, based largely on the survey program.

Histories of Weeden Island studies and overviews of previous interpretations have been offered elsewhere (e.g., Milanich 1980b; Milanich and Fairbanks 1980:89–143; Willey 1945,

1949:15–34). Consequently, in this volume we do not dwell too much on such studies, except where they are germane to an understanding of Weeden Island, such as in our discussion of the development of the concept of Weeden Island. Our interpretations, of course, rely heavily on our own findings as well as on other data, including those from northwestern Florida collected by David S. Brose and George Percy and their colleagues and students. We also use data and interpretations provided by Gordon R. Willey and William H. Sears, in some instances supplementing their information with newer data. We have sought a readable overview of the Weeden Island culture (though not a compendium of traits), one that will be of use both to archaeologists and to other individuals interested in the history of aboriginal peoples in Florida and the Southeast United States.

GEOGRAPHIC AND TEMPORAL DISTRIBUTION

The prehistoric people whose archaeological remains have been grouped under the generic term Weeden Island culture were distributed over much of the Gulf coastal plain in Alabama, Florida, and Georgia during the latter two thirds of the first millennium A.D. Possibly, the archaeological ceramic assemblage termed Weeden Island developed out of the earlier Swift Creek assemblage by A.D. 200 in the lower Chattahoochee–Apalachicola river drainage. Sites like Kolomoki and Fairchild's Landing in Georgia (Caldwell 1978; Sears 1956) and Aspalaga and Bird Hammock in Northwest Florida (Bense 1969; Moore 1903a:481–488; Penton 1970) present evidence for a gradual development from Swift Creek into Weeden Island in those areas. It is important to note that Swift Creek Complicated Stamped ceramics are present throughout most of the early Weeden Island period, especially west and northwest of

North Florida (see Figure 2.1 for a map of the Weeden Island culture region).

By A.D. 200, Weeden Island ceramics appear in North Florida; at the McKeithen site they overlay a small Deptford component. (No Swift Creek sites have yet been found in that portion of North Florida occupied by the McKeithen Weeden Island culture described in this volume.) The earliest dates for the Weeden Island culture are from the McKeithen site in North Florida, although no ceramic developmental continuum out of Deptford has been recognized. Village sites and burial mounds containing Weeden Island ceramics that probably date shortly after A.D. 200 are found as far east as the Okeefenokee Swamp in southeast Georgia (Trowell 1979:14–17, 1980) and as far westward from the Chattahoochee–Apalachicola drainage as Mobile Bay and the Tombigbee River (Moore 1905:253–262; Trickey 1958). Occasional sites are also found in the coastal plain of southern Georgia (e.g., on the Ocmulgee River in Coffee County; see Snow 1977:10) and southeastern Alabama (e.g., on the Alabama River in Dallas County; see Nance 1976:194).

To the north, Weeden Island sites extend along the Chattahoochee River to the fall line at Columbus (Chase 1967); southward, Weeden Island ceramics are found in mounds all of the way to Sarasota County, Florida, just below Tampa Bay—the location of the type site for Weeden Island located in Pinellas County. This distribution (see Figure 2.1) forms a hemispherical region centered on the tristate region where Alabama, Georgia, and Florida intersect. Outside this annular region, occasional Weeden Island potsherds are recognized in ceramic collections from south and east Florida, the Atlantic Coast of Georgia, and the Lower Mississippi Valley.

The Weeden Island ceramic complex changes through time, allowing us to differentiate an early period, ca. A.D. 250–700, from a later period, A.D. 700–900/1000 (there are apparently

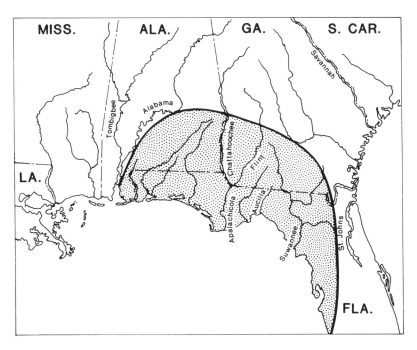

Figure 2.1 Region of the Weeden Island culture.

some exceptions to this terminal date of A.D. 900/1000, such as in North Florida). Willey (1949:396–397) has called these two periods *Weeden Island I* (characterized by ceramics with punctated, incised, plain, and complicated stamped decorations) and *Weeden Island II* (characterized by plain and check stamped decorations).

During the Weeden Island I period the densest distribution of sites is more restricted than it is in the Weeden Island II period, when there is a marked increase in the number and distribution of sites. These later sites, especially villages, are found both within the Weeden Island I region in locales and environmental zones that were less densely inhabited previously and in locations outside of the major Weeden Island I destribution. Such Weeden Island II villages appear in large numbers in southeastern Alabama and in smaller numbers in southern Georgia. In the latter area, however, village sites characterized by cord marked pottery appear to predominate, with Weeden Is-

land II villages present as apparent intrusions into the river valleys. The increase in the number of late Weeden Island sites over sites of the early period is documented by Willey's survey of the Florida Gulf Coast and White's (1981a) survey of the Lake Seminole area within the tristate region (see Table 2.1). This growth, apparent throughout the Southeast, is even greater than indicated by these data, because the Weeden Island I period lasts 450 years, while the later period is only 200–300 years long.

Circumstantial evidence suggests that this expansion in the number of sites and in the total area occupied is due to larger populations almost certainly associated with increased importance of agriculture during Weeden Island II times. The only maize recovered from a Florida Weeden Island site is from a Weeden Island II site, Sycamore, adjacent to the Apalachicola River and dating to the ninth century A.D. (Milanich 1974:15). It is possible that sites were placed in locations to which maize production

Table 2.1

Increase in Numbers of Late Weeden Island Sites and Components over Earlier Periods[a]

Site or component	Florida Gulf Coast	Lake Seminole
Swift Creek	17	18
Weeden Island I (includes mixed late Swift Creek and early Weeden Island)	32	38
Weeden Island II	48	103

[a]Gulf Coast data from Willey (1949:367, 397–399); Lake Seminole data from White (1981a:Tables 22–24). Both sets of figures include mound and midden sites.

was well suited. This would have resulted in larger numbers of sites and in the sites being located in areas not inhabited by earlier Weeden Island I villagers; both of these conditions appear to exist, especially in Northwest Flor-ida, where agricultural Mississippian cultures are found after A.D. 1000.

The Weeden Island II period might best be viewed as a transition from the settlement, subsistence, and social systems of the Weeden Island I people into the life-style known as Mississippian. In fact, it might be more correct to think of Weeden Island II as proto-Mississippian. Research in Northwest Florida in the Apalachicola Valley (Scarry 1980, 1981) documents the *in situ* development of Weeden Island II into the Fort Walton Mississippian culture. This development certainly occurred in Northwest Florida at about A.D. 900–1000 and is supported by numerous radiocarbon dates (see Table 2.2, which lists selected radiocarbon dates for Weeden Island period cultures, pre–Weeden Island cultures, and post–Weeden Island Mississippian cultures). A similar A.D. 900 development, in this case Weeden Island II into

Table 2.2

Selected Radiocarbon Dates[a]

Period	Northwest Florida	Peninsular Florida	Southeast Alabama and Southwest Georgia
Mississippian A.D. 1500–1000	A.D. 1400 ± 200 8-Ja-5, Fort Walton culture (Bullen 1958:348) 1190 ± 50 Curlee site, Fort Walton culture (White 1981b:25) 950 ± 70, 1010 ± 145, 1050 ± 100, 1110 ± 65, 1180 ± 60 Cayson site, Fort Walton culture (Scarry 1981:20, see also 1980) 915 ± 80, 925 ± 80, 1235 ± 80, 1585 ± 80 Lake Jackson, Fort Walton culture (Jones 1982:20–21) 840 ± 70, 920 ± 105, 1020 ± 105, 1050 ± 120, 1310 ± 70 Yon site, Fort Walton culture (Scarry 1981:20, see also 1980)	A.D. 775 ± 50, 905 ± 65, 1010 ± 60 Aqui Esta mound, early Safety Harbor (Luer and Almy 1982:53; see also Luer 1980)	A.D. 1555 ± 60, 1425 ± 55, 1320 ± 125, 1230 ± 70, 1200 ± 60, 1185 ± 55, 1160 ± 55, 1080 ± 90, 1055 ± 55, 1010 ± 55, 995 ± 55, 990 ± 80, 980 ± 55, 945 ± 70, 930 ± 60, 895 ± 65, 850 ± 60, 710 ± 95 Cemochechobee mounds (Knight 1981; see also Schnell et al., 1981)

Table 2.2 (*Continued*)

Period	Northwest Florida	Peninsular Florida	Southeast Alabama and Southwest Georgia
Weeden Island II A.D. 1000–700	A.D. 805 ± 85, 825 ± 85, 860 ± 85, 860 ± 85, 895 ± 85, 955 ± 85 Sycamore site, Wakulla culture (late Weeden Island; Milanich 1974:35)	A.D. 850 ± 105 Palmer burial mound, Weeden Island–related (Bullen and Bullen 1976:41)	A.D. 920 ± 105 Bear Creek site, Autauga phase (Weeden Island–related; Dickens 1971:64)
Weeden Island I A.D. 700–250	A.D. 800 ± 150 Basin Bayou mound, Weeden Island I (RDA 12266[b]; see also Willey 1949:223)	A.D. 720 ± 75 Roberts Bay site, late Manasota culture (Luer 1977b:127) 700 ± 70 Old Oak site, late Manasota culture (Luer and Almy 1982:216; see also Luer 1977a)	
			A.D. 530 Henderson site, Henderson phase (Weeden Island–related; Dickens 1971:58)
		490 ± 70, 275 ± 65, 210 ± 70 Hawthorne site, Cades Pond culture (UM-1781-83; see also Milanich 1978c) 220 ± 90 Melton site, Cades Pond culture (Milanich 1978c:163; see also Cumbaa 1972)	405 ± 25, 385 ± 75 Kolomoki village (I-482, 482-c; Karl Steinen, personal communication, 1980; see also Sears 1956)
		400 ± 50 Sarasota County mound Manasota culture (Bullen 1971:13) 400 ± 130 Weeden Island site, Manasota culture (Sears 1971:56)	390 ± 70, 370 ± 65, 365 ± 70, 310 ± 65, 265 ± 75, 260 ± 85, 250 ± 65, 245 ± 70, 175 ± 120, 150 ± 65, 140 ± 70, 110 ± 70, 90 ± 65, 35 ± 70 Mandeville site, early Swift Creek (Smith 1979:186–187)
Swift Creek and pre–Weeden Island A.D. 250–B.C.	A.D. 600 ± 75, 460 ± 75 Third Gulf Breeze site, late Swift Creek (Phelps 1969:18) 350 ± 250 8-Ja-63, late Swift Creek (Bullen 1958:327–331)	A.D. 180 ± 85 River Styx mound, early Cades Pond–late Deptford (Milanich 1978c:162) 30 B.C. ± 100 Crystal River mound, Yent complex (RDA 19451[b]; see also Sears 1962b)	70 B.C. ± 150 Halloca Creek site, early Swift Creek (RDA 6325)[b]

[a]All radiocarbon dates throughout this volume are uncorrected for recent tree ring calibrations.

[b]Radiocarbon Dates Association, Inc. serial number for unisort, edge-punch card with published radiocarbon date information.

the Rood culture, is suggested for the upper portion of the lower Chattahoochee River valley (Schnell 1981; Schnell *et al.* 1981:240–241, 248).

Because the Weeden Island II period has been viewed historically as associated with a pre-Mississippian cultural manifestation, investigation of sites from that period has been done by Weeden Island researchers rather than Mississippian researchers. Consequently, we have not in the past asked the correct questions regarding evolutionary processes, and our understanding of the emergence of Mississippian lifestyles in the Weeden Island region has been hindered (Scarry's [1980,1981] work is a notable exception).

It is not at all certain that the appearance of check stamped pottery and the hypothesized increase in agriculture during the Weeden Island II period occurred originally in the Weeden Island region proper. At least one check-stamped-pottery-making culture is present in the eastern coastal plain of Alabama prior to A.D. 700 (Henderson phase; Dickens 1971). Other Weeden Island II period check-stamped-pottery-making cultures are well distributed over much of the Alabama coastal plain, for example, McLeod (Walthall 1980:167–171) and Autauga (Dickens 1971; Nance 1976). Jeter (1977) has established that Henderson and Autauga are a developmental sequence, and he has also suggested diffusion southward to the Weeden Island region.

In North Florida the presence of Weeden Island I and II period sites is well documented as a result of our work in Columbia and Suwannee counties. This work, especially the program of surveys and site testing carried out by Sigler-Lavelle (1980a, 1980b) and by Loucks (1979; Loucks' research centered on early historic period aboriginal populations), also suggested that Swift Creek and Fort Walton sites are not present in those counties. Nor have any private collections that have been examined contained

materials from anything that could be called a Swift Creek or a Fort Walton site component. Although negative evidence is not the best, in this case it leaves us in the position of having to explain the apparent absence of such components in sites.

The explanation is simple: They are not present. At the McKeithen site the Weeden Island I component overlays a small Deptford component along the creek bank. The Swift Creek sites that are distributed across portions of west central Georgia and into eastern Alabama reached down into Northwest Florida (following the Flint and Chattahochee river drainage?) but did not extend into North or peninsular Florida. In North Florida, Weeden Island I follows Deptford.

Mississippian archaeological complexes also never developed or diffused into North Florida (the region east of the Aucilla River and north of the Santa Fe River between the Atlantic and Gulf coastal flatlands; see Figure 2.2). It is interesting that in the early historic period, the Aucilla River was the dividing line between the Muskhogean-speaking Apalachee (associated with the Fort Walton archaeological culture) and the Timucuan-speaking tribes, Yustega and Utina, (probable descendants of earlier Weeden Island peoples and associated with a different material culture). Perhaps this ethnic boundary persisted back 500 years to A.D. 1000. Indeed, the meager evidence suggests that a Weeden Island II ceramic complex—one different from that found in Northwest Florida—was present in North Florida from about A.D. 700 until the fifteenth century. Such different developments during Weeden Island II and subsequent times might explain historic period linguistic and cultural differences.

Peninsular Florida presents still another problem, albeit perhaps only a semantic one. Although Weeden Island pottery is found in mounds along the peninsular Gulf Coast from the big bend area of Florida south to below Tam-

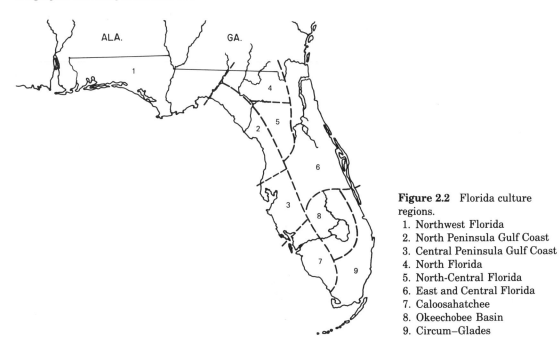

Figure 2.2 Florida culture regions.
1. Northwest Florida
2. North Peninsula Gulf Coast
3. Central Peninsula Gulf Coast
4. North Florida
5. North-Central Florida
6. East and Central Florida
7. Caloosahatchee
8. Okeechobee Basin
9. Circum–Glades

pa Bay, it is present in village ceramic collections in only very small amounts, ranging from about 10% in Taylor County in the north to less than 1% in Manatee County. Along that coast the vast majority of village pottery is undecorated.

The same is true in North-Central Florida. At village sites of the Cades Pond culture more than 90% of the ceramics are undecorated and Weeden Island pottery occurs only infrequently in the mounds. In both North-Central Florida and along the Gulf Coast, the distribution of Weeden Island pottery in mounds is not in eastside caches like in the more northern portions of the Weeden Island region, indicating different burial ritual.

This raises something of a dilemma: Should the Cades Pond and Peninsular Gulf Coast cultures dating from the Weeden Island I period be called Weeden Island, even though Weeden Island pottery has not been found in the villages (but has been found in mounds) and the burial

ritual associated with the mounds appears to differ? On the other hand, in some traits—coastal subsistence and settlement patterns, the presence of mound–village complexes, and so forth—the peninsular and the northern Weeden Island cultures are alike. Our definition of Weeden Island could be made large enough to include these "atypical cultures" (the type site for Weeden Island is a peninsular coastal site). One solution, employed here, is simply to call these atypical archaeological complexes *Weeden Island–related cultures,* allowing us to reserve judgment on what is and what is not a Weeden Island culture until more evidence has been examined.

A similar problem exists for the Weeden Island II check-stamped-pottery-making cultures in the eastern coastal plain of Alabama. Here, however, the reverse situation may exist. Although the village pottery is of the dominant type found throughout the Weeden Island region during that period, it is not at all certain that mounds contain Weeden Island pottery (and, in truth, it is not at all certain what ceramics a Weeden Island II mound does contain). It seems best to also think of the Alabama Henderson, Autauga, and McLeod complexes as Weeden Island–related cultures.

In summary, the Weeden Island I ceramic complex (at this point in our narrative still not fully defined) appears to have begun to develop out of the earlier Swift Creek ceramic complex by about A.D. 200 in the Chattahoochee and Apalachicola river drainages (though we recognize that the earliest dates obtained thus far for a pure Weeden Island I component are from the McKeithen site in North Florida). A number of archaeological sites in Northwest Florida demonstrate a very gradual replacement of the distinctive Swift Creek Complicated Stamped pottery by the incised and punctated Weeden Island pottery. (Complicated stamping remained a form of decoration throughout most if not all of the Weeden Island I period.)

The Weeden Island complex apparently spread outward into adjacent parts of northern and northwestern Florida, into the coastal plain of Alabama and Georgia. This geographic area, characterized by the Weeden Island I archaeological complex, is often referred to as the *heartland region*. Beginning about A.D. 700 this gradual expansion became a very rapid one. Ceramic styles changed and check stamping became the most popular form of decoration for village pottery. During the A.D. 700–900 period, Weeden Island II peoples moved into zones that previously had been occupied only seldomly. One hypothesis, supported by some evidence (Percy and Brose 1974:19–21), is that this expansion represents the adoption of maize farming by those Weeden Island peoples who later evolved into Mississippian populations. The evolutionary process differed in North Florida and the regions of the peninsular Florida Weeden Island–related cultures.

This period of expansion and change marked the transition from the life-styles of the earlier Weeden Island peoples into those known as Mississippian. The Weeden Island II culture(s) in the heartland region (excepting North Florida) evolved into regional Mississippian cultures such as Fort Walton and Pensacola (together located across the Gulf coastal plain from the Aucilla River at least as far west as Pascagoula, Mississippi) and Roods (located along the lower Chattahoochee River). In North Florida a late Weeden Island archaeological complex, rather than a fully Mississippian one, was apparently present into the sixteenth century. These differences between North and Northwest Florida are reflected in the respective Weeden Island II period settlement patterns, which, as we shall see, perhaps reflect somewhat different environmental configurations.

From the heartland region, Weeden Island traits also spread southward into peninsular Florida. Along the Gulf Coast (north of Charlotte Harbor), however, Weeden Island pottery is found almost exclusively in mounds and is very rare in village contexts. The name Weeden Island–related has been suggested for these and other "aberrant" Weeden Island cultures.

THE DEVELOPMENT OF THE WEEDEN ISLAND CONCEPT

To some readers it may seem ludicrous to discuss the temporal and spatial distributions of an archaeological complex without first defining that complex and explaining how it is unique and how it is recognized. However, defining Weeden Island is one of the major goals of this book. At this point, suffice it to say that the Weeden Island archaeological complex is best recognized by archaeologists on the basis of its distinctively decorated pottery.

Such attributes are easy to describe for the Weeden Island I period cultures but are less unique and easily recognized for the check stamped and other pottery of the Weeden Island II period. Although we can today characterize the process of distinguishing Santa Rosa, Swift Creek, Weeden Island I, Weeden Island II, Fort Walton, and Pensacola pottery complexes as easy, such a statement does not convey our reliance on modern stratigraphic information in making these differentiations. For example, in the nineteenth and early twentieth centuries, early archaeologists, such as Clarence B. Moore (who excavated more than 50 Weeden Island sites, mainly mounds) and W. H. Holmes (who described the pottery of the Northwest Florida and peninsular Gulf coasts, 1903:104–114, 125–128), could differentiate among stamped, incised (sometimes Holmes referred to incising as engraving), and undecorated pottery; but neither Moore nor Holmes had much information on temporal distribution. Holmes guessed that different tribes or people from different linguistic families might have visited the same sites over time, accounting for the varieties of ceramics found on specific sites.

During the winter, 1923–1924, archaeologists from the Smithsonian Institution, under the direction of J. Walter Fewkes, excavated portions of the Weeden Island site located in Old Tampa Bay in Pinellas County (Fewkes 1924). These excavations investigated both village middens and a burial mound. The latter contained an array of Weeden Island I ceramics, including whole vessels and sherds. Fewkes' work served to identify a distinctive Weeden Island mound ceramic complex and, along with the investigations of Moore, who dug in Florida sites from the early 1890s until almost 1920, provided a firm base for modern archaeologists to begin synthesizing the concept of Weeden Island and delineating its temporal and spatial attributes. Fewkes (1924:23–26) concluded correctly that the ceramic complex and the Weeden Island site were prehistoric and were related to more northerly materials and sites rather than those of the Caribbean.

Modern studies of the concept of Weeden Island began in Florida in the summer of 1940 when Gordon R. Willey and Richard Woodbury, then students from Columbia University, undertook a reconnaissance of aboriginal sites in Northwest Florida. Willey and Woodbury sought to use the information recorded by previous researchers, such as Moore and Holmes, as well as their own observations to establish a chronological outline for that region. And they accomplished their goal (Willey and Woodbury 1942:Figure 25; not only that, but their paper was written by December, 1940; unfortunately this standard of research and rapid report preparation has not been maintained by all of us Weeden Island researchers).

In that initial paper, Willey and Woodbury began to describe formally the Weeden Island ceramic complex, recognizing the Weeden Island I pottery type (Weeden Island Incised), the Weeden Island II type (Wakulla Check Stamped), as well as Weeden Island Plain. Thus, a major contribution was made to the concept of Weeden Island: the recognition that temporally sequential ceramic series could be defined. The study also placed the Weeden Island ceramic complex within the chronological sequence for Northwest Florida and the peninsular Gulf Coast north of lower Tampa Bay relative to earlier and later developments.

Willey and Woodbury (1942) sought to define other Weeden Island traits besides the ceramic complex, and they assembled information on subsistence (Weeden Islanders relied on wild foods within the coastal environment; agriculture may have been present, but probably was not intensive due to the sandy coastal soils), settlement patterns and types of sites (numerous coastal sites were distributed evenly along the Northwest coast in which conical sand burial mounds were found and the contents of the village middens were much like those of earlier periods), and other artifacts of the archaeological complex (mounds might contain shell pendants, quartz crystal fragments, mica, and greenstone celts; middens contained stemmed points). The concept of Weeden Island was born.

Willey continued to flesh out the concept of Weeden Island. In 1945 he published a synthesis of "a major portion of the existing data concerning the Weeden Island complex of the Florida Gulf Coast" (1945:225). That paper discussed the spatial distribution of Weeden Island mounds, the artifacts and other traits present in 56 mounds (mainly excavated by Moore), and the relations of Weeden Island to the remainder of the Southeast. Because Weeden Island studies were still in their nascent period, the emphasis was on traits.

An interesting and still debated point raised by Willey in these two studies (1945; Willey and Woodbury 1942) is the similarity in some ceramic decorations present in the Weeden Island ceramic complex with decorations in the ceramic complexes of the Baytown (Willey called this Troyville, which was common usage at that time) and Coles Creek archaeological cultures of the Lower Mississippi River Valley. Other, later archaeologists have also noted similarities for these two regions during both Weeden Island I and II periods (e.g., Belmont and Williams 1981; Brown 1982; Sears 1956: 74–83).

That ideas and even specific decorative motifs with their associated meanings might be spread across the coastal plain from Louisiana into Florida is not surprising, especially when we consider that the distance from the McKeithen site in North Florida to Pensacola, Florida is about 675 km while the distance from Pensacola to New Orleans is only about 290 km. Our problem, and one that still exists, is explaining the significance of these similarities and the nature of the contact that they imply. Are they indicative of the diffusion of aspects of culture other than pottery decoration, a relatively insignificant feature? Or are they a result of both Baytown and Weeden Island I ceramics

and motifs developing out of the ceramics of earlier cultures that shared similar Hopewellian-related beliefs?

In 1948 Willey published still another paper relevant to the concept of Weeden Island that focused on an area we refer to today as the Manasota region, which ranges from just north of Tampa Bay southward to Charlotte Harbor and which Willey referred to as Central Gulf Coast and Manatee. Using previously excavated data, Willey documented the presence of Weeden Island ceramics in burial mounds (but not in village middens) as far south as the Manasota region. Willey noted that Weeden Island was followed by Safety Harbor in the Manasota region. He also noted that the Weeden Island II complex was apparently not present in his Manatee region and that sites of the Glades cultural tradition were. Additionally, an Englewood period and ceramic complex was included between Weeden Island and Safety Harbor in the area south of Tampa Bay.

As already noted, Willey's Manatee region as an archaeological construct has been revised (he originally noted that it was "still open to verification," 1948:210). Luer and Almy (1979, 1982) have provided the basis for the present view of the extent of the area encompassed by the Manasota region (or Central Peninsular Gulf Coast). The Manasota culture is viewed as dating from about 500 B.C. to A.D. 900 or slightly later, at which time it evolved into the Safety Harbor complex. During its early portion (up to about A.D. 300), Manasota is contemporary with the Deptford and Swift Creek cultures found to the north. The burial mounds containing Weeden Island pottery found along that central portion of the peninsular Gulf Coast (including the original Weeden Island site itself) are a ceremonial assemblage associated with the late Manasota secular life-style. Thus, late Manasota is a Weeden Island–related culture, at least in terms of a portion of its ceremonial activities.

Willey's discussion of the presence of the Glades cultural tradition and a culture called Perico Island is now known to be incorrect. Those village archaeological assemblages have been subsumed by Manasota, and the pottery in that region (undecorated ware) that was once designated as Glades is now known to be the undecorated village pottery manufactured by the Manasota peoples. Perico pottery is now also known to have been associated with the Manasota culture (limestone-tempered pottery is much more prevalent north of Tampa Bay on the peninsular Gulf Coast, where it was also manufactured by Weeden Island–related villagers and earlier peoples, such as at the Crystal River site).

The fact that the Weeden Island–related cultures of peninsular Florida maintained one ceramic complex in their villages and another in their mounds led early archaeologists to misinterpret the culture sequences of that geographic area. Since the publication of Sears' article pointing out the presence of secular (village) and sacred (ceremonial, most frequently found in mounds) ceramic assemblages (1973), we have had to rethink data from the peninsular Gulf Coast and from North-Central Florida. We return to this important point later in this chapter.

The year 1949 saw the publication of Willey's synthesis *Archeology of the Florida Gulf Coast.* This excellent compendium of previous research along the coast from Charlotte Harbor northward still remains a mainstay of Florida archaeology, although some of the interpretations and all of the culture sequences have been updated or altered. At the time the manuscript went to press in 1949, not a single radiocarbon date from Florida was yet available.

Included in the synthesis are excellent data on Weeden Island, including a listing of all known sites by period (village middens, burial mounds, and other mounds); brief discussions of settlement patterns, subsistence patterns,

other artifacts, population estimates, and mortuary traits; and formal type descriptions for the entire Weeden Island ceramic complex, then composed of 31 types (Willey 1949:396–452; 510–512). The volume also elaborated the sequence of cultures for the Gulf Coast, and discussed relations to other Southeast cultures. Put quite simply, Willey's study laid the essential groundwork for all future Weeden Island studies as well as for much of the archaeology carried out since then in Florida and the coastal plain regions of Alabama and Georgia. One wonders what our progress would have been without his contributions.

Another monumental contribution to our understanding of the concept of Weeden Island is Sears' work at the Kolomoki site, located 26 km east of the Chattahoochee River in Early County, Georgia. Sears began five seasons of excavation at the 120-ha site in 1948. His data and conclusions were promptly published in three preliminary reports and a final overview (Sears 1951a, 1951b, 1953, 1956). In retrospect, it is somewhat incredible that Sears' project was the first major field investigation of a Weeden Island village–mound site in a quarter century; 25 years had intervened between the commencement of excavations at Kolomoki and Fewkes' (1924) project at the Weeden Island site. It is even more incredible to realize that between the start of work at Kolomoki and the start of the McKeithen project, 28 years would elapse. Kolomoki remains the largest excavated site containing a Weeden Island component.

Kolomoki is a particularly complex site with components from Swift Creek, Weeden Island, and Lamar cultures (the last is a Mississippian culture now referred to in that region as Bull Creek). At the time of excavation, Sears (1956:22) chose to give the name Kolomoki culture to the Weeden Island sacred assemblage associated with the mounds at the site. He also assigned Kolomoki to the complicated stamped, secular, village ceramic assemblage, differentiating that assemblage from the Weeden Island I ceramic assemblage also found in portions of the village (Sears 1956:30–31). Based on differences between the Kolomoki secular assemblage and Swift Creek ceramic assemblages from Florida and Georgia, and on excavated information from the village midden, Sears chose to place the Kolomoki culture (both sacred and secular ceramic complexes) after Weeden Island I, equating them temporally with early Mississippian cultures (Sears 1951a:14–16, 38, 1956:80). Other factors influencing this decision were the lack of a Weeden Island II (check-stamped-pottery-associated) component at the site and the similarities between some of the Kolomoki sacred ceramics and ceramic vessels from Mississippian sites (Sears 1951a:38–40, 1956:84–92).

Sears' temporal placement of the Kolomoki culture and his association of the complicated stamped pottery village component with the Weeden Island I sacred assemblage have been questioned by other archaeologists. Today, based on the new data from McKeithen, Cemochechobee, and other sites, it seems best to reinterpret the temporal placement of the Kolomoki site sacred and secular assemblages. The major village occupation at the site apparently dates from the late Swift Creek and Weeden Island I periods (temporally overlapping the McKeithen site Weeden Island I occupation). Ceramics from both Swift Creek and Weeden Island I complexes are mixed in some village deposits, suggesting a transitional ceramic complex, as would be expected if Weeden Island material culture developed out of Swift Creek.

Seven or eight mounds (A–H; G may not be an aboriginal mound) are present at the site, one of which (Mound A) is a very large (100- by 61-m base, 17.2 m tall) truncated pyramid that seems to be out of place with the other mounds known for Swift Creek and Weeden Island sites.

Some archaeologists have suggested that the temple mound was constructed either over earlier structures by the Bull Creek Mississippian peoples or was built from scratch during that later period, probably incorporating midden material from the earlier Swift Creek–Weeden Island occupation as construction fill. A Bull Creek phase village lies on the opposite side of Mound A from the Swift Creek–Weeden Island village.

On the basis of the chronology for Swift Creek and Weeden Island used in this volume, it is probable that the Kolomoki site was occupied from about A.D. 100 until about A.D. 500, with at least some of the mounds (D and E, which contained Weeden Island I ceramic vessels) being constructed and used during the period A.D. 300–500. These dates are consistent with radiocarbon dates from the village (A.D. 385 and A.D. 405; see Table 2.2). The later, Mississippian occupation was probably after ca. A.D. 1400.

Despite reinterpretation of the cultural sequence and temporal placement of the Swift Creek–Kolomoki component at Kolomoki, the data obtained by Sears from the mounds at the site are critical to an understanding of the concept of Weeden Island. In later chapters, we use those data to help develop our description and understanding of Weeden Island.

Stimulated by his work at Kolomoki, Sears raised questions that are crucial to our understanding of Weeden Island. In several articles Sears (1952, 1954, 1962a) draws parallels between the social organization and ceremonial life of the Kolomoki Weeden Island peoples and the historic Natchez. He also cites evidence for similar levels of complex social organization and ceremonialism among other historic and prehistoric groups in the Southeast United States. According to Sears, such complex societies had stratified social classes.

Archaeologists today recognize that such systems, usually called chiefdoms, formed the sociopolitical foundation of Mississippian so-

Table 2.3
Sacred and Secular Archaeological Complexes in Northwest Florida

	A.D. 1000	900	800	700	600	500	400	300	200	100	A.D./B.C.	100	200	300	400	500 B.C.
Secular culture	Weeden Island II			Weeden Island I					Swift Creek				Deptford			
Sacred complex					Weeden Island ?___			Green Point		Yent						

cieties. That a chiefdom-type system might have developed at the Kolomoki site in pre-Mississippian times seems likely, based on Sears' data. However, such a system was probably restricted to that immediate region; there are no data supporting the contention that the entire Weeden Island heartland region was unified into a single polity with a hierarchic settlement system. The evidence from McKeithen points toward ranking of social statuses at that site, not stratification. Comparisons of Kolomoki Weeden Island and McKeithen Weeden Island, made in Chapter 9, provide an interesting contrast that is pertinent to our understanding of the reasons why chiefdoms might have appeared briefly at sites such as Kolomoki but did not become the prevalent system until Mississippian times.

Another contribution by Sears is his study of the temporal relation between the ceremonial (sacred) complexes associated with the Weeden Island I culture and the earlier Yent and Green Point complexes, both associated to some degree with the pan–eastern United States Hopewellian ceremonial complex (Sears 1962a). Brose (1979) and Ruhl (1981) have also examined the relation of the Weeden Island I ceremonial (sacred) complex to Yent and Green Point. Although not all of these archaeologists would agree on the involvement of the populations associated with these sacred complexes in the Hopewellian interaction sphere, they do agree that the Yent (associated mainly with late Deptford peoples in Northwest Florida, ca. 100 B.C.–A.D. 100), Green Point (associated with early Swift Creek and very early Weeden Island I peoples in the Weeden Island region, ca. A.D. 100–300), and the Weeden Island I (ca. A.D. 300–500 or later) ceremonial complexes represent an evolutionary continuum. This evolution certainly occurred in the heartland region, the same region in which the Weeden Island secular ceramic assemblage originated. A chart showing this sacred–secular dual evolutionary scheme is presented as Table 2.3.

Sears fully developed the sacred–secular ceramic dichotomy in a 1973 paper in which he also raised the issue of the dual nature of archaeological assemblages throughout the Southeast. The concept is now implicit in our thinking about the evolution of prehistoric peoples in the Southeast, and it is reflected in our taxonomies. We speak of a Hopewellian complex—specific artifacts and ceremonial practices associated with burial mounds—that is present among diverse populations from Florida northward to the Great Lakes and west to the Mississippi River. A village site, excavated by one archaeologist and associated with one ceramic assemblage, might be given one name, while a burial mound of the same people, excavated by a different archaeologist and associated with another ceramic assemblage, might be called something else (e.g., the Gunterland

III secular assemblage and the Copena sacred assemblage along the Tennessee River in northern Alabama; Walthall 1972:143–144). In some cases it has been only since the late 1970s that it was realized that the same people were responsible for both sites and both ceramic assemblages.

The same sacred–secular dichotomy was also present in Mississippian times, when great uniformity existed in ceremonial paraphenalia, mound construction, and even the patterns of settlement hierarchy over much of the Southeast and Midwest. But again, differences in secular, village assemblages were present.

Although the sacred–secular dichotomy is a useful taxonomic designation, we should remember that such a division was not necessarily recognized by the Southeast aborigines. What we classify as mundane or holy might have had different meanings to them.

The concept of Weeden Island might best be thought of on the same taxonomic level as Hopewellianism and Mississippianism (although like those two terms, Weeden Islandism" is a mouthful). In other words, we have a sacred complex, known mainly through the excavations of mound sites, that is called Weeden Island and that developed out of the earlier Yent and Green Point, Hopewellian-related complexes. The Weeden Island I sacred complex is best known from the many sites excavated by Moore, from the Weeden Island type site in Pinellas County, from the Kolomoki site, and now from the McKeithen site. That complex dates between ca. A.D. 300 and 600, although a later terminal date may be possible. Within the region in which the sacred complex was present, there was some geographic variation, such as along the Florida peninsular Gulf Coast.

The following are the working names assigned to the various secular assemblages found in the villages associated with Weeden Island I mound complexes in both the heartland and

peninsular regions. These cultures are Weeden Island I period cultures and most evolved *in situ* into Weeden Island II period cultures (Milanich 1980b:13–14; Milanich and Fairbanks 1980:96).

1. Cades Pond is a Weeden Island I culture located in North-Central Florida that evolved from an earlier Deptford culture. This Weeden Island–related culture was replaced about A.D. 700 by the intrusive Alachua tradition (Milanich 1971).

2. The late Manasota culture located within the Central Peninsular Gulf Coast is a Weeden Island I and II culture (with none of the secular ceramics) that developed out of the early Manasota culture. A Weeden Island–related culture, Manasota probably evolved into the Mississippian period Safety Harbor archaeological culture.

3. The North Peninsula Gulf Coast Weeden Island–related culture is a Weeden Island I and II culture found along that coast from Pasco County to the Big Bend area of Florida (Taylor County). Its secular assemblage apparently evolved out of the earlier Deptford assemblage and developed into Mississippian period assemblage(s) related to Safety Harbor. At the Crystal River site a Yent and Weeden Island burial mound is present as well as later temple mounds of the Mississippian period.

4. The McKeithen culture is a Weeden Island I and II assemblage in North Florida that may persist in time well after other Weeden Island II cultures. It is associated with the heartland variant of the sacred assemblage.

5. Northwest Weeden Island is a Weeden Island I and II culture found in the panhandle region, especially along the coast and extending inland up the river valleys.

6. Kolomoki Weeden Island is a Weeden Is-

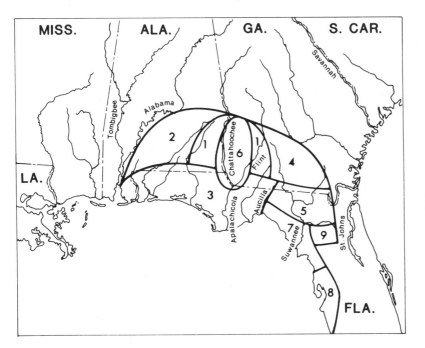

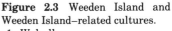

Figure 2.3 Weeden Island and Weeden Island–related cultures.
1. Wakulla
2. Southeast Alabama
3. Northwest Florida
4. Southwest Georgia
5. McKeithen
6. Kolomoki
7. North Peninsula Gulf Coast
8. Manasota
9. Cades Pond

land I culture in the lower Chattahoochee Valley and probably encompasses sites in adjacent parts of Alabama and Georgia.

We might add one other culture, Wakulla Weeden Island, a Weeden Island II culture that apparently was present in the upper portion of the Apalachicola River Valley, extending up the Flint River and into southeastern Alabama. As already noted, the check stamped Weeden Island pottery characteristic of this culture may have come from southeastern Alabama where the check stamped ceramic complexes have received several names. We might also add to this list the undefined Southeast Alabama and Southwest Georgia Weeden Island cultures, which have received little study outside the Kolomoki and Wakulla regions. The preceding list is summarized graphically in Figure 2.3.

Obviously, these are working taxonomic terms; most of these Weeden Island and Weeden Island–related secular cultures have received little study (see Milanich and Fairbanks 1980:96–105, 115–117, 124–131, for summaries of life-styles practiced by the Cades Pond, Wakulla, and various coastal-dwelling Weeden Island peoples).

In short, Weeden Island is several things. It is a secular ceramic complex found at most village sites in the heartland region, a complex that changed through time. It is also a sacred or ceremonial complex found within the heartland region with variations present in the west and north-central portions of peninsular Florida. This Weeden Island sacred complex might be thought of as a system that evolved from earlier, Hopewellian-affiliated belief and behavior patterns held by many peoples in the Southeast and Midwest. Weeden Island and Weeden Island–related cultures are those archaeological cultures that participated in this sacred, socioreligious system, whether or not their potters decorated all of their vessels with Weeden Island designs.

Weeden Island also represents a time period, A.D. 200–900 (but with variations), within a geographic region. When we reach the fringes of those temporal and geographic distributions, there is increased variation. Most likely the people living on the fringes of the Weeden Island territory in Alabama at A.D. 500, or those living at the Weeden Island site itself at A.D. 500, did not even realize they were on the verge of being taxonomically excised right out of the scope of this book.

At this point it might be fair for any of our readers to say, "Gee, for almost a century of work (including more than four decades of modern archaeology), you have not developed the concept much." But we can blame that on sampling error (an excuse akin to computer error); we simply have not presented all of the known data on Weeden Island in this chapter. We will try to weave portions of it into discussions in subsequent chapters, using the McKeithen Weeden Island culture as a case study against which to compare those data. Even though North Florida was not the center of the Weeden Island universe (although it was in the heartland region, positioned in the lateral portion of the left ventricle), the relative recentness of the work at the McKeithen site makes it a useful measure against which we can compare other sites and cultures, thereby helping to bring the concept of Weeden Island to adulthood.

3

Patterns of Site Location and Prehistoric Occupation

To many readers, the name Florida conjures up visions of sawgrass-filled everglades, white sand beaches with swaying palm trees, tropical flowers, and walking catfish. Although these features are present in portions of the state, especially the southernmost quarter, they are not found in the Weeden Island region and they are certainly not present in North Florida. (There are some Gulf Coast beaches, but their distribution is much more restricted than on the Atlantic Coast; there is nothing comparable to Daytona Beach on the Gulf Coast of Florida.) In North Florida, as well as in most other non-coastal locales within the Weeden Island heartland region, pine or mixed pine and hardwood forests with their associated animal and plant populations predominated in the past.

Interspersed among the forests in North, North-Central, and Northwest Florida (especially the Tallahassee Red Hills region east of the Apalachicola River) are numerous lakes. Tucked among these lakes within western North-Central Florida are wide expanses of freshwater prairies and marshes, habitats of major importance to the Cades Pond Weeden Island–related culture (Cumbaa 1972; Milanich and Fairbanks 1980:96–111). Such ecological differences within the Weeden Island re-

gion, including the coastal salt marshes used by a very small proportion of all the Weeden Island peoples, were a major factor in the differences that existed among the Weeden Island villagers. Life-styles, especially among the Weeden Island I peoples to whom agriculture apparently was not of great relative importance, depended on the natural environment. People living within different physiographic regions evolved different subsistence strategies with appropriate material culture assemblages. It is not such a coincidence, then, that village artifact assemblages, including ceramic complexes, differed among Weeden Island peoples.

Coastal Weeden Island peoples constituted only a very small percentage of the total Weeden Island population, probably less than 5% based on total geographic area occupied. And although those coastal peoples took a number of species of shellfish and fish from the shallow, inshore waters of the Gulf of Mexico and the adjacent salt marshes, they were still very dependent on plants and animals of the coastal strand, oak–magnolia hammocks. It is perhaps no coincidence that the dense distribution of coastal shell middens along the Florida peninsular coast in Levy, Citrus, and Hernando counties, including the famous Crystal River site, correlates with this coastal distribution of hardwood hammocks.

As a consequence of their geographic and environmental distribution, the Weeden Island peoples may be characterized as users of forest and freshwater habitats and the resources of those habitats, though a small percentage relied on resources of saltmarsh and marine habitats. Often inland sites are within a few kilometers of lakes, creeks, marshes, or swamps. Rarely are sites found on the banks of major rivers, like the Apalachicola, Chattahoochee, and Suwannee. Rather, sites tend to be adjacent to small creeks or springheads that empty into those larger waterways. Even along the Gulf of Mexico, most village sites are situated next to spring-fed creeks that empty into the marshes. From such locales, villagers had access to a variety of environmental habitats within only a few kilometers. Much of the Weeden Island region is an environmental mosaic of terrestrial and aquatic habitats—a jigsaw puzzle of overlapping resources rather than a system of broad, dispersed zones.

Thus, like nearly all of the aboriginal inhabitants of the southeastern United States during the first millenium A.D., the Weeden Island peoples lived adjacent to freshwater sources, often near other aquatic habitats, that provided fish, shellfish, and other animals. Their villages were usually located in deciduous or mixed pine and deciduous forests, from which the largest variety and amount of foods could be extracted.

NORTH FLORIDA: REGION OF THE McKEITHEN WEEDEN ISLAND CULTURE

Prior to the initiation of our project in 1976, almost nothing was known about the archaeology of the region now called North Florida. As noted in Chapter 1, the only published accounts were those of Goggin (1950), regarding an early lithic site in Suwannee County (Paleoindian and Early Archaic period?), and Deagan (1972), who described the collections from a Spanish mission (seventeenth century) site located in Columbia County (which had been excavated by Goggin). Based largely on linguistic data gleaned from ethnohistorical documentation (Milanich and Sturtevant 1972) and the recognition of the environmental zone known as the Middle Florida Hammock Belt (Harper 1914: 254–265), it had been surmised that the present regions of North and North-Central Florida together should constitute one culture region. That area was the same as the sixteenth-century territory of the various western Timucuan groups, the aboriginal inhabitants of that region at historic contact. Originally, Goggin (1947) had named this region Central Florida, while Milanich (1971:1) later referred to it as North-Central Florida. The eastern boundary was demarcated by the region of the St. Johns tradition (Goggin 1952) and the western boundary by the coastal flatlands. The northern edge was the Florida–Georgia state line; the region extended southward to Lake County.

When we began our project, it became immediately evident, based on examination of ceramic collections and site reconnaissance, that the region that we eventually named North Florida needed to be separated from the more southerly North-Central Florida region (Milanich and Fairbanks 1980:30–33). Our evidence for the uniqueness of North Florida comes from physiographic, archaeological, and ethnohistorical data. The desire to define North Florida as a discrete unit also came from a heuristic need to define our project region; and future research, especially work in the Madison County part of the region, is needed to better define the northwestern boundary. The Aucilla River is an arbitrary marker between the North and Northwest regions; as yet we do not have sufficient information on differences between the Weeden Island I cultures east and west of the

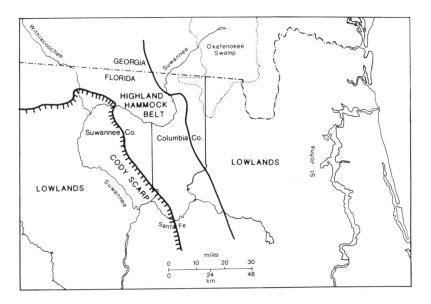

Figure 3.1 Natural features of Columbia and Suwannee counties and adjacent portions of North Florida.

river to decide where to divide the continuum. Indeed, our own work in Columbia County shows differences between the Weeden Island I village pottery assemblage in the northernmost portion of the county and the general McKeithen site locale, suggesting that still finer divisions may be needed in the future.

In our present definition of North Florida, the Santa Fe River, which originates in Lake Santa Fe in northeasternmost Alachua County and progresses westerly, ultimately emptying into the Suwannee River, is the southern boundary (Figure 3.1). Several small streams—New River, Olustee Creek, and Ichetucknee River—flow into the Santa Fe, which forms the present-day political boundary between Alachua and Gilchrist counties to the south (in North-Central Florida) and Suwannee, Columbia, Union, and Bradford counties to the north (in North Florida). Its status as a political boundary seems to go back in time almost 2000 years. During the post-Deptford, Weeden Island I period, after about A.D. 200, the river served as a boundary between the Cades Pond culture to the south and the McKeithen Weeden Island I

culture in the north. After about A.D. 700, the Alachua tradition peoples were in North-Central Florida (Milanich and Fairbanks 1980: 169–180), while the late McKeithen Weeden Island peoples lived to the north. In the sixteenth and seventeenth centuries the river was the territorial division between the Timucuan-speaking Potano in Alachua County and their linguistic relatives, the Utina, in Suwannee and Columbia counties (Milanich 1978d: 69–81). This is quite remarkable since even by Florida standards the Santa Fe is not a large river.

The eastern boundary of North Florida, separating it from the St. Johns region (also called East Florida), is not as well demarcated. A north–south line from Macclenny, Florida to Lake Santa Fe, marking the halfway point between Lake City and the St. Johns River, almost evenly divides the coastal lowlands of that region. These lowlands are mainly composed of pine forests with scrub oaks, saw palmetto, and other species as understory. Portions contain marshes and cypress and bay swamps. They were not prime habitat for aboriginal hunting and gathering or agriculture and even today are not densely inhabited. The relative number of archaeological sites in these lowlands is not as high as in certain other Florida habitats.

On the other hand, west of Lake City, in the central part of North Florida, and to the east along the St. Johns River, there are numerous archaeological sites of the McKeithen Weeden Island culture and the St. Johns culture, respectively. The intervening pine forests—Lake City to the St. Johns valley—apparently constituted a little-inhabited buffer zone between those two cultural regions. The farther east or west from our boundary line, the more sites there are. Although archaeological surveys in Baker, Bradford, and Clay counties have been rare, the available evidence (including negative evidence: a lack of collections from those counties brought to the Florida State Museum) substantiates the claim that this was a buffer zone. One survey by Ruple (1976) of 8000 acres along the remnant littoral feature called Trail Ridge, which runs north–south through the McKeithen Weeden Island–St. Johns region buffer zone (located about 32 km west of the St. Johns River), revealed 10 archaeological sites (1 per 32.5 km^2. A total of only 29 potsherds was recovered from the surfaces of the 8 ceramic-bearing sites; 7 of the sites may be single-episode camps and one site may have been used over a slightly longer period of time. When viewed as a single complex, the potsherds from all 8 sites are very similar to McKeithen Weeden Island II collections made in North Florida.

The northern boundary of North Florida is placed at an east–west line drawn through Valdosta, Georgia, in Lowndes County. This is the ecotone between the Middle Florida hammock land, which extends north from Madison and Hamilton counties in Florida, and the pine–wire grass region of south-central Georgia. North of this boundary as far as the Ocmulgee River big bend area, almost nothing is known archaeologically. Larson (1980:35–65) has noted that the pine barrens were little inhab-

ited by argriculturalists during the Mississippian period; and, other than the river valleys, the same seems to be true during earlier times. A survey by Marrinan (1976) of a limited portion of the Little Satilla watershed in Wayne and Appling counties (within the pine barrens) in southeast Georgia failed to reveal a single camp or village of any period; only one chert tool was found. Local residents also knew of almost no sites in the area. Like the buffer zone to the east of North Florida, the immediate region to the north also seems to have been little occupied by aborigines.

Most of the southwestern boundary of North Florida also is demarcated by a change in vegetation with the accompanying changes in soils, topography, and underlying geological strata. This change is much more abrupt, however, than the environmental changes to the north and east and is marked by the transition from pine–oak forest to the Gulf Coast pine forests of the coastal lowlands. Like the lowlands to the east of North Florida, this zone was relatively uninhabited by aboriginal peoples. The lowlands begin east of the Suwannee River; west of the river the lowlands are very poorly drained. Even today few roads cross the wet lowlands and few people live in the piney woods portions of Taylor and Lafayette counties, except in the local, slightly higher areas where pockets of hardwood are present.

An exception to the general settlement pattern is along the Fenholloway River and Spring Warrior Creek near Perry, Florida, in Taylor County, where Weeden Island sites have been found by local collectors. These sites, like the Crystal River site to the south, are located in the locally more numerous hammocks that extend from Perry to the coast and down the coast for about 30 km.

Completing our circumnavigation of North Florida is the western boundary, which is placed tentatively at the Aucilla River separating Jefferson and Madison counties. This is the

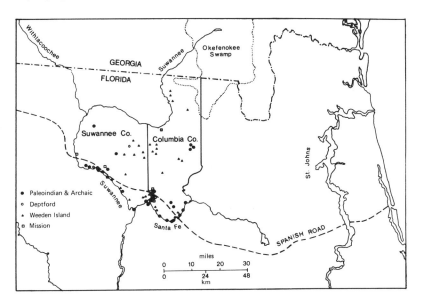

Figure 3.2 Site locations in Columbia and Suwannee counties. Some symbols represent closely spaced sites.

location where the mixed hardwood and pine forests of the Tallahassee Red Hills of Northwest Florida, aboriginal home of the Muskhogean-speaking Apalachee, meet the forests of North Florida, home of Timucuan peoples. Fort Walton Mississippian period sites are not known from east of the river, nor are Swift Creek sites. However, the archaeology of prehistoric Madison County is also almost totally unknown, and this western boundary may eventually be shifted, perhaps eastward to the Suwannee River. Having skirted North Florida and recounted aspects of its cultural environment, it is now time to penetrate the region and to examine the distribution of natural features within it.

PHYSIOGRAPHY

Even from across the room a glance at the 3- by 3.5-m composite, color map of Suwannee and Columbia counties that hangs on the wall of Milanich's office reveals three things. (The map is made up of individual United States Geo-

logical Survey (USGS) $7\frac{1}{2}'$ quadrangle sheets showing topography and other features; some of these features are shown in Figure 3.2.) First, the Suwannee River, flowing south out of the Okeefenokee Swamp in southeastern Georgia, does not flow directly to the Gulf of Mexico. Once it passes the hamlet of Purvis Still, about 25 km south of the Georgia–Florida state line, it acts like a North Florida tourist, turning west, then northwest, south, east, and southeast before tiring out and flowing more sedately to the Gulf. The result of this wandering is a dromedary-like hump that, appropriately enough, is Suwannee County.

An explanation for this behavior is simple. Where the river flows out of the lowlands toward Suwannee County it has an elevation of about 25 m above mean sea level (AMSL), much lower than the highlands in northern Suwannee and southeast Columbia counties with their elevations from 60 to 45 m AMSL. The river simply flows around the highlands, eventually reaching the Gulf coastal lowlands and the wet flatwoods where it again flows almost due south to the Gulf of Mexico.

The second physiographic feature apparent from the composite map is a natural division that runs from northwest Suwannee County southeast across that county and on across southernmost Columbia County down into North-Central Florida. That line represents the Cody Scarp, a relict marine shoreline that separates the Middle Florida Hammock Belt (the central highlands) from the beginning of the slope to the Gulf Coast (the lowlands). The portions of Columbia and Suwannee counties below this scarp are characterized by karst topography and numerous sinkholes, which are formed by solution of the underlying Miocene Hawthorne formation, composed of phosphatic limestone, sand, clay, marl, and fuller's earth. In general the region above the scarp, both in North and North-Central Florida, is characterized by more hardwoods mixed with pines and by richer soils and good drainage. The Tallahassee Red Hills in Northwest Florida also are located in the highlands above the escarpment.

Finally, the map clearly illustrates the presence of a longitudinal band of higher land with numerous lakes and marshes that runs through the central portion of North Florida. At its widest, this band—the northern portion of the hammock belt—is about 30 km across, narrowing as it leaves Suwannee and Columbia counties into Hamilton County and eventually disappearing as the wire grass region of south-central Georgia is reached. This band of land, which we refer to as the North Florida highlands, has on its eastern edge the town of Lake City and on its western the town of Live Oak. It was a prime area for settlers to establish farmsteads in the early nineteenth century when that area was first permanently occupied by whites.

This highland zone can be differentiated from the lowlands on both the east and west sides. The latter are drained poorly and, as we have seen in our discussion of the boundaries of North Florida, extend beyond the Suwannee River in the west and beyond the town of Lake City in the east. Anyone knowledgeable about aboriginal subsistence patterns could easily rank these three zones—the highlands and lowlands in North Florida and the wetter lowlands that lie outside that region and closer to the coast—in terms of relative suitability (and popularity) for aboriginal habitation. We would expect the best zone to be the highland hammock belt, the narrow band extending north between Lake City and Live Oak. Less desirable would be the lowlands on each side; almost never inhabited, in fact quite unsuitable for year-round use, are the coastal lowlands that remain wet much of the year. The aboriginal settlement pattern that we have begun to reconstruct corroborates this ranking; however, we found the numbers of sites in the drier lowlands to be higher than expected. This can be explained by the realization that elevation is not the major factor in determining vegetative communities. More important is the underlying geological substrate; in our North Florida case the same limestone formations underlie both the highlands and the lowlands. Because of this, most of the same floral and faunal communities (and resources) are found in both the highlands and the lowlands, making them almost equal as valued settlement areas.

NATURAL ENVIRONMENT

The casual visitor to Florida, traveling by automobile along Interstate 75 on the way to Disney World or the beaches to the south, regards North Florida as a prolonged inconvenience. To the motorist jaded by the heroic proportions of the Appalachians, then lulled by the undulating piedmont, the coastal plain of Georgia and Florida may seem flat and featureless. Tourists who venture beyond their car windows to observe the still rural landscape more closely will, however, discover that North Florida harbors a mosaic of distinctive habitats.

Habitats within this North Florida environmental mosaic, like most of the northern interior of peninsular Florida, fall into two categories: freshwater aquatic and terrestrial. These in turn can be divided into separate habitats or communities. Wetland habitats include permanent and intermittent creeks, the Suwannee River and its major tributaries, ponds, lakes, marshes, and swamps (Berner 1950). The variety of aquatic habitats is perhaps most dramatic in the highlands. The underlying Hawthorne limestone stratum is porous and allows water to percolate downward through it into the underground natural reservoir. Thus, rather than being drained by a dentric stream system that eventually flows to the ocean, a system common to most of the Southeast, the subregion is distinguished by a number of freshwater habitats the water volumes of which vary according to rainfall and subsurface water table conditions. Such habitats also occur in the lowlands, products of a similar limestone stratum.

Local residents in Live Oak and Lake City and the rural farmsteads between are in almost uniform agreement that groundwater levels are greatly reduced today from, say, 25 years ago. Agriculture, mining, and other activities apparently have used up freshwater supplies, lowering surface-water levels. Lakes that contained water 10 years ago are in some cases dry today. By implication, North Florida contained larger areas of aquatic habitats during aboriginal times than it does presently.

The highland area of North Florida between Live Oak and Lake City and surrounding the McKeithen site does contain numerous aquatic habitats even today. Some of them are: Workman Lake, Dexter Lake, Lake Louise, Campground Lake, Johnson Pond, Sistrunk Pond, Tank Pond, Little Hell Lake, Gum Slough, White Lake, Peacock Lake, Batchelor Lake, Tiger Lake, Scott Pond, Brim Pond, Sand Pond, Brandy Lake, Blue Lake, Button Push Pond, Flag Pond, Deep Lake, Crab Lake, Crawford Lake, Lake Wilson, Lake Lona, Hancock Lake, Lake Jeffery, Alligator Lake, Lake Hamburg, Lake DeSoto, Low Lake, McClelland Pond, Classy Lake, Wellborn Lake, Grissom Hole, Bethea Lake, Bell Lake, Bell Prairie, Long Pond, Lake Ogden, Indian Pond, Johns Pond, Orange Pond, and Indian Mound Swamp. Topography suggests that with higher water tables, many of these lakes, ponds, and marshes would have been connected. A local resident told Kohler that during a flood in 1928 it was possible to go by boat from the McKeithen site to White Springs on the Suwannee River.

Small creeks flow between some of the ponds and swamps, draining higher ones into lower ones. Such systems are not common, and they apparently were valued locales for early Weeden Island villages. In a few instances, such as with the Rocky Creek system, the creeks flow into the Suwannee River. The McKeithen site itself is situated adjacent to Orange Creek, which flows eastward from the town of Wellborn into Orange Pond. Until recent times, when a dam was built on it, Orange Creek was a small, but active stream winding through a floodplain and bordered by bluffs several meters high. The creek, which serves as the north boundary of the McKeithen site, is typical of such creeks in North Florida.

The wetland habitats are home to a variety of fish, reptile, and amphibian species as well as an attraction for wading birds and other birds that feed off fish and other aquatic animals. Species identified among the poorly preserved and very rare faunal materials from the McKeithen site include mudfish (*Amia calva*), catfish (*Ictalurus* sp.), largemouth bass (*Micropterus salmoides*), mud turtles (*Kinosternon* spp.), soft-shelled turtle (*Trionyx ferox*), chicken turtle (*Deirochelys reticularia*), and alligator (*Alligator mississipiensis*).

A more detailed picture of aquatic resources

used by early Weeden Island peoples was developed from a Weeden Island I period Cades Pond culture site in eastern North-Central Florida reported by Cumbaa (1972). The site, located adjacent to several extensive aquatic habitats in Alachua County, produced a rich assortment of well-preserved animal remains, including the following fish, reptiles, and amphibians (in addition to those just mentioned for the McKeithen site): garfish, gizzard shad, chain pickerel, lake chubsucker, sunfish, warmouth, speckled perch, toad, frog (*Rana* sp.), Southern leopard frog, amphiuma, greater siren, additional species of mud turtle, musk turtle, pond turtle, and 10 species of snake, many of which are found in or around water. Species of water birds from the Cades Pond site were white ibis, sandhill crane, coot, egret, and two species of heron. Pond snails were also present at the site, while freshwater clams were recovered from McKeithen. Eventually, we hope to locate a Weeden Island site in North Florida with similar excellent preservation to verify and quantify the importance of the aquatic animal species to the Weeden Island peoples in that region.

As varied as the aquatic habitats are the terrestrial vegetative communities in North Florida, which include several types of pine and mixed pine and deciduous forests (Snedaker *et al.* 1972). Local geological conditions and past and present human activities, as well as natural fires, all affect the types and succession of vegetative communities. Sand pine scrub forests, the overstory of which is dominated by a dense growth of the sand pine (*Pinus clausa*), are generally found on infertile, drier sands. Scrub oak (*Quercus virginiana* var. *maritima,* a dwarfed variety of the true live oak), myrtle oak (*Q. myrtifolia*), and Chapman oak (*Q. chapmanii*) along with saw palmetto (*Serenoa repens*) and scrub palmetto (*Sabal etonia*) comprise the majority of understory species.

Sandhill communities are much more open and parklike than the scrub. They contain long-leaf pine (*P. palustris*) along with mainly turkey oak (*Q. laevis*) and several other species of oaks. Today the longleaf pines are heavily timbered out. Wire grasses (*Aristida stricta* and *Sporobolus* spp.) form abundant ground cover. Fire, which kills the oaks but does not affect the fire-resistent pine seedlings, is necessary to the growth of the longleaf pine forest. Without fire, such communities climax as hammocks.

Found both in the highland and lowland portions of North Florida are the flatwoods, forests of slash pine (*P. elliottii*), longleaf pine, and pond pine (*P. serotina*) with some hardwood scattered throughout (e.g., oaks, magnolias, and a variety of other species). Such communities are typically found on flat topography with poorly drained, generally acidic soils. The understory of the flatwoods is often quite dense.

Interspersed among these forests are hammocks dominated by deciduous tree species. In the Middle Florida Hammock Belt, including much of North Florida, such hammocks were extensive in aboriginal times. Hammocks represent a successionary climax. The rich diversity of plant and animal species within these hammocks made them valued for settlement by aboriginal populations. The relative amounts of wetness with a hammock determines the constellation of plant species present and allows the classification of the hammock as xeric, mesic, or hydric. Typical of the overstory of most of the hammocks are laurel oak (*Q. laurifolia*), live oak (*Q. virginiana*), palm (*S. palmetto*), hickory (*Carya glabra*), and magnolia (*Magnolia grandiflora*). Frequency of these and other species vary according to relative wetness. Xeric hammocks are most often associated with scrub and sandhill communities, while hydric hammocks are often found in flatwoods where drainage is poor.

The most diverse vegetative community and undoubtedly the most important to Weeden Island peoples is the mesic hammock. Portions of the McKeithen site that have not been disturbed are typical of such hammocks in North Florida. By modern aesthetic standards the live oak–hickory–magnolia mesic hammocks with their diversity of plant and animal life are magnificent. At the McKeithen site, in addition to the triad of oak–hickory–magnolia species, other important plants include water oak (*Q. nigra*), American holly (*Ilex opaca*), smilax (*Smilax* spp.), wild grape (*Vitis* spp.), dogwood (*Cornus* spp.), wild plum and cherry (*Prunus* spp.), persimmon (*Diospyros virginiana*), blueberry (*Vaccinium* spp.), and huckleberries (*Gaylussacia* sp.). In addition, a host of other shrubs and trees are present. By any standard, mesic hammocks are a valuable resource.

The aboriginal vegetative communities of North Florida have been severely reduced in area by modern timbering and farming. (Another glance at Milanich's wall map shows the vast extent of land under cultivation.) And the effects of more than 150 years of white settlement in North Florida have been just as traumatic for the animal populations that inhabited the forests (and some of the aquatic habitats) as for the forests themselves. Increases in human settlement have decreased the animals' habitats, resulting in a decimation of some animal populations. Prior to the nineteenth century, the primarily carnivorous faunal population of the North Florida forests included panther (*Felis concolor*) and alligator, red wolf (*Canis niger*) and grey fox (*Urocyon cinereoargenteus*), bobcat (*Lynx rufus*), mink (*Mustela vison*), muskrat (*Ondatra zibethicus*), otter (*Lutra canadensis*), and a variety of raptorial birds and snakes (mink, muskrat, and otter inhabited aquatic habitats.)

Although all of these animals were probably used by the Weeden Island villagers (and all are represented in faunal assemblages from other Florida sites), they were not as important in the diet as the herbivores, including a variety of aquatic fishes and turtles in addition to the hammock-dwelling species. Rabbits (*Sylvilagus*

floridanus and *S. palustris*), several species of squirrel (*Sciurus* spp.), opossum (*Didelphis virginiana*), raccoon (*Procyon lotor*), and black bear (*Ursus americanus*) all have been identified from other northern Florida aboriginal sites and are known to have been inhabitants of the McKeithen region.

The largest amount of faunal bone of a single species recovered from the McKeithen site, as at every inland site in northern Florida, is white-tailed deer (*Odocoileus virginianus*). This efficient herbivore, a dietary mainstay, could turn the North Florida vegetation into meat protein for the Weeden Island villagers. During our research project in Suwanee and Columbia counties, deer, snakes, rabbits, squirrels, raccoon, and opossum were the only wild mammal species observed.

We can speculate that the subsistence system of the early McKeithen Weeden Island peoples, like that of nearly all Weeden Island I peoples, was a generalized one dependent on a variety of plant and animal species that could be obtained in many habitats. Such a system would be less susceptable to environmental fluctuations than a system that was more specialized. We would also expect this system to be more stable and less likely to change through time. An interesting question for future research is the role of this stability between ecosystem and subsistence in preventing the adoption of a fully Mississippian life-style (as represented by a Mississippian archaeological assemblage, e.g., Fort Walton) in North Florida. Why is it that the McKeithen Weeden Island peoples did not evolve into a more ecologically specialized Mississippian-type culture with settlement hierarchies and social stratification? The same question may also be asked of much of the Florida peninsula where habitats are also arranged in a mosaic as in North Florida. We return to this question at the end of this chapter.

Before examining the settlement system of the McKeithen Weeden Island peoples in more detail, a quick look at temperature and rainfall and a short discussion of Weeden Island agriculture is needed. The climate of North Florida is said to be temperate, with freezing temperatures occurring only about 15 times a year; but that information does not reflect the true day-to-day fluctuations. Temperatures can easily range from −10°C to as high as 38°C. Modern farmers can plant in March (sometimes very early in March) and harvest as late as September or even early October. North Florida, on an average, has plenty of rainfall for agriculture. The highest average monthly rainfall is 190 mm, which occurs in July (the middle of the growing season), while the lowest rainfall, 25 mm, is in November. Yearly average, measured in Lake City, is 1300 mm. This amount exceeds the average annual potential evapotranspiration (PET) by about 20%, a comfortable surplus when it is noted that the months of highest PET are also the months of greatest precipitation.

Again, average figures belie the fact that devastating droughts do occur. In the summer of 1977, for example, a drought occurred throughout the entire growing season and corn crops withered in the fields despite the best irrigation efforts of modern agribusiness. A less severe drought also occurred in the summer of 1981, and many crops in specific locales were damaged. Because groundwater levels are lower today than in the past, farmers must rely on irrigation systems to provide sufficient water during dry spells. It is possible that even under wetter conditions the aboriginal farmers, without benefit of irrigation, may have been more restricted than modern farmers in the locales in which they could plant crops and be able to assure sufficient ground moisture in dry times. Such better watered locations occur in both the highlands and lowlands in North Florida, including some lowland locations in northeastern Columbia County where it was thought such conditions would not be found.

Did the McKeithen Weeden Island peoples and other Weeden Island groups practice agriculture, and to what extent? At the present time we have no direct evidence for agriculture (i.e., actual food remains) from any Weeden Island or Weeden Island–related site of the Weeden Island I period. Maize kernels have been recovered from one well-dated Weeden Island II site on the Apalachicola River, the Sycamore site, dated at ca. A.D. 860 (Milanich 1974).

Negative evidence is not always the best. However, despite extensive recovery efforts at a number of Weeden Island and Weeden Island–related sites—including McKeithen, 8-A-169 (which produced numerous examples of charred plant remains; Cumbaa 1972), Garden Patch in Dixie County (Kohler 1975), and other North-Central and North Florida sites—no Weeden Island I cultigens have been found. This strongly suggests that cultigens were not present in very large amounts, especially when we compare the Weeden Island data with that of the Fort Walton culture, which includes maize remains from at least six sites (Milanich and Fairbanks 1980:197). Charred maize cobs numbering in the hundreds have also been recovered from an early historic period Spanish–Utina mission in southern Suwannee County (Loucks 1979:233–236).

These data are consistent with similar information on maize presence or absence elsewhere in the Southeast. Maize is much rarer at pre–Mississippian sites than at later sites. The implication is, of course, that the appearance of Mississippian archaeological cultures with their associated complex, stratified sociopolitical system occurred along with increased agriculture. The generalized subsistence system of most Weeden Island I peoples, and those of many other contemporary societies in the Southeast, evolved into more specialized systems. Such changes probably took place during the Weeden Island II period, ca. A.D. 700–900, throughout much of the Southeast.

Although we do not have direct evidence of Weeden Island I agriculture, we can surmise that some agriculture was present (and squash and gourd ceramic effigies have been found in Weeden Island I burial mounds; Moore 1902:Figure 337, 1903a:Figure 106; Willey 1949:410–411. Evidence for maize has been recovered from contemporary archaeological cultures elsewhere in the Southeast, including South Florida (Sears 1982; Sears and Sears 1976). But the nature of such Weeden Island agriculture still remains to be investigated.

SITE DISTRIBUTION DATA FROM NORTH FLORIDA

Comparison of the distribution of archaeological sites in North Florida with environmental data allows us to begin to understand the cultural ecology of the aboriginal peoples who inhabited that region. During the past two millennia, the period encompassing the Weeden Island peoples, we are certain that there have been no major environmental changes in North Florida (recognizing the many changes since the mid-1800s caused by white settlement, especially the clearing of the virgin forests and the lowering of groundwater). Consequently, we can be reasonably sure that our knowledge of the present-day environment can be used to help interpret Weeden Island settlement patterns. This is true throughout all of the Weeden Island region: The environment of the Weeden Island peoples was essentially the same as that encountered in the early nineteenth century.

Our knowledge of the distribution of archaeological sites in Columbia and Suwannee counties comes from several sources. The largest numbers of sites have been found by recreational divers (in some cases waders rather than divers) interested in collecting arrowheads and other artifacts. Undoubtedly, the greatest

quantities of Paleoindian points and other lithic tools in the state have come from the North Florida rivers, especially the Santa Fe, Aucilla, and Ichetucknee. Because of the mineral content of the water, bones of animals and bone artifacts are also preserved in the rivers. Included among the bones are extinct species of elephant, horse, camel, cat, bison, and other animals that date from Pleistocene and immediately post-Pleistocene times.

A second source of information on site locations is the Henry H. Simpson family of High Springs, Florida, who recorded locations of a number of northern Florida sites over a 40-year period beginning in the 1920s. One son, the late Mr. J. Clarence Simpson, worked almost continuously as an archaeologist for the Florida Geological Survey from 1930 until his death in 1952. In 1966 Mrs. H. H. Simpson presented the family's collection of aboriginal artifacts to the Florida State Museum, along with records on locations of sites, excavations, and surface collections. This valuable resource contains nearly 13,000 artifacts, most from North and North-Central Florida, and includes information on both riverine lithic sites and mounds and village sites found away from the rivers and springs.

Included in the collection are more than 1000 bone and stone tools from the Paleoindian and Archaic periods; all of these artifacts were found in the Ichetucknee River. Most were collected with the aid of glass-bottomed pails (which could be pushed partially into the shallow water, allowing bottom visibility) or an ingenious glass-bottomed rowboat. Portions of the collection have been described or tabulated (Jenks and Simpson 1941; Milanich 1968; Simpson 1948).

Both the collections made by sport divers and those made by the Simpson family are very skewed, since interest was not in obtaining a total sample of artifacts from a specific site. Consequently, all of the components at a specific site may not be represented in our museum collections.

Another source of settlement information is the often extensive knowledge of the region, including locations of archaeological sites, shared by local residents. Many of the mound–village sites of the Weeden Island period in Columbia and Suwannee counties that we visited and investigated were brought to our attention by local residents.

During 1972, archaeologists working for the Florida Division of Archives, History and Records Management (FDAHRM) carried out informal surveys in two North Florida areas. Calvin Jones found several sites in southwestern Suwannee County as a part of his long-term research interest in Spanish mission sites. Most of the Apalachee and Timucuan mission sites lie along the aboriginal trail, later the Bellamy Road, which extended from St. Augustine across to Leon County (the region of the Apalachee peoples) and into the panhandle. The trail passed through southern Suwannee and Columbia counties, roughly paralleling the Suwannee and Santa Fe rivers. James Miller, another FDAHRM archaeologist, visited several sites in the Osceola National Forest and adjacent areas, recording them in the state site files. Two of the sites are in east-central Columbia County.

Lastly, site distributional data also come from two additional sources, both programs of survey and testing carried out in the late 1970s in conjunction with University of Florida and Florida State Museum archaeological projects in North Florida. During fall 1977, Loucks (1978a, 1978b, 1979), then a graduate student at the University of Florida, began an investigation into mission period aboriginal populations in southern Suwannee County, part of the territory of the Utina, a Timucuan group. Loucks wished to compare prehistoric and historic settlement patterns to see what changes, if any, might be attributed to the Spanish presence.

Surveys, including surface reconnaissance and systematic subsurface tests, were carried out in two randomly selected 800- by 160-m tracts, a third similar tract placed adjacent to a known Spanish–aborigine mission or *visita* (the Baptizing Spring site), and a fourth tract located immediately adjacent to the Suwannee River. These surveys located 12 sites of varying size and cultural affiliations.

The second survey was carried out by Sigler-Lavelle (1980a, 1980b) during a 9-month period in 1978 as a part of the overall McKeithen project. Within the context of the project, Sigler-Lavelle wished to develop a sociopolitical model for Weeden Island society in North Florida. On a more general level, it was felt that such a model would help in our understanding of the process by which societies evolved (or did not evolve) from egalitarian into ranked systems; that is, our understanding of the development of Mississippian social and political structure in the Southeast.

Sigler-Lavelle sought to determine the spatial and temporal distributions of Weeden Island sites, the types of sites present, and, as much as possible, the functional relations among sites. It was hoped that these distributions could be explained in terms of observed social and ecological factors. As it turned out, Sigler-Lavelle's survey and testing work did just that. It provides a model for human ecology in both North Florida and regions in peninsular Florida that can explain the configuration of observed prehistoric cultures, including the lack of fully Mississippian cultures (viz., Fort Walton in Northwest Florida) in those regions.

The field investigations undertaken by Sigler-Lavelle turned up 24 additional archaeological sites, most of which are from the Weeden Island period. Some of the sites contain both a mound and a village midden; others consist only of a mound or a village midden. Clusters of small sites around a single mound may reflect a community.

When we tally all of the site file information of Columbia and Suwannee counties, we find that there are 97 aboriginal sites the locations, and cultural components of which are reasonably well known (Figure 3.2). Forty-five of the sites are in Suwannee County and 52 are in Columbia County. Thirty-two of the total are riverine or spring sites; all riverine and spring sites contain Paleoindian or Archaic lithic artifacts, and less than one quarter of those contain some potsherds. An additional 15 nonriverine, nonspring sites contain lithic artifacts associated with the Paleoindian or Archaic periods.

The 50 remaining sites can be separated into the following: 10 mission period, 27 Weeden Island period (including 11 mound or mound and village sites), 3 Deptford period, and 10 probable Weeden Island period (including 3 mounds and 7 nonmound sites; small ceramic samples or, in the case of mounds, no ceramic samples are present for these latter 10 recorded sites, leaving their exact cultural association in doubt). This tally includes only major components; it ignores the fact that at 3 of the Weeden Island sites (including McKeithen), small Deptford components are present and that Weeden Island sherds are found in some of the Mission period aboriginal collections. Several of the recorded mounds have been totally destroyed and their cultural affiliations are uncertain. However, greenstone celts from 2 of those mounds strongly suggest a Weeden Island period affiliation. Indeed, there are no North Florida mounds associated with any culture other than Weeden Island.

Ninety-seven sites is a relatively small number for two northern Florida counties. By way of comparison, Alachua County (2345 km^2 in area) has 489 aboriginal sites located; in locales where 100% surveys have been carried out, site density is 3.1/km^2. The reason for the larger number of known sites in Alachua County is simple: Recording of sites and site surveys began in the late 1940s at the University of Florida. In Columbia and Suwannee counties, surveys did not begin in earnest until the 1970s.

The destruction of archaeological sites in all three counties has been phenomenal. Agriculture and land clearing for planting pines and constructing subdivisions have taken a heavy toll. If we use a site density figure for Alachua County of only 2/km^2 (for *all* periods), we can conclude that prior to nineteenth- and twentieth-century progress (the first white settlers came into the region in the first quarter of the nineteenth century), as many as 4600 sites were present. An even lower site density figure of 1.5/km^2 for Columbia and Suwannee counties (with larger zones of flatlands) yields a total of 5880 sites; clearly our 97 sites is a very small sample, about 2%.

In the following section the information that can be gleaned from these 97 North Florida sites, especially the 50 Deptford, Weeden Island, and Mission period sites, is presented along with Sigler-Lavelle's interpretations regarding McKeithen Weeden Island.

McKeithen Weeden Island Settlement Patterns

Sigler-Lavelle's research focused on Columbia County, although some sites in Suwannee County and two in Lafayette County were included in her study. Investigations began with a literature search intended to provide information on Weeden Island culture and the environment of North Florida, especially data regarding geology, hydrology, vegetation, and other factors influencing human occupation of the region.

Using these data, three prevalent vegetative communities were noted within the region. These are (1) pine flatwoods, (2) mesic hammock, and (3) sand hills. Also present were several types of aquatic habitats: (1) marshes or wet prairies with fluctuating water levels, (2) permanently watered lakes and ponds, some of which are sinkhole ponds, (3) permanently watered streams or creeks, (4) wooded swamps, and (5) the poorly drained flatwoods that occasionally are wet.

Background data also suggested that Weeden Island villages were generally associated with mounds. Thus, by using the mounds as foci, adjacent villages could be located for investigation.

A multiphase sampling scheme was devised on the basis of environmental information and mound locales, and 9 months in 1978 were spent surveying portions of North Florida. The first step was to locate, visit, and map mound sites, largely using local informants to obtain locations (thereby saving a great deal of field time). It is very doubtful if any mounds exist in Columbia and Suwannee counties for which locations are not well known to local residents (it is also doubtful that any mounds are present that have not been the recipient of at least several potholes).

Of the 11 Weeden Island mound sites, 6 are located in the highland hammock belt region between Lake City and Live Oak (Peacock Lake with 2 mounds, McKeithen with 3, and Rocky Creek, Leslie, Turkey Prairie, and Indian Mound Swamp all with 1 mound; 4 are located in the lowlands in northern Columbia County within several kilometers of the Suwannee River (Carter Mounds 1–3, each a single mound and village site, and Little Creek); and 1 mound (which is now totally destroyed) is in the lowlands near Branford in southern Suwannee County within a kilometer of the Suwannee River. Three mounds believed to have been Weeden Island are all located in the lowlands within a kilometer of either the Santa Fe or Ichetucknee rivers in southernmost Columbia County; all have been destroyed.

Seven of the 11 mound sites were selected for more intensive testing, 3 in the highlands (Peacock Lake, Rocky Creek, and Leslie Mound) and 4 in the lowlands (Little Creek and 3 Carter mounds). At each a series of 60- by 80-cm test pits were excavated on line in the four cardinal directions from the mound 25 m apart in order to locate the village midden. Middens were found on the east side of 6 of the mounds. No midden at all was found for the Rocky Creek mound in any direction and it was concluded that the construction of Interstate Highway 10 had destroyed the village (which would have been north or northeast of the mound). Each of the 6 villages was further delimited by cutting across it with a line of north–south tests perpendicular to the original line of tests that had intersected the village. In this fashion both the east–west and north–south dimensions were determined and a sample of cultural materials from the respective village sites was secured.

The next phase of the sampling sought to survey a portion of the highland region characterized by a high density of mound and village sites (all of the highland mounds were in an area roughly 16 km east–west and 8 km north–south). A transect was defined that would intersect a portion of this high–density region and, by extending the transect to the east, would also intersect portions of all 4 aquatic habitats.

This 3- by 10-mi transect (defined on USGS quadrangle maps by using sections) in Columbia County was not intended to locate or survey the mounds and their associated villages, since this had already been done. Rather, the survey was to determine the range of site types peripheral to mound and village complexes and to determine preferred types of environmental locations for sites. Each of the thirty, 1-mi^2 (2.56-km^2) sections was divided into quarter sections (120 total) and a sample of 15% was drawn. Within the targeted quarter section, a diagonal line of test pits was placed at 25- to 30-m intervals. When a site was encountered, further testing was carried out to delimit it and to gather artifact collections.

The final stage of the survey intensively sampled the locale around several of the mound and village sites. The first two sampling phases revealed some differences in artifacts between sites in northern and central Columbia County. A larger sample was needed to help determine whether these variations might be due to ethnicity, temporal differences, environmental differences (e.g., vegetation, distance to water, elevation, soils, and distance to critical resources such as those needed for subsistence or pottery making), or even intersite spacing.

Three mound areas were selected for the more intensive sampling. At the Carter Mound 1 and Little Creek sites, the surrounding 3.2–4 km were divided into quarter sections and tests were placed along diagonal transects in each section in the same fashion as the second phase of the survey. Both of these sites are in the lowlands on discontinuous sand ridges surrounded by other ridges and lowland swamps. The locale around another mound site, Rocky Creek, was similarly tested. Rocky Creek, located in the highlands, is in the north-central portion of the dense distribution of Weeden Island mound sites.

In addition to the program of testing carried out in conjunction with Sigler-Lavelle's multiphase survey and the extensive work carried out at the McKeithen site in both the mounds and village areas, Milanich and Sigler-Lavelle also tested two burial mounds (Carter Mound 1 and Leslie Mound, both in the highlands) and one village (Sam's site, located in the highlands immediately east of the McKeithen site).

The focus of this North Florida research was, of course, on the Weeden Island sites, which can be divided into several types:

1. continuous-use sand burial mounds with no evidence that would indicate an adjacent village; these are thought to result from the destruction of formerly adjacent villages;

2. continuous-use sand burial mounds with an adjacent village;

3. mound complexes (i.e., two or more mounds) each with an associated village;

4. outlying villages that together with a burial mound(s) and village (Type 2) formed a *community;* these were determined to occur within a 4.5-km distance from the mound site;

5. task-specific sites that apparently resulted from hunting or resource processing;

6. stone quarries;

7. clay exposures, which are listed as possible sites due to the lack of direct evidence of aboriginal use.

The three-stage program of survey in North Florida indicated that all of the habitation sites exhibit the same constraints on location, suggesting that such locales were more desirable than were others due to

1. access to permanent water sources (potable water);

2. location in a mesic hammock;

3. location within a distance of 0.8 km to aquatic habitats (ponds, creeks, wet prairies or marshes, swamps);

4. good site drainage;

5. location within a distance of 1.6 km to the total range of vegetation diversity;

6. location within a distance of 3–5 km to a burial mound

The results of this survey and testing program along with comparisons of other settlement data allow several general observations to be made regarding McKeithen Weeden Island settlement systems in North Florida. Foremost is the recognition that the sites that have been recorded in Suwannee and Columbia counties are only very few of the sites that probably existed prior to nineteenth- and twentieth-century settlement, construction, and farming activities, including pine farming. The sample with which we have to deal is estimated at 2% of the total, and it may be even less. Certainly a relatively large number of sites exist that are not included in this discussion; perhaps as many as 90% of all sites have been destroyed or severely disturbed. What exists today is only the bare bones of the archaeological resource.

Our sample of 97 sites is very skewed. Forty-eight percent of the total are predominantly Paleoindian or Archaic and nearly 70% of those are underwater (where they have been somewhat protected prior to discovery and recording). The remaining 50 sites are all post-500 B.C. and are of the Deptford (500 B.C.-A.D. 200), Weeden Island (A.D. 200–historic period[?]), and historic (post-1539) periods. As noted previously, the North Florida culture sequence is quite different from the sequences found to the south in North-Central Florida and to the west in Northwest Florida. For instance, no Swift Creek components or sites have been found in the McKeithen region. At the 3 Weeden Island sites that have small Deptford components (McKeithen site and 2 others), a continuum from Deptford into Weeden Island I is suggested (but not proven).

Our chronology for North Florida is tentative. The date of 1539 for the beginning of the historic period is based on the date of the passage of the de Soto entrada through the region north to Lake City and west to the Suwannee River. Using the historic period to mark the termination of the Weeden Island period is a decision that flies in the face of hard data from other Weeden Island regions. But at this time the evidence from North Florida is that the late Weeden Island ceramic complex is followed directly by the Leon–Jefferson ceramic complex. Historic period sites, some with late Weeden Island pottery, cluster along the Spanish road that passed through portions of southern Suwannee and Columbia counties. To date, only one site with Leon–Jefferson ceramics has been recognized in the northern half of either county.

Clearly a shift in settlement locales toward the south took place by the time the first Spanish *visitas* were established in the late 1580s. The Utina, almost certainly the descendants of the late McKeithen Weeden Island peoples, apparently deserted the locales that had served as village areas for nearly 1000 years, both highland and lowland locations in the upper two thirds of the region, to establish villages at and near the Spanish missions.

A working hypothesis is that the change from the late Weeden Island ceramic complex to that of the Leon–Jefferson complex that occurred by the 1580s is somehow a result of changes brought about by contact with the Europeans. The shift southward may have been due to Spanish attempts to relocate native populations in controllable mission-related villages along the major transportation route through the region. This hypothesis needs to be tested as future work in North Florida is carried out. A similar shift in settlement areas and change in ceramic complexes also apparently occurred at about the same time in Northwest Florida, the territory of the historic period Apalachee people (Fryman 1971).

Can a model be suggested that explains the observed nature of the McKeithen Weeden Island sites? Such a model should also try to explain the great variation between the densely occupied McKeithen site and other sites, such as Sam's site, which have much less dense and smaller middens. In subsequent chapters we examine the model set forth below, examining it in light of the excavated data from the McKeithen site.

The location of McKeithen Weeden Island habitation sites show a marked preference for locales adjacent to permanent water sources and to mesic hammocks. Most likely this is related to the frequency of task repetition, for example, the need to have very frequent access to potable water and to have easy (seasonal) access to hardwood nut- and fruit-bearing trees (oak, hickory, wild plum, wild cherry, etc.) as well as to a variety of aquatic habitats.

A distance of 0.8 km to multiple aquatic habitats—ponds, lakes, marshes or wet prairies, creeks, and swamps—puts the resources of those habitats in easy reach, minimizing travel and pursuit or search time and reducing risk. A distance of 1.6 km to a variety of vegetative communities also means easy access to the animal and plant resources of those habitats, minimizing effort and allowing a greater degree of sedentism for dispersed households.

It is clear to us that there is only superficial resemblance between this model and models generated and in some cases tested for Mississippian cultures (e.g., Smith 1978). Mississippian models emphasize social factors such as distance to primary and secondary civic–ceremonial centers); a pyramidal hierarchical arrangement of sites (such as primary center, secondary center, village, hamlet, farmstead, camp); and ecological factors (such as access to oxbow lakes and their fish resources, waterfowl flyways, and flood-renewed river valley agricultural soils). Some researchers have ranked Mississippian settlements according to size or distance to mound centers or even on the basis of volume of soil in mounds within a village, presumably a reflection of labor imput and importance.

At first glance, it appears that our model might rank McKeithen Weeden Island settlements as having a hierarchy similar to that suggested for Mississippian settlements. We might have a primary center (McKeithen site with three mounds), a secondary center (Peacock Lake with two mounds), outlying villages (villages with a single mound each), hamlets (villages with no mounds), camps, and so forth. However, we do not think that the evidence justifies such a model. The presence of villages with a single mound each and other villages without mounds can better be explained by a budding process due to size and subsistence factors than to a culturally defined political hier-

archy. And the actual size of both villages and mounds in the McKeithen Weeden Island region is much less than almost anything found in Mississippian cultures (colleagues from Harvard Peabody Museum's Lower Mississippi Survey once actually sneered at slides of our 1-m-high platform mounds at the McKeithen site). The McKeithen Weeden Island settlement system does not warrant a model predicting a level of cultural complexity found in Mississippian cultures. We would expect this outcome, especially if Weeden Island cultures with their generalized subsistence economies and little reliance on agriculture, preceded Mississippian cultures.

An alternative explanation of social and cultural organization for McKeithen Weeden Island, one we endorse, emphasizes the presence of small villages composed of households that together formed an interacting community of related families. As villages grew in population, reaching a size culturally and ecologically outside of an acceptable norm, new villages (consisting of one or more households) budded off and settled in locales ecologically similar to the parent village. However, our data regarding aboriginal subsistence vis-à-vis the natural environment is so poor that we cannot begin to determine these norms.

Burial in a mound adjacent to a village probably represents the physical manifestation of the lineal descent principle. The evidence for continuous-use mounds is provided by the Leslie Mound and Carter Mound 1. Burials from each of these mounds were nearly all secondary interments, and were probably stored in charnel houses or similar structures that were periodically cleaned out. Individuals in a new village, one recently budded off, might have been returned to the original village for interment. Later a burial mound at the new village might have been established.

Burial in a mound may be a permanent confirmation of lineage membership and it would allow the physical centralization of ritual obligations for lineage descendants. Religious ritual associated with lineage burial and other religious obligations provided the basis for power held by religious specialists. Periodic performance of the rituals continually reinforced that power. Such a phenomenon could have provided the base for manipulation and periodic control of religious ideology that resulted in the legitimization of nonkin social positions.

The model suggests that the system of social organization characteristic of McKeithen Weeden Island culture was somewhere between the egalitarianism of the prehistoric hunter–gatherers of the Archaic period and the chiefdoms of the Mississippian period cultures. Based on relative dating in the Southeast, that is exactly what one might expect.

Other implications of the model include the following:

1. Mound burial was guaranteed for all lineage members and burial treatment should reflect a pattern common to an egalitarian society; that is, status is differentiated on the basis of age and gender only.
2. Special status achieved by the religious specialist provided, in effect, an entrepreneurial niche for the manipulation of religion-oriented commodity production.
3. Lineage segments within environments that exhibit increased density of resources and a decrease in the distances between resources would have a competitive edge in their ability to host communitywide feasts and rituals. (Religious specialists of such villages might have had high status, analogous to a "big man," as the term is used in Harris 1977:70–73.)
4. The link between environment and production just cited is influential in the development of social differentiation between lineages and within lineage segments.
5. Mound village sites are the focus of intra-lineage interaction and would have the highest probability historically of becoming the centers of interlineage exchange systems (and of becoming the largest villages in size and complexity).
6. The importance of any one such center would diminish over time as a result of population fissioning; the splitting of village populations and the budding off of new villages are related to production, optimal density limits, and the stage of settlement expansion within the locale.

It should be clear that items 3–6 are important to our promised explanation of the differences in midden density and size between the McKeithen site and other habitation sites in North Florida. Based on the information from the McKeithen site, we argue that what we are seeing preserved archaeologically at that site is a village that grew in importance, becoming for a time a complex village that served as a center for intra- and interlineage activities and at which some ranking of lineages probably existed.

One of the McKeithen site *religious specialists* (a term used here to define a position that might have been any combination of priest, civil leader, and war leader) achieved high status, and he and his activities received special treatment and status. During that period, perhaps only one generation or even a few years, the individual was truly a "big man" who undoubtedly was supported by his own (higher ranking) lineage members and, perhaps, by other individuals. They provided support for him, of which the mounds at the site may be one observable manifestation. Also during that same period the McKeithen site was a true center, albeit a short-lived one.

The appearance and decline of such centers must have occurred at other times during the Weeden Island period. Undoubtedly sites like Aspalaga in Gadsden County in Northwest

Florida and Kolomoki in Georgia also represent such centers (Kolomoki's reputation among Weeden Island peoples must have dwarfed those of McKeithen and Aspalaga.)

It is easy to suggest that such centers and their religious specialists grew in importance as extensive agriculture and rituals related to farming increased in importance. This is perhaps what occurred at many locations in the Southeast between A.D. 700 and 1000, the evolution of existing social, political, and religious structure and ideology into those phenomena associated with Mississippian cultures and their economic systems. In other words, social and political complexity became incorporated into agricultural groups. The autochthonal models for the origins of Mississippian cultures (presently enjoying popularity, as opposed to the older migration theories) fit with these speculations.

We have one more chore before leaving this chapter, which has grown to encompass more than simply a discussion of settlement patterns, that is, an explanation for why the McKeithen Weeden Island culture did not become Mississippianized. In one sense, the North Florida aborigines did become quasi-Mississippian, or at least they became "Southeasternized." At the time of historic contact in the sixteenth century, these Weeden Island descendants shared many traits with other Southeast aborigines, including the peoples later known as Creeks. The Utina in North Florida spoke a Timucuan language quite different from the Muskhogean languages, but they shared very similar words for chiefly statuses, such as *holata* and *inihama* (which are cognates with the Creek words *holahta* and *heniha*). They also shared aspects of ideology and social and political structure (Milanich and Fairbanks 1980:216–227; Milanich and Sturtevant 1972:23–48). In the sixteenth century the Utina and other Timucuan societies certainly appear to have been chiefdoms with ranked social statuses. Living for 500 years adjacent to Mississippian peoples

might have provided the opportunity for many Southeast traits, including many Mississippian sociopolitical patterns, to diffuse into the North Florida, post–A.D. 1000 Weeden Island populations.

But North Florida with its mosaic environment and long history of a generalized subsistence pattern simply was not suited to adopting or adjusting to a fully Mississippian social and economic system with all of its associated cultural traits. Those ecological factors that Smith (1978:480–488) has defined as necessary for the maintenance of Mississippian systems are not present in North Florida. The harnessable energy from the forests of that region in Weeden Island and later aboriginal times simply does not reach the levels produced in Southeast river valleys that were accessible to Mississippian peoples.

Although we do see changes in the McKeithen Weeden Island ceramic complex between Weeden Island I and II times (the appearance of check stamped and cord marked surface treatments and the disappearance or reduction in popularity of many older decorative motifs), we do not see any abrupt changes in settlement systems. Agriculture, especially the growing of maize, might well have increased in importance in North Florida after A.D. 700. as it apparently did in many regions of the Southeast. In the McKeithen region the change must have been slow and was tacked on to the existing economic system rather than replacing it.

However, the presence of agriculture alone was not sufficient for the development of a Mississippian culture. Simply put, the resources of the North Florida environment could not support a fully Mississippian life-style.

North Florida (and North-Central Florida where the Potano, also Timucuan speakers, likewise had chiefly statuses called *inihama* without ever having had ancestors who built temple mounds or used Southern Cult paraphernalia) does provide an interesting laboratory for the study of the processes that took place in late prehistoric times and that account for the many similar cultural traits shared by the historic Southeastern Native Americans. Such information could be important to an understanding of the nature and evolution of the Mississippian cultural phenomenon.

The next several chapters examine the evidence from the McKeithen site and present our interpretations of those data, at times testing our model against those data. Chapter 9 summarized our conclusions within the context of other Weeden Island cultures and against the fabric of southeastern prehistory.

4

The McKeithen Village

This chapter presents the results of 30 weeks of research carried out by Kohler in the village at the McKeithen site. It might be pointed out, not to his credit, that he originally suggested the title "Here They Once Stewed" for this chapter (with apologies to Boyd, *et al.* 1951).

Excavations in the village had two purposes. First of all, we wished to test the hypothesis that the site represents the remains of a society in which there was some degree of inequality, or ranking, among the villagers. A second, but not less important, goal was to provide as much detail as possible concerning other aspects of the village occupation within the constraints of the available time and funding.

While the hypothesis we wished to test is hardly innovative, the examination of its test implications in the habitation area, rather than in burial or regional settlement pattern contexts, is a departure from the usual method applied to Southeast studies. It also serves to examine in greater detail several aspects of the model developed in the previous chapter. The major interest of such an approach is that it focuses attention on elites in their everyday life rather than in their special roles. The study of what distinguishes the daily life of emerging elites from their fellows promises to shed as much light on the processes of hierarchical status differentiation as does the study of how

these individuals were differentially treated in death.

The first portion of this chapter establishes a method for testing the hypothesis in a habitation area; this is then followed by a description of the archaeological remains themselves. Our discussion of test implications may appear tedious, but it is a necessary exercise in achieving some degree of understanding of the Weeden Island culture and the evolution of Southeast societies. Finally, after developing a chronology for the village, we are then in a position to return to the hypothesis and a more general discussion of McKeithen village life during the first millennium A.D.

GENERATING TEST IMPLICATIONS

To test our hypothesis, we searched ethnohistorical, ethnoarchaeological, ethnological, and historical archaeological studies for situations bearing analogous relations to the archaeological problem and group under study. An effort was made to associate aspects of society that are visible archaeologically (those that are preserved in the ground) with those—such as social organization—that cannot be directly perceived archaeologically (those that are not preserved). This could be considered an attempt to calibrate the archaeological record. For our village study, two sources of analogous relations—ethnohistory and historical archaeology—were consulted to provide such a calibration for the McKeithen Weeden Island culture. From these sources we can define archaeologically recoverable data pertinent to our study of status differentiation among the villagers.

Ethnohistory

The sixteenth-century Spanish and French explorers of *La Florida* (as a large portion of southeastern North America was then known) documented the hierarchial ranking present in aboriginal political and social systems in the Southeast. The first French chronicles from the 1560s described the North Florida Timucuan leaders and their first wives as "kings" and "queens"; the other members of the community were described as "their subjects." The French reported that as many as 40 of these kings served as vassals tied by kinship or friendship to another, more powerful lord, for example the "much respected Olata Ouae Outina Utina" of North Florida. The Spanish occasionally differentiated between these two levels of political leadership by describing the overlords as "caciques" and their vassals as "mico." Among other privileges, these political leaders had the right to have more than one wife, to assemble and direct council from a seat more elevated than the others, to enlist groups of workers for planting and harvesting, and to conduct warfare against neighboring groups. Caciques were so much the official spokesmen for their people that their villages and the surrounding areas took on their names (e.g., Potano was chief of the people whom the Spanish called the Potano and he lived in the village known as Potano. "Priests and elders," the *iaruars,* were differentiated from the king but were of sufficient

status to address him in council. On the death of one of these leaders, several days and nights of mourning were observed, and the chief's dwelling and all of his prized possessions were burned. (The preceding was summarized from René de Laudonnière in Lussagnet 1958.)

The hierarchical ranking noted in these and other reports on the Timucua represent a common pattern of aboriginal sociopolitical organization in the Southeast at the time of contact. Both more and less elaborate systems existed, however; for instance, the Natchez organization possibly was more highly centralized (Swanton 1911:100–108), while de Soto's expedition met with relatively egalitarian tribes on the western margins of the Southeast.

Among the Timucua, village leadership centered on one individual, usually a male, who enjoyed privileges not available to everyone. Villages were integrated into a more or less unsteady alliance under the leadership of a more powerful figure in another, usually larger, village, a pattern prevalent in the Southeast at the time of earliest European contact (Hudson 1976:202–213). In these organizations the power of the father was inherited by the son. Referring to the Timucua, de Laudonnière (in Lussagnet 1958:44; Kohler translation) observed that "Each man takes a wife; while Kings may have two or three, only the first is honored as the Queen, and only her children inherit the King's power and property." Swanton (1946:641–653) cites examples of such ascribed authority among the Chitimacha, Natchez, Creek, Chickasaw, coastal Algonquians, and piedmont-dwelling eastern Siouans.

High status was identified in both material and nonmaterial ways. Some symbols of rank or achievement leave no archaeological trace. Among various southeastern groups in early historic times, such symbols included tattoos, location of seat in council, and respect due an individual. Material correlates of ascribed status included possession of exotic clothing items such as the "marten" or "sable" robes reported by Elvas and Biedma (in Swanton 1946:440); feather mantles of duck down made by Natchez women for women of the honored class (Le Page du Pratz in Swanton 1911:63); and the crowns of swan feathers, which (according to the same source) could be worn exclusively by the sovereign. In reference to the Yuchi, Speck states that fans of wild turkey feathers were "The proper possession of . . . older men and chiefs who spend much of their time in leisure. . . . During ceremonies to carry the fan is a sign of leadership" (in Swanton 1946:456).

Even in cases where personal ornaments were not reserved exclusively for high-status use, important individuals (and perhaps their lineages) may have possessed such items in greater quantities or of higher quality. This category includes beads, pearls, copper gorgets, and gold or silver ornaments. It appears that high-status persons also monopolized expensive objects, that is, those that were manufactured with a great deal of effort, or from a nonlocal or scarce natural resource. Even symbols of rank that were not exotic or expensive, and that would theoretically have been available equally to all, were controlled with strong sanctions. Thus Adair (in Hudson 1976:203) says that bearers of unearned tattoos would be forced to remove them, and anyone taking a seat in council above his rank would be the object of public derision.

Status was also reflected by the size, features, and locations of dwellings. The Gentleman of Elvas, who accompanied the de Soto expedition, described the residences of the principal men of a town called Toalli (probably in present-day southwestern Georgia) as follows:

> The difference between the houses of the masters, or principal men, and those of the common people is, besides being larger than the others, they have deep balconies on the front side, with cane seats, like benches; and about are many large barbacoas, in

> which they bring together the tribute their people give them of maize, skins of deer, and blankets of the country. (Smith 1968:52)

In some cases the principal residences appear to have been elevated. When seen by de Soto, the town of Osachile, which Swanton (1946:41) locates between the Suwannee and Aucilla rivers in North Florida, contained dwellings on an earth platform for "the lord and his family and the people of his service." A plaza was immediately adjacent to the platform. Although the wording of the secondhand report is ambiguous, it seems as though the dwellings "of the noblest and most important personages" were characterized by frontage on the plaza and location adjacent to the earthen platform (Garcilaso 1962:170–171).

Alliance and warfare seem to have played important roles in the society of the Timucua, who are analogous in geography and environment to North Florida Weeden Island groups. Town headmen maintained a series of peaceful alliances against a set of enemies. Warfare was frequent, often resulting in the loss of male life and the enslavement of women and children; according to de Laudonnière, it was always conducted by surprise attack. It evidently provided an opportunity for social advancement for the warriors and for recruitment of a subclass of enslaved persons. If the early 1560s experience of the French at Fort Caroline in Northeast Florida was representative, alliances appear to have been initiated and maintained by mutual exchange of finely crafted items and valuable materials among village headmen.

Even such a highly selective review of the most relevant ethnohistoric evidence suggests several important points.

1. By the sixteenth century, North Florida groups were organized into ranked but stateless societies in which status was accompanied by both material and symbolic correlates.

2. Material correlates of high status included finely crafted clothes of exotic materials, and differential access to (or even total monopoly of) a variety of goods, including those made of scarce or nonlocal materials such as silver or pearls, and labor-intensive items such as the "curiously-made ceramic vessels" mentioned by de Laudonnière (in Lussagnet 1958).
3. Size and location of dwellings apparently varied with status.
4. The roles of priest, magician, and curer were often combined in the same person, but were distinguished from the major political leader.
5. Warfare was common and alliances were necessary for group survival. Alliances were cemented, at least in part, by high-level exchange of the same material items that served as status markers.

Historical Archaeology

Historical archaeology, like ethnohistory, has the potential to provide calibrated models for prehistoric archaeology. Although it is less useful than ethnohistorical models in a direct historical approach to the archaeology of aboriginal communities, historical archaeology can provide a test of the assumptions made when generalizing ethnographic models to a different time or place.

Using data from a well-documented nineteenth-century context, Otto (1975) attempted to prove some of the assumptions habitually made by prehistoric archaeologists in their reconstruction of social systems. On Cannon's Point, St. Simons Island, Georgia, Otto excavated portions of several slave cabins, an overseer's house, and the refuse associated with the main planter's house. Historical documents confirmed that these units had been occupied by individuals of different ethnic, social, and economic statuses (Otto 1975:7–16), but all were

from a contemporaneous context. Through subsequent analysis, Otto identified categories of material remains that best differentiated the three units. While the economic and cultural setting of the Couper Plantation is not directly comparable to aboriginal North Florida, Otto's reflections concerning elements shared by all stratified societies are of interest:

> In stratified societies, status positions associated with social roles or activities are ranked in hierarchies. Upper status individuals enjoy greater prestige and have preferred access to the resources of the natural and social environments. People occupying lower status positions have less prestige and suffer impaired access to resources. . . . Some members of a stratified community are relatively affluent, though others live in relative poverty. (Otto 1975:8)

In the context of the nineteenth-century plantation, Otto clearly demonstrates that it is possible to distinguish status differences on the basis of material remains. The best indicator of difference between the free whites and the Black slaves was their housing. Both planter and white overseer components were far superior to those of the slaves in terms of "available living space; number of specialized rooms; the features available to occupants; the quality of construction materials; and expected durability" (Otto 1975:360). Most nonceramic artifacts could not be used to differentiate between the three groups; certain bone and iron button types and pipes were an exception, all of which were more frequent in the lower-status refuse. Faunal remains also reflected status differences, with higher-status levels consuming a wider range of vertebrate species.

For our purposes, however, the most important category of status indicators identified by Otto are the ceramics. He concludes that the range of ceramic types increases with status represented by the refuse component, and that certain types are especially good indicators of social status. In particular, banded wares were characteristic of the slave and overseer sites, and transfer printed wares were characteristic of the elite plantation owners. These differences may have been due to the sources of supply available to each social segment. The planter's kitchen was stocked with ceramics supplied by a factor who obtained his goods from Europe via New York packet lines. The slaves and overseers, on the other hand, may have acquired some of their ceramics from local shopkeepers who stocked the more traditional folk pattern banded wares, possibly as a response to customer preference; or the planter may have supplied them with a limited range of inexpensive, utilitarian crockery. Otto further demonstrates that the highest-status proveniences also have the highest diversity of vessel form (as measured by the Shannon–Weiner $\bar{H}$ index; see Kohler 1978b:27–28).

While the specifics of Otto's work in historic planter–slave systems on the Georgia coast cannot be directly compared to aboriginal cultures in North Florida, analogies can be drawn from the generalities true of both. In both situations, refuse of high-status components can be expected to contain a greater percentage of elite goods. We have already seen that at the time of contact such goods included objects requiring a great deal of time and effort for their manufacture; objects made of a scarce or nonlocal resource; and objects needed for specialized functions not performed by lower-status individuals—for example, in mortuary ritual. Just as the relative frequencies of banded versus transfer printed ware provided a status-group index for refuse in Otto's study, ceramic types can be found that differentiate status-group residences at an aboriginal site. Sears' (1973) sacred ceramics, which were highly correlated with ranking individuals in mounds, are good candidates for identification as elite goods. Like the banded ware bowls of Otto's study, an open, undecorated bowl form can be expected to appear in higher relative percent-

ages in the lower-status areas of the aboriginal site. Both are purely utilitarian items fulfilling everyday functions.

In addition to their obvious function of marking status, do these exotic, high-cost items have any "hidden" roles in a complex aboriginal society? Some archaeologists would argue that such items regulate trade networks and could have been exchanged for foodstuffs, and so acted as insurance against poor local conditions. Others believe that exchange of these "primitive valuables," as Dalton (1977:197–198) called them, were mainly sidelines to important exchanges of information between neighboring leaders, as in the alliance-cementing exchanges documented for the Timucua. A third explanation for the role of these items is that their owners may also be considered to have esoteric knowledge, and with that knowledge power (Helms 1979:3). Whichever of these theories might be correct for the covert social role of the items, each predicts monopolization, or at least preferential access, of exotic items by an elite, a circumstance documented time after time in many different societies.

In summary, based on ethnohistorical and historical archaeological data, we have identified five major characteristics that may be recovered in the archaeological record and that ought to be correlated with the presence of status differences, if any, at the McKeithen site. First, high-status areas of the site should be differentiated by higher concentrations of nonlocal ceramics. Assumptions pertinent to this characteristic include (1) The village "big man" and his lineage control most nonlocal exchange represented by the presence of exotic ceramics, and (2) more of these nonlocal ceramics are retained within the high-status lineage or lineages than are redistributed to other occupants of the site.

Second, it should be possible to distinguish high-status areas within the site by a greater concentration of elite pottery. This assumes that the village elite have preferential access to nonutilitarian vessel forms and to utilitarian ceramics that are more elaborate than necessity demands. We also assume that since the village elite perform functions reflecting their elite political and religious roles, they may also possess ceramics necessary to those functions. Elaborate vessels or vessels with totemistic or other special motif representations are possible examples of such vessels.

Third, as a corollary of the first two implications, high-status areas should be marked by a higher ceramic type diversity than other areas of the site. This assumes that the pottery typology assigned by archaeologists reflects the aboriginal culture's actual formal and functional ideals to some degree (cf. Deetz 1967:43–65), although some archaeologists argue that the type concept is simply a construct imposed on aboriginal ceramics (Rouse 1960:318).

Fourth, in addition to imported ceramics, materials such as bone, shell, and lithics that are not readily available locally should be more abundant in elite residential areas. (See the assumptions on which the first and second implications are based.)

Fifth, it should be possible to differentiate high-status areas by larger size and by location next to public buildings or public spaces.

To these five we can add a sixth characteristic, the correlation between settlement size and predicted social differentiation. This line of inquiry comes largely from the work of Blau (1977) who has attempted to derive a theory of social structure. Beginning with the assumption that community size and density correlate positively with social differentiation, he makes several predictions concerning the kinds of social changes that occur as size and density increase. These changes include increased intergroup conflict within a village, inequality of power, more complex division of labor, and increased concentration of authority and economic power. As community size and density increase, social roles within a village becomes more differentiated and the village as a whole becomes more important in terms of authority and economic power relative to other, nearby settlements. To examine this characteristic through archaeology, we must be concerned with estimating the size of the resident population at the McKeithen village through time and the relation of the McKeithen village to surrounding, contemporaneous settlements.

FIELD INVESTIGATIONS

Setting of the Site

As noted in Chapter 3, the principal lakes and hammocks in North Florida's highlands can be found within the Middle Florida Hammock Belt, a strip some 30 km long trending northwest to southeast along a line drawn between present-day Live Oak and Lake City. The McKeithen site is in the middle of this band of lakes and ponds, ideally situated to serve as the focus for a series of communities heavily dependent on these aquatic and hammock resources. Orange Creek forms the north border of the site. Until the 1960s when dams were erected upstream from the site, Orange Creek was a small but active stream bordered on its south bank by 2–3-m bluffs and winding through a floodplain varying from 10 to 30 m in width.

The meander belt of the creek and the protected bluffs, typical of such hammock belt locales, support mesic hammock and floodplain vegetation dominated by magnolia, hickory, water oak, American holly, and two species of dogwood. The McKeithen site itself sits on this set of small bluffs south of Orange Creek and on the sandy, well-drained soils of the Blanton and Lakeland association south of the creek that support a slightly more xeric vegetation dominated by various oaks and pines, especially slash pine, loblolly pine, laurel oak, and live

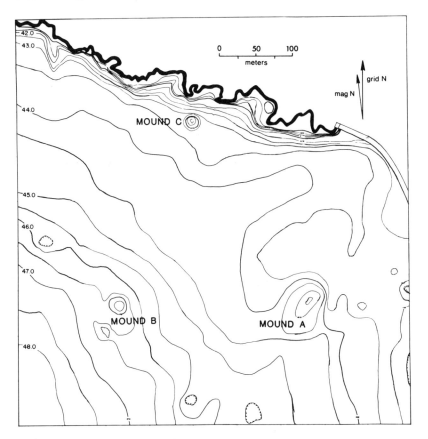

Figure 4.1 Topographic map of the McKeithen site. Contour interval is 0.5 m.

oak. Longleaf pine, once an important species on the site, was selectively removed in the 1950s.

Most of the major disturbances to the site occurred in its southern two thirds, which was used for watermelon cultivation in the 1920s and thereafter for pasture until the 1950s, when slash pines were planted. At the time of our excavation, these pines covered the southeastern two thirds of the site.

Away from the creek, the land is nearly level, with a general, gentle upward gradient toward the southwest (see Figure 4.1). Slight cultural modification of this plan can be seen in the ridge that arcs from east to west to the south of Mounds A and B, in the slight ridge that runs from north-northeast to south-southwest start-

ing just southeast of Mound A, and in the slight ridge that runs from west-northwest to east-southeast south of Mound C. These linear ridges are made up primarily of the accumulated deposits of several hundred years of human occupation. Except for the large depression at the extreme southeast of Figure 4.1, the mapped depressions appear to be borrow areas for the three mounds and possibly for the ridges marking the habitation areas.

Sampling Techniques

The test implications outlined in the preceding section demanded a great deal of information on the distribution of artifacts at the McKeithen site, which covers nearly 20 ha.

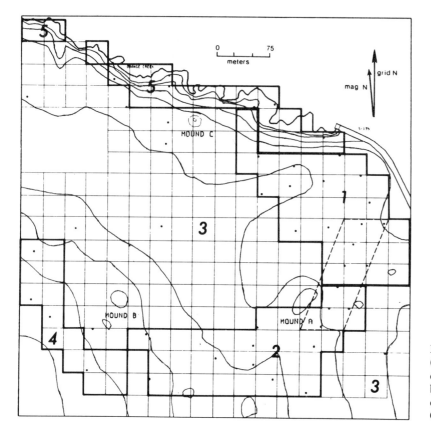

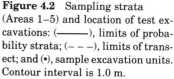

Figure 4.2 Sampling strata (Areas 1–5) and location of test excavations: (———), limits of probability strata; (– – –), limits of transect; and (▪), sample excavation units. Contour interval is 1.0 m.

Therefore, a multistage plan was initiated in the summer of 1976 that called for a low-level sample over the entire site plus more intensive excavations in limited areas. Crews of four to eight members spent three 10-week seasons mapping and sampling the village area. A grid was laid out over the entire site as the initial step in obtaining horizontal control. All village excavations were done in arbitrary 10-cm levels within natural zones and excavated soil was sifted through ¼-in. screening.

To help determine excavation strategy, an initial surface collection was made over a random sample of one third of the site. Since amounts of

disturbance and depth of forest litter varied greatly across the site, each collector was asked to rank the surface collection conditions from 1 (good) to 4 (poor). These ranks were then multiplied by the number of surface artifacts collected in each large grid unit (the collection units were 30 by 30 m in size). The resulting *richness values* provided a rough correction for the different surface collection conditions across the site.

Five sampling areas were then identified on the basis of this surface collection (Figure 4.2). Areas 1 and 2 appeared to be the primary midden areas, Area 3 appeared to be nearly sterile, and Areas 4 and 5 appeared to be fringe midden areas of low artifact concentration. The four midden areas, which were of maximum interest, were sampled at a proportion of 0.001 (thirty 2- by 2-m squares altogether). Area 3, of less intrinsic interest, was sampled at a proportion of 0.0003 (ten 2- by 2-m squares). A random numbers table was used to select these squares (for more detail see Kohler 1978b:42–81, 88–92). All the squares excavated during this sampling phase are referred to as the *probability sample.* Later, a line of nine squares was added to this sample in the critical boundary area between Areas 1 and 2 (see Figure 4.2).

The next step in the last field season was to undertake large block excavations in the northeast, east, and southwest portions of the midden. These areas were chosen on the basis of dated features (hearths, postmolds, etc.) previously encountered in the probability sample to provide the greatest possible chronological range of village materials and to investigate areas of the site that contained different assembages of decorated pottery as determined by cluster analyses (see Kohler 1978b:62–66). These more extensive excavations were also located in areas of deep midden in order to provide a large sample of pottery from stratified contexts for seriation.

Stratigraphy

The sandy, terrace-deposited sediments on the site appear to result from Pleistocene reworking of the underlying Miocene *Hawthorne formation,* a complex marine deposit rich in sand, clay, marl, limestone, fuller's earth, and phosphates (Rowland and Powell 1965:94–98). Across the site, the soils in general are either sandy clay loams or sands, both with either weak, very fine granular structure or no structure.

Three large, natural vertical zones were normally specified during excavation and in the drawn profiles: Zone I, consisting either of a dark gray plow zone or of a surface layer of gray fine sand in unplowed areas; Zone II, the area of greatest artifact concentration, which was frequently subdivided to reflect cultural depositional events; and Zone III, below the occupation and devoid of artifacts except those that had been moved downward by agents of disturbance, which included roots, gopher tortoises, and pocket gophers. (Milanich once observed a pocket gopher, whose burrow intersected an excavation unit profile, push one bushel of soil, including artifacts, out of the burrow in 40 minutes.) The artifact-bearing strata ranged in depth from 10 cm or less to 1.5 m in a few places on the creek bluffs and the southern midden ridge.

Site Size, Plan, and Materials

The general plan of the village, which appears to have remained stable over several hundred years of occupation, was a horseshoe encompassing the three mounds open to the west-northwest and with a plaza area devoid of artifacts in the center. Total size of the village, including the plaza, is 19 ha. Figure 4.3 is a SYMAP plot of the densities of all subsurface artifacts per cubic meter. A *SYMAP plot* is a computerized mapping technique with which hot spots, or areas within the village having high relative frequencies of a data category, can be identified. Where structures were intercepted, they seem to have been located on old midden, with later refuse piled on top of them; therefore it appears that Figure 4.3 represents not only the distribution of refuse but also the general location of the residences as well.

Surprisingly little attention has been paid to the total layout of prehistoric southeastern communities. Although some have attributed the development of the concept of a plaza ringed

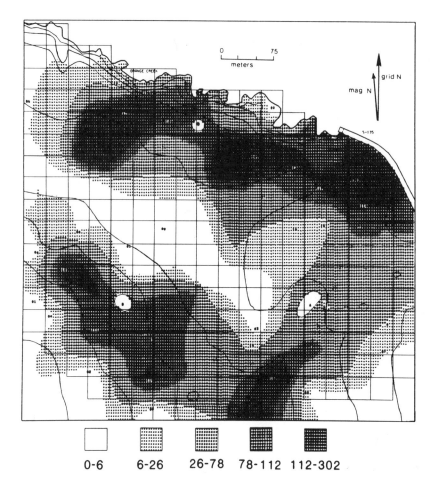

Figure 4.3 Artifact density (SYM-AP) per cubic meter. Contour interval is 1.0 m.

0-6   6-26   26-78   78-112   112-302

by residences and mounds to the Late Woodland and Mississippian periods, the McKeithen village plan indicates that this is certainly not the case. In fact, such horseshoe-shaped village schemes have been recorded for Kolomoki (Sears 1956:7–8) and other Swift Creek and Weeden Island sites (for Aspalaga, see Sears n.d.; for Snow Beach, see Phelps 1969:14–15). Lower densities of material in the eastern midden area seems to indicate that it either was occupied for a shorter period of time, or by fewer households. This leaves two primary residential areas—one adjacent to the creek, the other south of Mounds A and B—facing each other

across the plaza. Figure 4.3 shows the high artifact density in these two areas in contrast to the somewhat lower densities in the arc to the east of Mound A.

Intriguing and consistent differences between the two primary midden areas were revealed by a *discriminant analysis,* a multivariate statistical technique for distinguishing between two or more groups of observations. In this case the observations are artifact frequencies from the different village areas. Analysis clearly separated the northern, southern, and plaza areas from each other on the basis of a series of ceramic and lithic variables (see

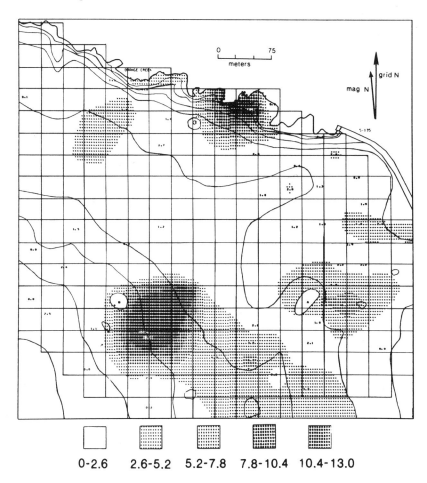

Figure 4.4 Ratio (SYMAP) of ceramic to lithic artifacts across the site. Contour interval is 1.0 m.

| 0-2.6 | 2.6-5.2 | 5.2-7.8 | 7.8-10.4 | 10.4-13.0 |

Kohler 1978b:49–56). Major differences between the three village areas that were noted include the following:

1. The northern midden has more lithic artifacts than the southern.
2. The southern midden has higher pottery counts.
3. Weeden Island Zoned Red, Weeden Island Punctated, and an unidentified punctated ceramic type are all relatively more common in the south than in the north.
4. A few pottery types such as Napier Complicated Stamped and a check stamped

type with 4–6 checks per in. are relatively more abundant in the north than in the south.

5. Silicified coral debitage also constitutes a higher percentage of the lithic materials in the northern midden area than in the southern.

Figure 4.4 displays the high ratios of ceramics to lithics east or southeast of each mound; ratio values were generally higher in the south and southeastern midden areas. Explanations for these trends can be suggested, but not proven. Perhaps detailed analysis of the lithic collections from McKeithen will suggest functional explanations for these differences.

Excavations in the Northern Midden Area

The northern midden area is bounded on one side by Orange Creek and on the other by the plaza area in the center of the site with few or no artifacts (see Figure 4.3). Two excavation units (part of the probability sample) located in the creek floodplain were sterile or nearly so, but yielded complex stratigraphies indicating that the creek actively meandered during and perhaps since the last occupation of the site.

The creek bluffs, wherever tested, yielded dense concentrations of artifacts. One excavation unit near the eastern end of the site about halfway down the creek bluff intercepted a staggered row of postmolds with extremely rich midden on one side suggesting a house structure. Two carbon samples from these features were radiocarbon dated to A.D. 640 ± 95 and A.D. 650 ± 70 (see Table 4.1). In the following season we returned to this spot to see if we could find more of this possible structure. Figure 4.5 shows a plan of extended excavations in this area and the original surface contours before excavation. Further excavation revealed that the northern and western portions had been destroyed by erosion, apparently during prehistoric times, while the center and a portion of the southern periphery could not be excavated due to large trees.

From the oval section of postmolds that remained, however, a structure measuring about 3 m north–south and 5 m east–west can be extrapolated. This is smaller than Deptford house structures reported by Milanich (1973) on Cumberland Island, Georgia, which ranged between 7 by 10 m and 4 by 8 m, and smaller too than a Weeden Island period house structure near the Apalachicola River in Northwest Florida, which was reported to be 6.2 by 8.9 m (Milanich 1974:13).

Table 4.1
Village Radiocarbon Dates and Contexts

Site and context	Lab number	Date in radiocarbon years
Northern midden		
Feature 2; probable	UM 929	A.D. 1390 ± 70
tree stump con-	UM 933	A.D. 1535 ± 70
tamination	UM 934	A.D. 1260 ± 65
Postmold associated		
with Feature 6	UM 930	A.D. 510 ± 75
Feature 9	UM 1092	A.D. 650 ± 70[a]
Feature 9 and		
postmold	UM 1091	A.D. 640 ± 95[a]
Feature 9D	UM 1257	A.D. 145 ± 100
Southern midden		
Postmold associated		
with burned sand	UM 930	A.D. 420 ± 95
Feature 12; proba-		
ble hearth	UM 1259	A.D. 245 ± 80
Feature 8	UM 931	30 ± 95 B.C.
Eastern midden		
Feature 10	UM 1093	A.D. 785 ± 75
Feature 10D	UM 1258	A.D. 265 ± 70

[a]These dates average A.D. 647 ± 55.

From the surface contours superimposed on the plan in Figure 4.5, it can be seen that the modern surface slants down towards the creek about 90 cm between the southernmost and northernmost postmolds, a slope of about 25°. There was also a slant—though of only 70 cm (20°)—while the structure was in use, raising a question as to whether it could have been used comfortably as a residence. No living floor was visible in the soil matrix, which was marked by traces of filled pocket gopher burrows and root molds. Feature 9 first became visible at about the level the postmolds bottomed out, suggesting that the interior area was dug out between 5 and 20 cm below the depth of the surrounding ground. The two radiocarbon dates from Feature 9 (see Table 4.1) can be averaged to A.D. 647 ± 55 (Long and Rippeteau 1974:209).

Features 9 and 9A both contained numerous fragments of bone, all of which were calcined;

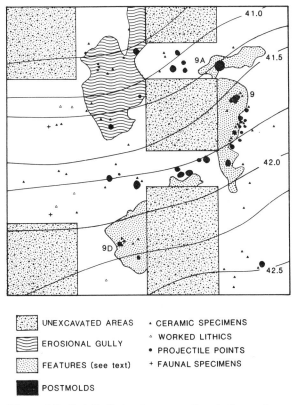

UNEXCAVATED AREAS   • CERAMIC SPECIMENS

                             ▵ WORKED LITHICS

 EROSIONAL GULLY   • PROJECTILE POINTS

FEATURES (see text)   + FAUNAL SPECIMENS

POSTMOLDS

Figure 4.5 Detail of intensive excavations in the northern midden. Area shown is 4 by 4 m.

one of these from Feature 9 was a fragmentary squirrel humerus, while the rest were identifiable only as mammal, or were not identifiable at all. Feature 9D, on the other hand, contained only six bone fragments, only half of which were burned or calcined. It likewise contained a higher ratio of pottery to lithics than the other two features.

In terms of its contents and placement relative to the structure, Feature 9 is reminiscent of features excavated inside the perimeter of a Potano house at Site 8-A-100 (Milanich 1972:44). Using ethnohistoric Timucuan parallels Milanich interpreted these as refuse from smudges under the benches or beds lining the interior walls of the house. On the other hand, at McKeithen these features could simply represent the

accumulation of debris swept off the central activity area.

The early radiocarbon date from Feature 9D (A.D. 145 ± 100) suggests that it was not associated with this structure at all. The large erosional gully shown in Figure 4.5 was active during the occupation of the site, suggesting that the creek bluff was deforested and unstable.

The symbols on the plan in Figure 4.5 indicate artifacts that were mapped in place. This was done for all sherds 5 by 5 cm or larger, worked lithic materials, and the larger faunal fragments. These bits of refuse seem to be concentrated along the row of postmolds and help define the original wall of the structure. One of the few mapped lithic materials in the eastern half of the excavations was a first-sized fragment of limestone. It was located to one side of the large northeastern postmold, and may have served as a wedge for the corner post. Judging from the poor definition of the postmolds and the absence of carbonized wood, the posts associated with the structure seem to have rotted in place rather than burned, making their identification more difficult. All were sectioned along two vertical planes to differentiate them from the numerous burrows and root traces. This section revealed that only a small proportion of the stains were found to be postmolds. It is possible that the western posts, of which no trace could be found, were salvaged for other uses after abandonment of the structures. However, their probable former placement can be estimated by continuing the arc of the existing postmolds through the areas having high concentrations of mapped specimens.

It is difficult to arrive at a satisfactory functional interpretation for this structure, partly due to the lack of preservation. On one hand its small size and placement on a slope suggest that it might have been a special-purpose structure for storage or some kind of processing. On the other hand, Feature 9 is similar in placement, shape, and composition to features seen in better-preserved but later structures in this area

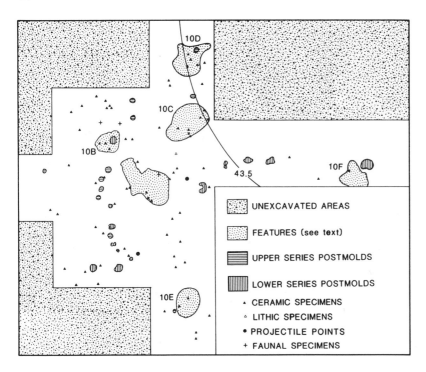

Figure 4.6 Detail of intensive excavations in the eastern midden. Area shown is 4 by 5 m.

that have been interpreted as residences. To resolve this question of function requires additional horizontally oriented excavations designed to recover structural information at similar sites.

The Midden Northeast of Mound A

The second area to be more intensively tested was the vicinity of a square with a linear feature yielding an A.D. 785 date (see Table 4.1). This was Square 350N416E, excavated as a part of the transect of the eastern midden area, and located 55 m east-southeast of the top of Mound A just west of a barrow pit (shown in Figure 4.6). The plow zone typically extended about 20 cm deep in this area, which is now planted with rows of pine but was once a watermelon patch. Altogether 52 m² of surface area were opened in this area. In several of the excavation units, postmolds were exposed at the top of Zone II

immediately below the plow zone. These postmolds are from structures that probably date to the final occupation of the site. Remains of these structures were fragmentary, and it seems likely that portions of the structure (or structures) were destroyed by plowing (see Figure 4.6). It is not certain that the radiocarbon date from Feature 10 adequately dates this construction, since the feature was first noted 10 cm below the bottoms of the postmolds and continued an additional 30 cm in depth. Features 10 and 10C were very similar in depth and size and shared an abundant lithic and faunal inventory as well as a high percentage of burned and calcined bones and an abundance of charred wood. More importantly, both features contained four small fragments of a daublike material that appeared to be partially fired clay, sometimes bearing impressions of what might be sticks or reeds. Features 10, 10C, and 10D also contained a concentration of large rim sherds along their sides and bottoms, though it would be an exaggeration to say that they were sherd lined. Features 10 and 10C may have been shallow earth ovens inside which foods were cooked with a smoldering fire. Features 10, 10B and 10C appear to be associated with a structure partially outlined by the upper series of postmolds in Figure 4.6. Feature 10D, which yielded a radiocarbon date of A.D. 265 (see Table 4.1), was 20–30 cm below these two features and below both series of postmolds appearing in Figure 4.6.

If these postmolds are from two structures, neither is complete and only the later one can be roughly estimated in size. When the incomplete arc of postmolds separating Feature 10 from 10B is extended to include 10C within the structure, as seems reasonable, it could not have been less than 5 m north–south, nor less than 3 m east–west. This is approximately the size of the structure adjacent to the creek, but once again its function cannot be identified because of its fragmentary nature. Feature 10E is on the same level as the two proposed interior features, and may have been an exterior feature associated with this possible structure. It was 15 cm deep and roughly basin shaped. Though it had relatively little cultural or faunal material, it contained higher percentages of undecorated pottery than either of the two interior features, both of which contained higher percentages of various decorated types (Kohler 1978b:75, Table 6). This and Feature 10B are also clearly distinguished from the interior features on the basis of a much higher ceramic to lithic ratio. The interior features had high amounts of debitage and few tools, while the exterior features had little debitage and a higher proportion of tools. The high proportion of calcined bone in the faunal materials from 10E once again suggests a food preparation function.

Feature 10B is somewhat lower than these three features, but like the interior features contains much higher than average amounts of decorated pottery. Feature 10F is at about the same level as the interior features, and could be associated with several of the lower series of postmolds that bottom out at that level. It is the only one of these features with more lithic than ceramic materials, and all of the recovered bone is calcined.

In summary, portions of more than one structure were intercepted in this area, which seems to have been in use relatively early in the occupation of the site (A.D. 265) as well as toward the end (A.D. 785). The most complete probable structure, which may date slightly after the A.D. 785 feature, seems to be about the same size and shape as the structure intercepted to the north on the bluffs of Orange Creek. The presence of an earlier structure is suggested by the line of probable burned posts running east–west to the north of Feature 10F. If this was a structure it may have been square or rectangular and oriented along the cardinal directions. Once again, a length of at least 5 m can be suggested for the only wall intercepted. Most of the features in this area cannot be assigned functions, although all except 10B contain some calcined bone and all contained evidence of burning. Features 10, 10C, and 10D are quite similar; ignoring irregularities at their upper elevations, all are much the same in outline with sides sloping downwards to form basin-shaped bottoms ranging from 20 to 40 cm in depth. Two of these contain daublike fragments, which may suggest an attempt to obtain reducing conditions or an earth-oven effect, or may simply indicate that daub was used in the construction of the associated structure. Percy (1976) has reported possible structural daub from 8-Ja-104, a Weeden Island site on the west side of the Apalachicola River in interior Northwest Florida that he dates to approximately A.D. 500–700.

The Southern Midden Ridge

The third area to be more intensively sampled was the vicinity of Square 312N133E where Feature 8, excavated in the course of the probability sample, yielded a radiocarbon date

Figure 4.7 Excavations in the southern midden. Note ridge in background.

of 30 B.C. (see Table 4.1). Feature 8 was a round, symmetrical pit nearly 1 m deep with straight, steep sides. This feature was definitely constructed early in the occupation of this area of the site, since the backdirt from the excavation of the pit clearly underlies, in profile, the main midden accumulation. Despite this excellent context, the date is open to question (and is probably in error) in view of its associated Weeden Island ceramic inventory (Kohler 1978b:80). Nevertheless, the relatively early occupation of this area of the site is supported by the A.D. 245 date from Feature 12, an apparent hearth in Square 306N133E 6 m south of Feature 8.

The original strategy for excavating this third midden area was to open up as much horizontal expanse as possible in all directions adja-

cent to Square 312N133E, in order to delimit the structure (if any) with which the feature may have been associated. However, after excavating 28 m² adjacent to this excavation unit, no clear structural evidence was found. The lack of a structure with this large, deep feature, its proximity to Mound B, and its unusually rich artifactual inventory with high proportions of nonlocal materials (including shark) and both animal and vegetal foodstuffs (including persimmon) suggest that this feature resulted from a public function such as a feast in public area. Sears (personal communication to Kohler, 1978) observed similar features at the Kolomoki site. Hally (1983) has observed that persimmon was harvested during several weeks in the fall but generally stored in processed form without seeds. Since it does not seem reasonable to interpret this as a trash-burning feature, it seems plausible that it was in use during the fall persimmon processing period—one of few seasonal indicators at the site.

It was then decided to excavate a transect across what appeared to be two low ridges south of Square 312N133E (Figure 4.7). Such a transect would allow us to determine whether the southern ridge marked the placement of a fortification or another habitation area. Altogether, twenty-seven 2- by 2-m tests were opened, most of them along the 133E line. For the northernmost 16 m, adjacent 2- by 2-m squares were excavated along this north–south line; over the next 29 m, every other possible 2- by 2-m unit along this line was excavated; and as the southernmost extreme of the midden was approached, tests were placed at approximate 10-m intervals. One of the southernmost tests was in a depression filled to a depth of 60 cm with a dark gray plow zone that elsewhere averages about 25 cm deep. This depression was apparently one of the three or four borrows for the construction of Mound B; it was partially filled during the years of cultivation earlier in this century. In general, the portions of the site now planted in pines have undergone considerable leveling. Local residents have said that both Mound A and the midden ridges were considerably higher and steeper in outline than they were at the time of excavation.

Both ridges proved to be areas of high artifact density (see Figure 4.8) and, presumably, habitation. However, no convincing structural evidence was found although several isolated postmolds were noted and mapped on the southern midden ridge. Only one other feature (Feature 12) was encountered. Feature 12, in Square 306N133E of the northern ridge, was round in plan, basin shaped in profile, and not quite 20 cm deep. It contained orange sand discolored by heat, portions of a deer humerus, and numerous flecks of carbon from which a date of A.D. 245 ±

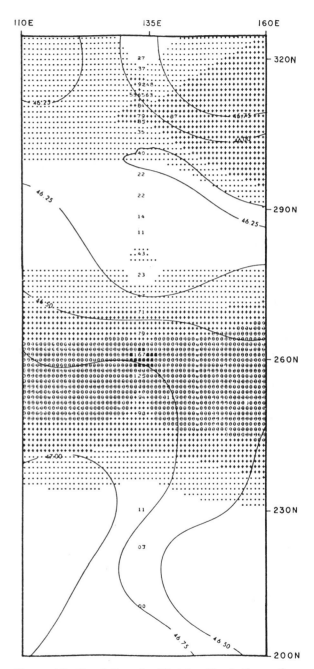

Figure 4.8 Correlation of artifact densities in the southern midden with the two ridges. Grid in meters; contours are meters AMSL.

80 was obtained (see Table 4.1). Seriation later demonstrated that the more southern of the two midden ridges in this area was later than the accumulation near Mound B that provided these two early dates. No evidence of fortification was found here or anywhere else at the site.

The only specimen of galena from McKeithen comes from a provenience 30 cm below the plow zone in the later, more southern midden ridge. This sample, analyzed by John A. Walthall (Chief Archaeologist, Illinois Department of Transportation, letter March 10, 1980), comes from the Potosi formation of southeastern Missouri, also the source for most of the galena in Middle Woodland sites in the Lower Illinois Valley and Twenhafel.

CERAMICS

As shown in Table 4.2, the McKeithen village ceramic collection consists almost entirely of Weeden Island complex types with a few sherds assignable to the earlier Deptford occupation. The latter came primarily from the lowest levels of a few deep squares along the bluffs of Orange Creek. A detailed analysis of 32 attributes was carried out on a sample of 366 large rim sherds selected from the total village collection. Sherds were selected that were large enough to allow estimation of vessel diameter and classification of design elements, if present.

The 32 traits examined in the attribute analysis include details of vessel form, decoration, paste characteristics, color, and surface characteristics. Most of these attributes are self-explanatory. Vessel shape categories included plate, dish, bowl, vase, and jar forms. These forms are generalized from Willey's (1949:496–506) study, and representative examples of some of the vessel shapes just listed may be found in his figures 69c (plate), 69a, b, d–j (bowl), 71h–n (vase, equivalent to Willey's beaker form) and 70a–d (jar). The dish form

used in this study is intermediate in profile between the open bowl and the plate forms; examples can be found in O'Brien (1972:56–72, Figures 34c, 56c) who refers to them as "shallow, pan-like bowls."

Measurements of wall and lip thickness, orifice diameter, vessel depth, spacing of incised lines, punctation size and spacing, land and groove width, and number of checks per 4-cm^2 area were made when applicable. Table 4.2 reports check stamped ceramics by number of checks per linear inch. This system was retained for the purpose of comparison with earlier work, for example Sears (1963). Nevertheless, for the attribute analysis the number of checks was measured by area to eliminate ambiguities about whether to measure checks along their long or narrow axis.

The following comments describe the ceramics at the site by type in terms of their most typical characteristics (the modal vessel). A range of characteristics is cited where (1) some characteristics are an important minority within a type, or (2) the observed frequency of an attribute for a type dramatically exceeds the expected frequency for that attribute in the total sample.

Weeden Island Series

Weeden Island Plain Modal vessel is a bowl with outslanting walls, a folded lip with a single incised line on the exterior, and smooth interior and exterior surfaces. The paste texture is fine with small but abundant sand inclusions; very sparse white inclusions; and a cross section that is dark throughout, with black exterior, interior and core. Mean wall thickness is 7.8 mm, mean lip thickness is 8.2 mm, and mean vessel diameter at orifice is 18.8 cm. Variations include a dish form (23.5 versus 11.8% for all types), inslanting wall profile (18.8%), a pointed lateral rim flange on one specimen, a burnished exterior on 21.2% (versus 12.8% for the total sample), and very sparse mica inclusions in 8.7% (versus 6.6% for the total sample). Burned external carbon encrustations were noted on 9.8% of the sample; fireclouding, usually on the exterior and often around the lip, was noted in 34.3% of the specimens. n (the sample size used in the attribute analysis) = 104.

Table 4.2
Number and Relative Ceramic Frequencies, Village Midden

	n	Relative[a] (%)	Estimated true relative[b] (%)		n	Relative[a] (%)	Estimated true relative[b] (%)
Weeden Island series				Complicated stamped ceramics			
Weeden Island Plain	432	3.28	2.54	Swift Creek Comp. Stamped	105	0.80	0.54
Weeden Island Red	87	0.66	0.94	Crooked River Comp. Stamped	28	0.21	0.13
Weeden Island Zoned Red	41	0.31	0.18	Old Bay Comp. Stamped	18	0.14	0.12
Weeden Island Punctated	169	1.28	1.49	Napier Comp. Stamped	14	0.11	0.18
Weeden Island Incised	206	1.56	1.16	Kolomoki Comp. Stamped	7	0.05	0.04
Carrabelle Punctated	273	2.07	1.84	St. Andrews Comp. Stamped	12	0.09	0.14
Carrabelle Incised	214	1.63	0.94	unidentified rectilinear	44	0.33	0.39
St. Petersburg Incised	4	0.03	0.04	unidentified curvilinear	80	0.61	0.67
Keith Incised	75	0.57	0.39	Pasco paste[c]			
Indian Pass Incised	24	0.18	0.08	Pasco Plain	26	0.20	0.16
Tucker Ridge-pinched	20	0.15	0.12	Residual categories			
St. Johns paste				smooth sand-tempered plain	3908	26.69	30.00
St. Johns Plain	242	1.84	1.86	grit-tempered plain	443	3.37	2.42
St. Johns Check Stamped	23	0.17	0.32	residual plain	6149	46.71	47.77
Papys Bayou Incised	10	0.08	0.05	residual red	121	0.92	0.92
Papys Bayou Punctated	39	0.30	0.05	unidentified incised	156	1.19	1.30
Other check stamped ceramics				unidentified punctated	29	0.22	0.18
4–6 checks/in.	41	0.31	0.37	other[d]	35	0.27	0.73
7–9 checks/in.	66	0.50	1.17		13164	100.0	99.77
10–12 checks/in.	19	0.14	0.49				
Deptford Linear Check Stamped	4	0.03	0.05				

[a]These values are based on all collections except those from the mounds.

[b]These values are point estimates of the true population proportion (100) based only on the probability sample.

[c]Subsequent intensive ceramic analysis has demonstrated that the white inclusions are not limestone but possibly fuller's earth.

[d]This category includes rare occurrences of simple stamped, cross simple stamped, cord marked, fabric impressed, Dunns Creek Red, St. Johns Complicated Stamped, St. Johns Incised, etc.

Weeden Island Red Although this type was described by Sears (1956:19) on the basis of a misunderstanding with Willey, it is substantially different from Weeden Island Zoned Red at McKeithen, so retention as a type is recommended. The modal vessel is a bowl with outslanting walls and a folded lip with no incision underneath. Slipping always occurs on the interior and usually on the exterior as well, covering the entire wall. Paste texture is fine with small but abundant sand inclusions and sparse black and red inclusions. In cross section the exterior surface is a medium to dark reddish brown to reddish gray, while the interior surface and the core is black. Mean wall thickness is 7.4 mm, mean lip thickness is 7.1 mm, and mean vessel diameter at orifice is 20 cm. Important variations include the presence of a single incised line under the lip on the exterior only. Plate and dish forms occur on 33.4% of the specimens, higher than the 13.8% for these forms in the total sample. Mica occurs in 28.6% of the specimens compared to 6.9% in the total sample. Two specimens exhibit external fire-clouding. $n = 7$.

Figure 4.9   Weeden Island series potsherds.
  A. Weeden Island Incised
  B. Weeden Island Incised
  C. Weeden Island Punctated dish
  D. Weeden Island Punctated collared bowl with interior decorated rim (8.0 cm long at rim)
  E. Weeden Island Zoned Red dish

Weeden Island Zoned Red The modal vessel is a dish or plate with a folded lip with a single incised line on both interior and exterior surfaces with red painting present on the interior and exterior. The painting is contained inside zones set off by a single fine incised line that may be straight or curvilinear. Paste texture is fine with small but abundant sand inclusions and very sparse red inclusions. In cross section the paste is light tan or light gray on both interior and exterior, with no distinct coring present. Mean wall thickness is 7.8 mm, mean lip thickness is 9.2 mm, and mean vessel diameter at orifice is 23.3 cm. Important variations include the dish form (represented by the sherd in Figure 4.9E), which occurs on less than 4% of the specimens, much higher than the 11.8% occurrence among all types taken together. Presence of mica was noted in 20% of the specimens versus 6.9% in the total sample. Two specimens exhibit external fire-clouding, and one external carbon encrustations. *n = 10*.

Weeden Island Punctated The modal vessel is a bowl with outslanting walls, a folded lip set off by more than one incised line and punctations on the exterior. The interior is smoothed, and the exterior is smoothed and burnished. The most common decoration is a series of 1- to 2-mm adjacent linear punctations on the exterior in a variety of arrangements. Paste texture is fine with small but abundant sand inclusions and very sparse red inclusions. In cross section the paste is black throughout, at the core and on both surfaces. Mean wall thickness is 7.3 mm, mean lip thickness is 7.5 mm, and mean vessel diameter at orifice is 16.4 cm. This type and Weeden Island Incised are highly variable in design and shape, but generally excellent in execution. Impor-

Figure 4.10 Carrabelle Punctated potsherds.
A. round to oblong
B. triangular (width 3.0 cm)
C. fingernail
D. hollow reed
E. linear
F. rectangular to square

tant variations include plate and dish forms (27.3 versus 13.8% in the total sample), a single row of punctations under the lip with no incised line (25 versus 13.8% in the total sample), compound wall profiles (16.7 versus 5.5% in the total sample), lips decorated on both the top and the exterior (25 versus 3% in the total sample), very fine paste texture (33.3 versus 9.1% in the total sample), and presence of mica inclusions (25 versus 6.9% in the total sample). Interior and exterior surfaces are light tan or light gray almost as frequently as they are black. Exterior fire-clouding and carbon encrustations occur on one specimen each. Lip additions of adornos (too fragmentary to characterize) or triangular lateral flanges occur on one specimen each. The interior decorated surface on the rim of a Weeden Island Punctated dish is illustrated in Figure 4.9C; the interior rim surface of a collared bowl is shown in Figure 4.9D. $n = 12$.

Weeden Island Incised The only vessel form in the sample is a bowl with either inslanting or incurving walls and a folded lip with one or more incised lines on the exterior. Interiors and exteriors are smoothed, and incised lines of medium width or of two distinct widths decorate the exterior. The motif is generally curvilinear and complex, usually in combination with 2- to 4-mm triangular punctations spaced 2–5 mm apart that occur in zones demarcated by the incisions. Paste texture is variable, ranging from very fine (25%) to coarse (37.5%) with fine-sand inclusions moderately abundant and red inclusions very sparse. Exterior surface in cross section is usually dark brown or dark gray to black; the interior surface is medium brown or medium gray to black, with no distinct core present. Mean wall thickness is 7.4 mm, mean lip thickness is 7.5 mm, and mean vessel diameter at orifice is 13.7 cm. Important variations include

lips that may be set off by both incised lines and punctations (12.5 versus 3.0% in the total sample), decorations that may occur on both the top of the lip and the exterior (12.5 versus 3.0% in the total sample), and several specimens that exhibit two different shapes of punctations—the small triangular form and a large round form. One specimen is entirely filmed with red, and two others show traces of red filming. Lateral triangular or rounded rim flanges occur on one specimen each; one specimen exhibits external carbon encrustations. Classic examples of this famous type are illustrated in Figure 4.9A–B. $n = 8$.

Carrabelle Punctated (See Figure 4.10.) The modal vessel is a bowl with incurving walls and a folded lip set off by a single incised line on the exterior. Interior is smoothed and undecorated; the exterior is smoothed, and where there is enough wall to ascertain the extent of the decoration, it is usually confined to a band below the rim. The decoration consists of a series of punctations, which for analysis were grouped into six main categories: round to oblong (13.3%; Figure 4.10A), triangular (26.7%; Figure 4.10B), fingernail (16.7%; Figure 4.10C), hollow reed (23.3%; Figure 4.10D), linear (10.0%; Figure 4.10E), and rectangular to square (3.3%; Figure 4.10F). Another 6.7% fit none of these categories. The modal punctation diameter is 4–6 mm, and the modal distance separating the punctations is 5–8 mm. Paste is either fine or intermediate in texture; sand inclusions are small but abundant. The paste cross section is most often dark throughout with a black exterior and a dark brown to dark gray interior surface. Mean wall thickness is 6.8 mm, mean lip thickness is 6.0 mm, and mean vessel diameter at orifice is 16.4 cm. Important variations include an occasional vase form (10.7 versus 1.7% in the total sam-

Figure 4.11 Other village potsherds.
  A. Keith Incised
  B. Carrabelle Incised
  C. Carrabelle Incised
  D. Crooked River Complicated Stamped (maximum width 5.5 cm)
  E. Old Bay Complicated Stamped
  F. Wakulla Check Stamped

ple) and some lips that are flattened on top (26.7 versus 20.0% in the total sample). Very sparse white inclusions in the paste occur in 41.9% of the specimens (versus 48.4% for the sample as a whole), while sparse to very abundant red inclusions can be found in 58.1% of the specimens (versus 50.5% in the total sample). External carbon encrustations occur on 25.8% of the specimens; external fire-clouding occurs on 12.9%. $n = 3$.

Carrabelle Incised The modal form is a bowl with in-slanting or incurving walls and a folded lip over a single incised line on the interior. Both the interior and exterior surfaces are smoothed; and where there is enough wall to determine the extent of the decoration, it is confined to a band below the rim. The most common decorative motif is composed of fine incised lines spaced 4–6 mm apart running in one direction diagonal to the rim. Paste texture is fine or intermediate with abundant fine-sand inclusions, sparse to very sparse white inclusions, and intermediate to very sparse red inclusions. In cross section a dark central core is surrounded by black interior and exterior surfaces. Mean wall thickness is 7.2 mm, mean lip thickness is 6.4 mm, and mean vessel diameter at orifice is 17.4 cm. Important variations include a jar form that was noted in 4.6% of the specimens (the only jars in the sample); occasional outslanting (17.9%) and compound (16.7%) wall profiles; lips that are brought to a thin leading edge (sharpened), which account for 21.9% of these specimens (versus 7.1% in the total sample); and triangular or rounded lateral flanges that occur on 3 specimens (7.9 versus 2.5% in the total sample). Other common decorative motifs are vertical lines (15.4%; Figure 4.11B) or diagonal lines in two directions separated by a single vertical line forming a series of "trees" (Figure 4.11C). A minority of sherds exhibit abundant sand inclusions of intermediate size (15.8%), and very sparse mica inclusions were noted in 7.9% of the specimens. Fire-clouding was noticeable on 13.2% of the specimens, and 15.8% exhibited carbon encrustations on the interior or exterior. $n = 38$.

Keith Incised The modal vessel is a bowl with inslanting walls and a rounded lip with a single incised line on the exterior. Both the interior and exterior surfaces are smoothed. Incised lines of medium width spaced at 6- to 10-mm intervals are placed diagonally to the rim in two directions, crossing at approximately 90° angles. Figure 4.11A illustrates a specimen with more closely packed lines. Paste is intermediate in texture, fine-sand inclusions are abundant, and white and red inclusions very sparse. Interior and exterior surface colors are variable with specimens equally distributed between light reddish brown and reddish grey tones and black tones. Most exhibit a black central core. Mean wall thickness is 8.2 mm, mean lip thickness is 6.4 mm, and mean vessel diameter at orifice is 21.5 cm. Fire-clouding and carbon encrustations were noted on one specimen each. $n = 5$.

St. Johns Series

St. Johns Plain The modal vessel is a bowl with inslanting walls and a folded lip that is undecorated. Interior and exterior surfaces are smoothed and the paste is fine in texture. Sand inclusions are generally small and sparse, while an abundance of sponge spicules ranges from intermediate to very dense. White inclusions are sparse, and reddish brown inclusions are very sparse. Paste is generally dark throughout with black interior and exterior surfaces. Mean wall thickness is only 6.5 mm, mean lip thickness is 6.8 mm, and mean vessel diameter at orifice is 14.7 cm. Important variations include outslanting walls on 30% of the specimens, a single incised line on the exterior under the lip in 40% of the specimens (versus 55.7% in the total sample), and dark brown to dark gray color on 20% of the exteriors and 30% of the interiors. Fire-clouding was noted on 40% of the sherds, and carbon encrustations on 20%. $n = 10$.

St. Johns Check Stamped The modal vessel form is a bowl with vertical walls and a sharpened (thinned) lip that may be either undecorated or set off by a single incised line on the exterior. Interior surfaces are smoothed, while the exterior seems to be paddle stamped over the entire surface. Checks are either square or parallelogram in shape with land and groove widths both normally 1–2 mm. Number of checks per 4 cm² area is highly variable, ranging from 0–9 to 50–79. Paste texture is fine with sparse, fine sand inclusions. Density of sponge spicules ranges from sparse to very abundant; white inclusions are sparse and reddish-brown inclusions are absent or very sparse. Interior and exterior surface colors have no mode in this small sample; a dark central core is generally present. Mean wall thickness is 7.0 mm, mean lip thickness is 6.8 mm, and mean vessel diameter at orifice is 25.3 cm. $n = 4$.

St. Johns Complicated Stamped This is not a formally defined type, but a logical appellation for a Swift Creek–like curvilinear complicated stamping on a St. Johns chalky paste. The only form represented is a bowl, usually with inslanting or incurving walls and a folded lip with no incision below. The interior surface is smoothed, and the exterior appears to be entirely paddle stamped. Motifs include *bull's-eyes,* concentric ovals or eyes set in a field of flowing lines, and a unique arrangement of circles filled with parallel, straight lands set in a field of check stamps. Land width is generally very narrow—less than or equal to 1 mm—and groove width is only slightly wider at 1–2 mm. Paste texture is fine, with sparse inclusions of fine sand, sparse to very abundant sponge spicules, and very sparse white inclusions. Exterior surfaces may be either light tan to light gray or dark brown to dark gray, interior surfaces are either black or dark brown to dark gray, and all have a dark central core. Mean wall thickness is 5.6 mm, mean lip thickness is 6.4 mm, and mean vessel diameter at orifice is 17.6 cm. Variants include outslanting walls (20%), a lip that is flattened (20%) or beveled towards the interior (20%), a single incised line on the exterior under the lip (40%), and very sparse reddish brown inclusions (40%). $n = 5$.

Other Checked Stamped Ceramics

Wakulla Check Stamped The modal form is a bowl with walls that are most commonly inslanting, culminating in a folded lip that is not usually set off from the paddle stamping covering the entire exterior. The interior surface is usually smoothed. Rectangular checks, as seen in Figure 4.11F, are more common than square. On one half of the rectangular specimens the lands in one direction are somewhat wider that the lands in the other direction. Land and groove width is most often 1–2 mm. Number of checks per 4-cm² area is bimodal, peaking at 10–19 and again at 40–49. Paste texture is intermediate with a moderate amount of fine-sand inclusions. Interior and exterior surface color is most often dark brown to dark gray with a dark central core. Mean wall thickness is 6.4 mm, mean lip thickness is 7.4 mm, and mean vessel diameter at orifice is 20.8 cm. Variations include compound wall profiles (25 versus 5% in the total sample), a single incised line under the lip on the exterior (33%), and sparse to very sparse white inclusions (44%). Two specimens exhibit carbon encrustations; fire-clouding was noted on one specimen. $n = 9$.

Other Complicated Stamped Ceramics

Swift Creek Complicated Stamped The only form represented is a bowl, usually with either outcurving or inslanting walls and folded lips not set off from the paddle stamped decoration (which usually covers the entire exterior of the vessel). Interiors are smoothed. The bull's-eye and the barred circle are common motifs. Land width is generally 1–2 mm and groove width 2–3 mm. Paste is intermediate in texture with abundant fine-sand inclusions. Exterior surface is most often dark gray, and the interior surface is black. Presence of coring is highly variable, equally split between none at all, a dark central core, and a dark central core adjoining a dark interior surface. Mean wall thickness is 7.3 mm, mean lip thickness is 6.4 mm, and mean vessel diameter at orifice is 23.8 cm. Variants include a flattened lip (25%), a single incised line on the exterior under the lip (37.5%), and sparse to very sparse red inclusions (50%). Internal and external fire-clouding was noted on one specimen and carbon encrustations on two. $n = 8$.

Crooked River Complicated Stamped The most frequent form is a bowl, generally with inslanting walls and a folded lip usually set off by a single incised line on the exterior. The interior surfaces are smoothed; on the exterior the rectilinear complicated stamp seems to cover the entire vessel. The common design element is the chevron (Figure 4.11D). Land width varies from 1–3 mm, while the groove width is generally 2–3 mm. Paste is fine in texture with abundant fine-sand inclusions and very sparse white and red inclusions. Exterior surface is generally black; the interior surface either black or medium brown to medium gray; and in cross section, the paste looks uniformly dark throughout. Mean wall thickness is 7.1 mm, mean lip thickness is 7.1 mm, and mean vessel diameter at orifice is 18.7 cm. Both a dish (14.3%) and a vase (14.3%) form were noted, as were incurving wall profiles (28.6%), undecorated lips (42.9%), and very sparse mica inclusions (14.3%). $n = 7$.

Old Bay Complicated Stamped The only form represented is a bowl with either vertical or inslanting walls and a flattened lip above a single incised line on the exterior. The interior surface is smoothed. The exterior paddle stamping covers the entire wall and possibly the entire exterior. The motif is a series of concentric circles or bull's-eyes set in a field of check stamps (Figure 4.11E). The land width is generally very narrow, less than or equal to 1 mm; the groove width is generally 1–2 mm. The checks are small, usually 50–79 per 4-cm^2 area, and the paste texture coarse with a moderate amount of intermediate size sand inclusions and sparse white inclusions. The exterior and interior surfaces are usually light tan to light gray surrounding a dark central core. Mean wall thickness is 8.0 mm, mean lip thickness is 7.3 mm, and mean vessel diameter at orifice is 18.0 cm. Variants include lips that are round or folded. The classifier of this collection (Kohler) found it impossible to distinguish between Willey's New River Complicated Stamped (1949:386) and his Old Bay Complicated Stamped (1949:437); thus only the latter is included here. $n = 4$.

Napier Complicated Stamped The only form represented is a bowl with outslanting, vertical, or incurving walls and a folded lip above a single incised line on the exterior. The interior surface is smoothed, while the exterior appears to be stamped on the walls only with a motif generally composed of parallel lands zoned into a diamond shape separated by three or more lands. The lands are generally narrow, from less than 1 to 2 mm in width, while the grooves range from 3 to 4 mm in width. The paste texture ranges from fine to coarse with abundant sand inclusions of intermediate size and very sparse red inclusions. Interior and exterior surface color is highly variable, ranging from a light gray or light tan to a dark gray or a dark brown with some darker coring towards the center and the interior surface usually present. Mean wall thickness is 7.0 mm, mean wall thickness is 5.8 mm, and mean vessel diameter at orifice is 19.3 cm. $n = 4$.

Other Ceramics

Plain This is a residual category that includes the smooth sand-tempered plain, grit-tempered plain, and re-

sidual plain groups listed in Table 4.2 but excludes named paste variants such as St. Johns Plain. The bowl is the overwhelmingly dominant form (90.5%), with the dish form (6.0%) next in frequency. Outslanting walls are most common (28.6%), followed by an incurving wall profile (23.8%). The most common treatment of the lip is flattening (29.8%), followed by a simple, unmodified round form (28.6%). The lip is rarely (7.1%) set off by a single incised line on the exterior, which is usually partly obliterated. The interior surface is generally smoothed (69%) but may be unsmoothed (29.8%). Likewise the exterior may be smoothed (53%) or unsmoothed (45.8%). The paste is intermediate in texture (40.5%) or fine (33.3%) with abundant inclusions of fine sand (34.5%) or a moderate amount of fine-sand inclusions (21.4%). Very sparse white inclusions occur in 60.7% of the specimens, very sparse black inclusions in 27.4%, and very sparse red inclusions in 44%. Exterior surface color is most frequently black (45.2%) or dark brown to dark gray (25%); likewise on the interior surface, black is the most common color (44%), followed by dark brown to dark gray (28.6%). The paste, then, is usually dark throughout (34.5%); but in 22.6%, a darker central core is present. Mean wall thickness is 7.4 mm, mean wall thickness is 6.5mm, and mean vessel diameter at orifice is 17.2 cm. $n = 84$.

Other The sample chosen for attribute analysis also included three sherds of Tucker Ridge-pinched, one Papys Bayou Incised, one Papys Bayou Punctated, one Basin Bayou Incised, one Kolomoki Complicated Stamped, one St. Andrews Complicated Stamped, one Deptford Simple or Cross Simple Stamped, one Savannah(?) Cord Marked, one Dunlap Fabric Impressed, one Gulf Check Stamped, and four unidentified sherds. The attribute analysis was carried out on these sherds and they are included in percentages that characterize the entire sample. The samples were too small to report individually. $n = 16$.

Discussion

The ceramic attribute analysis was used to help divide the pottery into different categories for further analysis. One dichotomy that can be drawn between types in the analysis is between local and nonlocal loci of origin, determined on the basis of both paste and design. The technological analysis indicated that clays easily exploitable in the vicinity of the site do not contain sponge spicules, and micaceous inclusions occur only in rare quantities in clay samples from Orange Creek and the immediate vicinity of the site (see Chapter 6). Ceramic types, which by definition contain high densities of sponge spicules, are St. Johns Plain, St. Johns Checked Stamped, St. Johns complicated stamped, Papys Bayou Punctated, and Papys Bayou Incised. Only a few ceramic types had a significant (noted in more than 10% of the specimens) incidence of micaceous inclusions. These include Weeden Island Red (28.6%), Weeden Island Zoned Red (20%), Weeden Island Punctated (25%), Weeden Island Incised (12.5%), and Crooked River Complicated Stamped (14.3%).

In other instances known regional distributions of ceramic types suggest a nonlocal origin. Such is the case with Kolomoki Complicated Stamped, which has a well-documented geographic distribution in the Chattahoochee River area of southwestern Georgia (Sears 1956; Steinen 1976). Likewise, Napier Complicated Stamped seems to have a piedmont Georgia center of distribution (Sears 1956; Wauchope 1966). Several other types (such as Old Bay and St. Andrews Complicated Stamped, Tucker Ridge-pinched, and Indian Pass Incised) have not been included in a nonlocal category because they are such minor types wherever they appear that it is difficult to pinpoint centers of high frequency.

A second dichotomy could be drawn between those types represented almost exclusively by the bowl form (which constitutes 83.6% of the sample) and those types in which more exotic forms are well represented, since vessel shape diversity may be greater in high-status areas. Pottery types that have more than 25% nonbowl forms (excluding types that are represented by less than five specimens), include Weeden Island Plain (26.4% nonbowl), Weeden Island Red (33.4% nonbowl), Weeden Island Zoned Red (37.5% nonbowl), Weeden Island Punctated (27.3% nonbowl), and Crooked River Complicated Stamped (28.6% nonbowl).

The presence of polishing or burnishing is an uncommon attribute state for surface finish in this sample. A list similar to that for nonbowl vessel forms results by isolating types for which exterior polishing or burnishing occurs on more than 25% of the specimens (again excluding rare types): Weeden Island Zoned Red (28.6% polished), Weeden Island Punctated (50% polished), and Weeden Island Incised (25% polished). Presence of lip additions such as adornos and lateral flanges add increased diversity to vessel form without obvious practical functions. These attributes occur in a frequency of 10% or higher in the following ceramic types: Weeden Island Zoned Red (10%), Weeden Island Plain (16.7%), and Weeden Island Incised (25%). Such lists could be continued using presence of other traits such as slipping or painting, interior surface burnishing, and extra fine paste texture. The four ceramic types that occur most frequently in all such lists are Weeden Island Red, Weeden Island Zoned Red, Weeden Island Punctated, and Weeden Island Incised. For convenience, this group is hereafter referred to as *elite* pottery, a term used as "a shorthand notation for special-purpose, status, or restricted good" (Rice 1981:236).

These types constitute what has been called the *sacred ceramic series* (Sears 1973); in the McKeithen habitation area the four make up only 3.8% of the total ceramics. In all cases in the village, these are either utilitarian forms or abstract forms (see Sears 1956:23 for definitions) that could have had a utilitarian function, even though some contain form modifications that have no clear utilitarian advantage. Effigy forms have not yet been identified from the village context, though they occur in Mounds B and C. Of all the ceramics in the village midden, these four types also have the highest *production step measure,* an index of the relative labor investment involved in ceramic manufacture devised by Feinman *et al.* (1981).

LITHIC MATERIALS

Worked or utilized stone comprises about 5% of the total lithic artifacts in the village (see Table 4.3). Worked stone is of two major mate-

Table 4.3

Raw and Relative Lithic Frequencies, Village Midden

Category	Raw	Relative[a] (%)	Estimated true relative[b] (%)
Chert			
worked or utilized	284	4.03	5.28
thermally altered	2405	34.11	30.75
other	3796	53.84	55.32
Silicified coral			
worked or utilized	24	0.34	0.51
thermally altered[c]	72	1.02	1.42
other	220	3.12	4.63
Mica	1	0.01	0.02
Other materials			
worked or utilized	32	0.45	0.62
not worked or utilized	217	3.08	1.45
	7051	100.00	100.00

[a]Data are based on all collections, except those from mounds.

[b]A point estimate of the true population proportions (100) based only on the probability sample.

[c]Excluding worked or utilized materials, which are included above.

rials: chert (used in the traditionally broad archaeological sense), which is locally available and is by far the more abundant, and silicified coral, which is available about 10 km from the site in and adjacent to the Suwannee River.

For analytical purposes the excavated series of reasonably complete projectile points was visually divided into 10 groups described in the following primarily on the basis of shape and secondarily on the basis of size characteristics. Although the projectile point taxonomies of Bullen (1975) or Cambron and Hulse (1975) have not been used in defining these groups, some of the groups do equate with published type names; others subdivide or crosscut existing types. If these typologies had been used, the general range of projectile points would include Bullen's Pinellas, Tampa, Ichetucknee, Florida Copena, Jackson, and Duval; with Florida Ar-

chaic Stemmed points and a possible fragmentary Santa Fe point from surface, creek, and plow zone collections; and Cambron and Hulse's Hamilton, Montgomery, Bradley Spike, Greeneville, Guntersville, Nodena, and Coosa point types. A single example of each of the 10 groups defined here is illustrated in Figure 4.12. The descriptive terminology follows Cambron and Hulse's pseudobotanical approach. No claim is made that these represent distinct functional groups.

Projectile Points

Group 1 These points have a concave base, biconvex or median ridged in cross section and a straight or incurvate blade (one is slightly excurvate). Three specimens have expanded, pointed auriculate bases. One specimen (Figure 4.12A) has serrated edges. Includes Bullen's Pinellas subtype 3. Length is 26 mm maximum and 19 mm minimum, width is 22 mm maximum and 13 mm minimum. Six are of chert, and of these, four appear to be thermally altered. One specimen is of silicified coral. $n = 7$.

Group 2 These have a base that is rounded or excurvate and biconvex or median ridged in cross section and a blade that is excurvate with an acute distal end. The sample includes Bullen's Tampa and Cambron and Hulse's Montgomery. Length is 49 mm maximum and 24 mm minimum. Width is 26 mm maximum and 13 mm minimum. One specimen is silicified coral and 9 are chert, of which 3 appear heat treated (Figure 4.12B). These points are concentrated in the upper levels of the northern midden area. $n = 10$.

Group 3 These have a base that is usually straight, biconvex or flattened in cross section, and a straight or slightly excurvate blade with an acute distal end (Figure 4.12C). The sample includes Pinellas variants and is similar to Group 7 but with a lower length-to-width ratio. Length is 39 mm maximum and 24 mm minimum. Width is 22 mm maximum and 12 mm minimum. Fourteen specimens are chert, 3 of which appear to be heat treated; 1 specimen is silicified coral, and 1 specimen is fine milky quartz. These points occur more frequently in the eastern and southern midden areas than do most of the points. $n = 16$.

Group 4 These are a group of crude and variable small points of which 4 are asymmetrical. Two specimens (Figure 4.12D) have a suggestion of short, rounded stems. Distal end may be obtuse or acute; blade is straight or recuvate. The

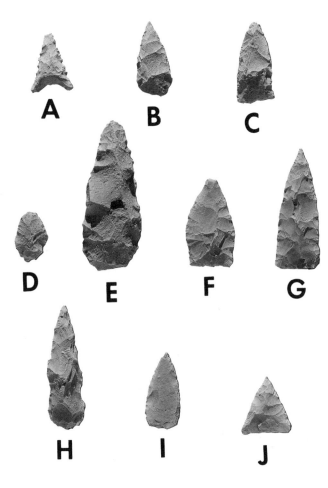

Figure 4.12   Excavated examples of village projectile point categories.

A. Group 1   F. Group 6
B. Group 2   G. Group 7
C. Group 3   H. Group 8
D. Group 4   I. Group 9
E. Group 5   J. Group 10 (length 22 mm)

sample includes Cambron and Hulse's Coosa point. Length is 23 mm maximum and 16 mm minimum. Width is 16 mm maximum and 10 mm minimum. Six specimens are chert, of which 2 appear to be heat treated; and 1 is silicified coral. They occur most frequently in the eastern midden. $n = 7$.

Group 5 These have a base that is usually straight, with a pronounced medial ridge in most specimens, and a blade that is straight or excurvate. Most of these are relatively long, thick, and crude; and 5 have portions of cortex remaining on the blade. The sample includes Cambron and Hulse's Bradley Spike type. Length is 56 mm maximum and 37 mm minimum. Width is 26 mm maximum and 18 mm minimum. Only 3 of the specimens are chert; 2 of these are a very poor grade stone, and one appears to be heat treated. The other 6 are made from silicified coral; this is the only group for which coral was the preferred raw material. Some of the

specimens (Figure 4.12E) resemble Bullen's Ichetucknee point in outline but fail to meet the "small, nicely made" criteria. $n = 19$.

Group 6 The important features of this group are the parallel sides and straight base; many bases are flattened in cross section. The blade may also be somewhat excurvate. The sample includes Bullen's Florida Copena and Cambron and Hulse's Greeneville. Length is 39 mm maximum and 25 mm minimum. Width is 27 mm maximum and 13 mm minimum. One specimen is a unique, high-quality olive green jasper, apparently nonlocal; 11 are more common chert, of which 4 appear to be heat treated; and 4 are silicified coral of which one (Figure 4.12F) appears thermally altered. Four to 6 of the specimens are only minimally altered. A disproportionate number of this category is found in the northern midden. $n = 16$.

Group 7 These are long and narrow, and well thinned with straight or slightly concave bases and straight, nearly parallel or slightly excurvate sides; specimens are basally thinned (Figure 4.12G). The distal points are very acute. The sample includes Bullen's Pinellas, especially Subtypes 1 and 2 and Cambron and Hulse's Gunterville. Length is 45 mm maximum and 34 mm minimum. Width is 18 mm maximum and 17 mm minimum. All species are chert; one appears to be heat treated. $n = 5$.

Group 8 These are quite narrow, thick, and short to medium in length, usually with a prominent medial ridge. Bases are variable, with most being straight and some convex; sides are straight or slightly excurvate. One specimen is basally thinned and has a concave base. Another specimen (Figure 4.12H) exhibits slight side-notching toward the base and might be classified as a Duval point using Bullen's (1975) typology. This side-notching may result from trying to remove mass from the center of the point and may not be intentional. Others appear to resemble Cambron and Hulse's Flint River Spike or Nodena points. Length is 46 mm maximum and 30 mm minimum. Width is 15 mm maximum and 11 mm minimum. All are chert; 2 appear to be thermally altered. A higher than expected number of these appear to be thermally altered. A higher than expected number of these appear in the eastern midden area. $n = 9$.

Group 9 These are a variable lot of small points with acute distal ends, all of which are beveled either on one edge or on two opposite sides and edges. One specimen (Figure 4.12I) would probably be classified as Ichetucknee in Bullen's typology; the remaining points may be Pinellas variations. Length is 32 mm maximum and 17 mm minimum. Width is 18 mm maximum and 11 mm minimum. All specimens are chert. $n = 6$.

Group 10 This is a relatively homogeneous group, more or less equilateral in form with straight or excurvate sides and usually biconvex or flattened in cross section (Figure 4.12J). Four have the remains of the striking platforms on one of the basal corners; another 4 have suggestions of very small auricles on one or both of the basal corners. Most would probably be classified as Bullen's Pinellas Subtype 4. Length is 25 mm maximum and 11 mm minimum. Width is 28 mm maximum and 16 mm minimum. Only 1 specimen is silicified coral; 1 is a poor-grade consolidated sandstonelike material. Others are chert; 6 of these appear to be heat treated. $n = 14$.

Three other groups were defined for the remaining specimens. Groups 11 and 13 are points from disturbed contexts and the creek and probably date to the Archaic and Paleoindian periods. Group 14 consists of 20 projectile points too fragmentary to classify. Most of the points seem more carefully executed than the other lithic implements from the village (described in the following). During analysis, Group 12 specimens were determined not to be projectile points; that group is discussed in the next section.

The identification of the small triangular projectile points in the sample as arrow points seems reasonable. Although several variants of the small triangular points are commonly termed Mississippian (Wauchope 1966:162–163), they appear at the McKeithen site in a pre-Mississippian context. Such points also appear in the Cades Pond Weeden Island–related culture in North Central Florida (Milanich 1978c:165).

Most of the projectile points appear to occur throughout the occupation, though perhaps changing slightly in relative frequency through time. This is also true of most of the Pinellas-like points (Bullen 1975:8). Only Group 1, the concave-based variant, seems to mark the late period of occupation at the site. If these small triangular points characteristic of the McKeithen collection mark the introduction of the bow and arrow to North Florida, then Brain's postulated Late Marksville period introduction of the bow and arrow to the Lower Mississippi River Valley can be seen as an approximately contemporaneous event (1976:59).

Other Worked Lithic Artifacts

Other worked lithic materials at the site were divided into 15 categories by shape, size, and presumed function. Since the comments that follow are made without the benefit of a use–wear analysis, all functional assignments are tentative and are based on shaky morphological criteria. At least one specimen of each of these categories is illustrated in Figure 4.13 or 4.14.

Figure 4.13 Categories of worked and utilized lithics excavated from the village.
A. Group 12 (length 28 mm)
B. Group 15
C. Group 16
D. Group 17
E. Group 18
F. Group 19
G. Group 20
H. Group 22
I. Group 23

Group 12 This is a group of possible drills and awls, sharing acuminate or mucronate distal ends, but otherwise exhibiting a variety of forms. Except for the thinned, elongated distal point, most could be classified as Pinellas variants. Eight specimens are chert, of which 2 appear to be heat treated; 1 is silicified coral (Figure 4.13A). $n = 9$.

Group 15 This is a diverse group of possibly hafted tools, perhaps knives. All are asymmetrical. One unusually fine specimen, of an apparently nonlocal jasper, is shown in Figure 4.13B). Six of the other specimens are chert; 1 of these appears to be heat treated. One specimen is silicified coral. This group is nearly absent from the southern midden area and occurs most frequently in the eastern and northeastern midden area. $n = 8$.

Group 16 This is a group of two different varieties. The first (16 specimens) may originate from a biface that was broken along its margin during manufacture or use, having one retouched side and one flat side (Figure 4.13C). The other 13 specimens are similar, but where as the first group is retouched along the blade edge, these show evidence of use but not of reworking. All the first variety are chert; 2 appear to be heat treated. The second group includes 3 silicified coral specimens and 10 chert, of which 3 appear to be heat treated. This group appears almost exclusively in the northern midden area. $n = 29$.

Group 17 This is a diverse group of side and end scrapers, some of which (Figure 4.13D) might alternatively be considered projectile point blanks. These are typically biconvex in cross section, but 3 have strong medial ridges on one or both sides. Four are unifacially flaked, while 9 are bifacially flaked. Cortex is present on 7 of the specimens; 3 are silicified coral, the other 10 are chert, of which only 1

appears to be heat treated. As with Group 16, this category appears almost solely in the northern midden area. $n = 13$.

Group 18 These may be crude scrapers or flakes from the early stages of reduction (Figure 4.13E); 1 may have been used as a hammerstone. Only one is bifacially flaked; another is unifacially flaked. All but 2 exhibit some cortex. Six of the 9 specimens were formed from large flakes; 2 of the 9 are silicified coral, of which 1 appears to be heat treated. These are somewhat more common in the southern midden than elsewhere. $n = 9$.

Group 19 This is a group of side scrapers, 2 of which are unifacially retouched and 3 of which are bifacially retouched. It is not a homogeneous group. Two specimens (Figure 4.13F) may be basally thinned for hafting, or may simply be formed from flakes of fortuitous shape. All are chert. $n = 5$.

Group 20 This is a group of scrapers with a peculiar asymmetrical form (Figure 4.13G). These apparently functioned as side or end scrapers but have a 1- to 2-cm spur projecting from one side, possibly for hafting. All are formed from flakes. Either the concave side or the distal end (if the spur is considered the proximal end) show signs of use as a scraper. Two specimens are silicified coral; the others are chert, 2 of which appear to be heat treated. Both this group and Group 16 resemble microflints from Poverty Point collections (Haag and Webb 1953:236). This group is found primarily in the northern midden area. $n = 11$.

Group 22 These are large-stemmed, asymmetrical knives, all of which are broken except for 1 (Figure 4.13H), which may well be a broken and subsequently reworked Florida Stemmed Archaic point. Four of the 5 are chert and of these, three appear to be heat treated. The other specimen

Figure 4.14 Categories of worked
and utilized lithics excavated from
the village.
   A. Group 24 (height 9 cm)
   B. Group 25
   C. Group 26
   D. Group 27

is silicified coral. So far this class has been found exclusively in the northern midden area. $n = 5$.

Group 23 These are bladelike flakes, unretouched but with slight to moderate edge wear; all have a strong medial ridge running parallel to the cutting edges; most have straight, parallel sides (Figure 4.13I). None have been thermally altered. As with Group 22, these have been found only in the northern midden area. $n = 5$.

Group 24 These are medium to large specimens, perhaps cores. Three show signs of heavy battering along one edge. These may represent the basic unit of chert brought to the site for further reduction before additional reduction took place (Figure 4.14A). $n = 4$.

Group 25 These are round or elongated (Figure 4.14B) quartz "pecking stones." The illustrated example has a flake missing from either end but otherwise is regular and smooth. These are presumably nonlocal in origin; a cache of 4 similar items, all with flakes removed from one or two ends, was found in Mound B. As with Group 24, these may well represent the unit by which pebble quartz is brought to the site for further reduction. If so, then the flakes often struck from one edge may represent an experiment at the place of acquisition to determine the quality of the material before exchange or transport to the village. $n = 3$.

Group 26 These are small quartzite pebbles, smoothed from use or water action (Figure 4.14C). Most are elongated and cylindrical, 2 are round, and 1 is disk shaped. These can be found in local stream beds, but do not seem to occur naturally in the matrix of the site. They could have been used for shaping, smoothing, or burnishing ceramics. They are most common in the eastern and southern midden areas. $n = 15$.

Group 27 These are flat stone disks possibly used as hones; the illustrated specimen bears two faint grooves on one side (Figure 4.14D). One of the 2 is made of a sandy limestone; the other is a quartzite. $n = 2$.

Two additional groups, one of 27 miscellaneous retouched flakes and one of 35 miscellaneous utilized flakes, complete the recognized inventory of worked lithic materials from all village excavations to date. Both categories are heavily concentrated in the northern midden area and are nearly absent in the southern midden.

Discussion

In this lithic assemblage, worked lithic objects that presumably shared similar scraping or cutting functions take on a bewildering variety of forms. It is as if the maker had casually selected any remotely suitable item and made it work for the purpose at hand. Among the non–projectile point worked lithics there is one apparent exception to this expediency. This is the class of large-stemmed asymetrical knives that are quite similar to each other in form (Group 22).

FLORAL AND FAUNAL REMAINS

Faunal preservation at the site was very poor. Fully 65% of the recovered fragments were preserved only because they had been partially burned or completely calcined, and these were always very fragmentary (average weight of the recovered bone fragments was only 0.25 g). Large identifiable bone fragments were treated after excavation with a mixture of Ethulose and Carbowax.

All identified species from the midden (excluding terrestrial snails and obviously modern inclusions) are listed in Table 4.4 by number of fragments per element. Identification of these fragments was carried out by Kohler in the Florida State Museum Zooarchaeology Laboratory under the supervision of Elizabeth S. Wing.

Due to the obvious preservational biases in the sample presented in Table 4.4 no attempt was made to quantify minimum number of individuals or amount of meat represented. The sample also seems unsuitable for providing indications of seasonality of occupation. It should be noted that all of the identified shells and the shark could not have been obtained locally (the oyster and *Busycon* shells and the shark tooth could have been brought to the site as tools). The freshwater mussels (Unionidae) might have been available in the Suwannee River no more than 10 km away; but the saltwater species must have originated in the Gulf of Mexico, the closest point being the Steinhatchee–Deadman Bay area 70 km distant or the Atlantic coast, possibly from the mouth of the St. Johns River, about 100 km away. Of the eight examples of nonlocal fauna, five were obtained from the midden directly southeast of Mound B in an

Table 4.4
Faunal Remains from Village Excavations

Animal species	Elements present
Mollusca	
cf. *Busycon* spp.	1 columella
cf. *Crassostrea virginica*	1 valve
cf. Unionidae	2 valves
unidentified	3 valves
Chondrichthyes	
Carcharhinus cf. *milberti*	1 tooth
Osteichthyes	
Amia calva	1 vertebra
Siluriformes cf. Ictaluridae	2 vertebrae, 1 spine
Ictalurus sp.	1 vertebra
Micropterus salmoides	1 vertebra
unidentified	1 vertebra, 1 spine
Reptilia	
Emydidae	6 carapace, 1 coracoid
Kinosternon spp.	5 carapace
Trionyx ferox	1 carapace
Deirochelys reticularia	1 carapace, 1 plastron
unidentified turtle	2 carapace
Alligator mississipiensis	1 scute
Aves	
unidentified	16 unidentified long bones
Mammalia	
cf. *Sciurus* spp.	1 femur
Odocoileus virginianus	11 vertebrae, 26 teeth, 2 auditory bullae, 1 scapula, 20 humeri, 2 radii, 1 metacarpal, 4 carpals, 7 femora, 15 tibiae, 7 metatarsals, 111 unidentified bones, 13 phalanges
unidentified	1462 fragments
Unidentified	1530 fragments

area representing less than one-third of the total excavated volume.

Because of preservation conditions, fish are very underrepresented in this sample. If the true proportions were known, it is likely that they would approximate those at a contemporaneous habitation site in North-Central Florida (8-A-169; Cumbaa 1972:48), where 90% of the identified specimens in the excavated faunal collection originated in swamp and aquatic ecosystems. Certainly the location of these two sites in relation to aquatic resources is very similar. Based on the composition of the fauna at 8-A-169, Cumbaa inferred a year-round occupation at that site. By analogy, this might also be inferred for the McKeithen village.

No bone that could be positively identified as human was found in the village midden areas. Nor were there any features interpretable as burial pits or cremations. Given the elaborate ritual surrounding disposal of the dead documented in Chapter 5, this is not surprising, except insofar as the number of burials in Mound C could not conceivably reflect the total death population at the site.

The only abundant floral remains at the site were (unidentified) wood charcoal and burned fragments of hickory (*Carya* spp.) shell. One carbonized persimmon seed (*Diospyros virginiana*) was recovered from a large pit feature southeast of Mound B. Early attempts to extract pollen from the midden and feature deposits showed that none had been preserved, and sampling for pollen was soon terminated.

Although it seems likely that at least squash and perhaps corn cultivation were known by the occupants of the site, there is no direct evidence for either plant. This lack of cultigens does not necessarily indicate an absence of cultivation. However, the pattern of Weeden Island settlements in North Florida is conditioned primarily by access to permanent water sources, mesic hammock environments, abundant aquatic fauna, and high vegetational diversity (see Chapter 3). This suggests that food production, though perhaps present, played only a minor role in the total subsistence effort. In assessing the role of agriculture in McKeithen Weeden Island culture, it is important to remember that the structure of the environment—and particularly the animal resources—little resembles

that of areas where agriculture developed early. Specifically, the relatively small seasonal fluctuations in temperature and moisture contributed to a year-round availability of fauna that itself is not undergoing dramatic seasonal cycles in its nutritive value or abundance. This lack of faunal seasonability contributes in turn to low storage requirements and hence little profit from embarking on a strategy to utilize intensively a resource (such as maize) for which storability is its chief advantage. Indeed, no storage features or structures were documented in the village. Although they could easily have been missed due to our small sample or due to faulty interpretation, we would not expect food storage to be an important part of the subsistence strategy.

BUILDING A CHRONOLOGY

With the completion of the midden investigations and the classification and analysis of the excavated materials, attempts to identify changes in the artifacts through time began in earnest. Four types of evidence were used: (1) the stratigraphic relations of excavated levels, (2) the radiocarbon dates, (3) the changes in relative frequency of the various ceramic and lithic material categories through time, and (4) the study of 32 attributes of the sample of potsherds from the midden excavations.

Considering the radiocarbon dates first, the averaged date of A.D. 1395 ± 40 from a shallow feature in the northern midden area seems obviously out of place in comparison to the other dates. It also seems out of place because the ceramic assemblage from the feature was similar to that for the site as a whole. The feature is believed to be contemporary with the upper portions of the occupation in the northern midden area, and it seems probable that some contaminating factor—such as a postoccupation tree—had interfered. On the early end of the spectrum, the 30 B.C. ± 95 date from deep within the southern midden near Mound B is too early given the associated artifacts. Based on the range of each of the dates in Table 4.1, we place the Weeden Island village occupation within the range A.D. 200–750, recognizing that a somewhat shorter time span is also possible.

To test the hypotheses concerning the village occupation outlined at the beginning of this chapter, we needed to establish rough contemporaneities between excavated levels all across the habitation area—a more difficult problem than merely assigning a range to the date of occupation. The method developed to achieve this requires many pages to describe in detail (see Kohler 1978b:130–177) but can be briefly characterized as follows:

1. Using an R-mode principal components analysis of the relative frequencies of selected pottery and lithic types, chronologically sensitive factors were discovered for each midden area through their success in replacing the excavated levels in their correct stratigraphic order on their factor scores.

2. The acceptable radiocarbon dates for each midden area were plotted along a time scale with one standard deviation around each date represented by a heavy bar to the left of the appropriate stratigraphic column (see Figure 4.15). The northern and southern midden each have three acceptable dates, and the eastern midden area has two.

3. Since each radiocarbon date is derived from a provenience that also has an associated factor score, the factor scores between two dates in each chronological column were approximately scaled in relation to the absolute time line.

4. The individual proveniences were plotted with triangles along the scaled pseudo–time line for each area on the basis of its factor scores.

5. Depth categories were created in each of the three midden areas by lumping adjacent vertical levels after discarding the plow zone. These depth categories (three in the eastern midden, and four in the deeper northern and southern middens) were used as groups for testing a series of nominal-, ordinal-, and interval-level ceramic attributes for change through time.

6. The depth categories were graphically scaled against the levels located on the time column through their factor scores by centering the middle of each depth category for each midden area on the median factor score for the levels comprising that depth category.

7. The salient characteristics for the pottery from each depth category as determined by the attribute analysis were listed in the appropriate depth category.

8. For the portions of each column extending above or below the extreme radiocarbon dates for that area, the depth categories were positioned relative to each other in the manner that creates the best accord between the ceramic attributes for the depth categories when the chart is read across the columns (that is, for any given period of time).

9. Finally, the ceramic and lithic types, which were important in forming the factors against which the levels were scored, were listed above (for late markers) and below (for early markers) each column. Due to the linear nature of the principal components technique used, these are categories that either regularly increase or decrease through time, or are present at only one end of the temporal sequence

The resultant chart (Figure 4.15) both describes the most obvious trends of change through time in the ceramic and lithic materials and establishes rough temporal equivalences across the site for further intrasite analysis.

In his well-known sequence, Willey separated the Weeden Island period into early and late divisions primarily on the replacement of

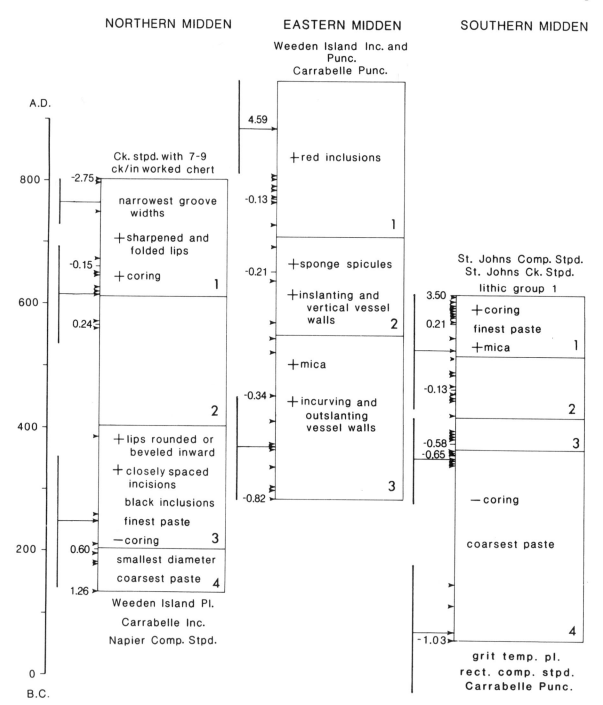

Figure 4.15   Village chronology. (+) indicates most (e.g., + coring is *most coring*); (−) indicates least.

Swift Creek Complicated Stamped pottery (late variety) by Wakulla Check Stamped pottery. He notes that

> the two periods, Weeden Island I and II, follow in that order after Santa Rosa–Swift Creek. Weeden Island I is noted by the first appearance of the Weeden Island series of pottery types. As now defined, Weeden Island Plain covers a great range of vessel forms, some of which first appear in the Santa Rosa–Swift Creek period. . . . Some types, such as Weeden Island Punctated, are more common in . . . Weeden Island II than in Weeden Island I. (1949:397)

Willey's dichotomy of the Weeden Island period has been further subdivided by Percy and Brose (1974) with additional specifications in Percy (1976). These subdivisions are as follows:

Weeden Island 1 This dominant ceramic type is late variety Swift Creek Complicated Stamped. Weeden Island types—including Weeden Island Incised, Keith Incised, Carrabelle Incised, and Carrabelle Punctated—appear for the first time. These were reported at Hall, Mound Field, Bird Hammock, Carrabelle (Pits III and IV), Fort Walton (Pit IV), and Parrish Lake (Area G).

Weeden Island 2 These other incised and punctated types in the Weeden Island series appear alongside those found during Weeden Island 1. These are represented at Bird Hammock, Hall, Carrabelle (Pits III and IV), Sowell (Pits III and IV), Fort Walton (Pits I and IV), and Stoutamire.

Weeden Island 3 This subdivision represents the introduction of check stamping coupled with a slight decline in importance of complicated stamping. These were reported at Hall, Sowell (Pits III and IV), Fort Walton (Pits I and VI), Stoutamire, and the southern end of Torreya site.

Weeden Island 4 During this period, complicated stamping disappears and check stamping increases in importance. These are represented at Sowell (Pits III and IV), Fort Walton (Pit VI), and Torreya (northern end).

Weeden Island 5 During this period cob marked pottery appears but checked stamped ceramics clearly dominate. Weeden Island series types have become less abundant.

Although the divisions are more specific than Willey's very general period assignments, the Percy and Brose scheme cannot be applied equally well to all the local Weeden Island cultures. Especially in North Florida and the North Peninsular Gulf coastal regions, it is doubtful that Wakulla Check Stamped was ever the dominant pottery type, even in very late Weeden Island period sites. In contrast to the 66% of total ceramics reported at 8-Li-8 (Percy 1976:81) or the 42% reported from Level 1 of Test 3 at the Tucker site (Sears 1963:10), Wakulla Check Stamped rarely exceeds 5% in the latest levels at the McKeithen site, which date between A.D. 600 and 750. It comprises 0–8% at later Weeden Island sites in North Florida (e.g., Johns Pond and Leslie Mound; see Appendix). The same is true for Swift Creek Complicated Stamped; the earliest levels at McKeithen contain far fewer examples of this type than do many sites to the west that are probably contemporaneous.

Despite these differences in relative abundance of the temporal markers, the general scheme of pottery change proposed by Willey (1949) for coastal sites and by Percy and Brose (1974) for the Florida Panhandle is reflected in several major trends of change at the North Florida McKeithen site. Certainly, small-check stamped pottery increases in later levels; this is represented by St. Johns Check Stamped in the eastern midden area and Wakulla Check Stamped in the northern midden. As predicted by Willey, Weeden Island Plain seems to show up quite early in the sequence, appearing as an early type in the northern midden seriation; Weeden Island Punctated, on the other hand, is more abundant in later levels than in earlier levels in the eastern midden area. Moreover, as predicted by both chronologies, Swift Creek Complicated Stamped (undifferentiated as to early or late) and large-check stamped ceramics have a weak tendency to occur in greater relative abundance toward the bottom (earlier levels) of midden deposits.

In general, all the rectilinear complicated

stamped types at McKeithen are slightly better represented in early levels than in late.
This should be no surprise as Willey
(1949:383–386) assigned both Crooked River
Complicated Stamped and St. Andrews Complicated Stamped to the Santa Rosa–Swift
Creek period.

Carrabelle Punctated is included in Figure
4.15 as an early type in the southern midden
area and a later type in the eastern midden
area. The early Carrabelle Punctated sherds
from the southern midden typically bear small,
well-spaced triangular punctations not unlike
those in the later type Weeden Island Punctated
though the paste is coarser. Small, round punctations also appear in early levels but are rather
uncommon. Over time, punctation styles pro-
liferate, with crescent and linear fingernail impressions and the donut like hollow reed impressions reaching highest relative frequencies
late in the occupation at McKeithen; this punctation style is characteristic of Carrabelle Punctated, which appears as a late marker in the
eastern midden area. Given the temporal differences for variants of Carrabelle Punctated
pottery, the establishment of a type–variety
system to formally recognize these variants
might prove very useful. Examination of Figure
4.15 suggests several other points:

1. The only time during which all three areas
   of the site were occupied was during the
   period A.D. 300–500 (compare the A.D.
   350–495 range for use of the mounds discussed in Chapter 5). In general, the earliest occupation of the site seems to have
   been along the northern and southern
   middens, while the last occupation at the
   site seems to have been along the east.
2. General trends in paste texture seem to
   have been from a coarse paste with gritty
   inclusions that had little or no unoxidized
   core, to a finer textured paste with a dark
   central core.

3. The frequency of micaceous inclusions in
   the ceramics was highest from about A.D.
   300–500, and lower toward the beginning
   and end of the occupation.
4. St. Johns paste types were infrequent at
   the beginning of the occupation and
   reached their peak frequencies after A.D.
   450.
5. As established by Willey, Weeden Island
   Plain appears as an early marker and
   Weeden Island Punctated and various
   check stamped types appear as late
   markers.
6. In general, land and groove width on both
   check stamped and complicated stamped
   ceramics narrowed through time.

Some other trends noted in either the principal components analysis or the attribute analysis, but which were not recorded in Table 4.3,
include

1. Relatively long projectile points, like those
   of Lithic Groups 5 and 7, decline in frequency relative to the small triangular
   points, especially those of Group 1, during
   the course of the occupation. The general
   stemless triangular form was already established, however, by the beginning of
   the occupation.
2. Weeden Island Red, and especially Weeden Island Zoned Red, decreased in relative frequency and perhaps disappeared
   after about A.D. 500; at this time, Weeden
   Island Incised and Weeden Island Punctated were increasing in relative frequency. The net effect, however, was a lower
   total percentage for these four types, taken
   together, by the end of the occupation.

This second point apparently reflects a trend
also noted for at least the southern portions of
the Lower Mississippi Valley and perhaps over
large portions of the Gulf coastal plain. In a

study of red painted pottery in the southern Lower Mississippi Valley, Belmont and Williams (1981) have identified two temporally successive and geographically widespread horizons that together span the period from about A.D. 300 to 600. After A.D. 600, elaborate zoned red and polychrome painting seem to disappear in that region. Some simple red slipping or washing—apparently the equivalent of what we call residual red at the McKeithen site—persists for a couple of centuries after A.D. 600 in some portions of the Lower Mississippi Valley and apparently in the Weeden Island area as well.

A RETURN TO THE HYPOTHESIS

After the construction of this total site seriation the chronological continuum was divided into three phases. The first consists of proveniences believed to have been deposited before about A.D. 300; the second from A.D. 300 to 500; and the third from A.D. 500 until the abandonment of the site, probably shortly after A.D. 750. Proveniences deposited during each of these phases could be identified by reference to the master chronological chart.

In the first part of this chapter, it was hypothesized that the McKeithen site represents the remains of a society characterized by a considerable degree of social inequality or ranking. The test implications suggested that high-status areas, if they existed, could be distinquished from the rest of the site on the basis of

1. greater concentration of elite pottery types;
2. greater concentrations of nonlocal ceramics;
3. greater ceramic type diversity;
4. greater frequencies of nonlocal bone, shell, and lithic materials;
5. dwellings of larger size, with more diverse

and elaborate features, located adjacent to public spaces.

In addition, from a regional perspective, the settlement pattern should be at least two tiered. The McKeithen village should be clearly larger than other contemporaneous villages if we also wish to interpret it as socially more complex. Absolute population estimates for the site should be derived if possible.

This last point has been partially addressed in the discussion of the survey results (see Chapter 3), and it is examined further in this section. It is obvious that there is presently not enough structural evidence from the village portion of the site to address the fifth test implication. Unfortunately, poor organic preservation in the site also makes it impossible to deal with distribution of bone and shell in a satisfactory manner. This leaves distribution of elite pottery types, distributions of nonlocal pottery, total ceramic type diversity, and distribution of nonlocal lithic artifacts along with estimates of village population size, as test implications for the hypothesis.

To address the first implication, the elite group of pottery types, as stated previously, is distinguished from other pottery on the basis of high vessel form diversity, high proportion of lip additions, smoothest surface finish, and finest paste. This group is composed of Weeden Island Incised, Weeden Island Punctated, Weeden Island Zoned Red, and Weeden Island Red. Even though not all of the sherds in this category display all of the just-mentioned attributes, these attributes reach their highest relative frequencies in the pottery of this group.

Next, the remaining pottery types, which have the highest proportion of paste attributes and design characteristics (suggesting nonlocal manufacture), were identified. Excluding the Weeden Island series, this group includes St. Johns paste ceramics (and Papys Bayou series), Crooked River Complicated Stamped, Kolomo-

Table 4.5
Variation over Time in the Test Variables Calculated for Pottery

Test variables[a]	Early phase	Middle phase	Late phase
Elite ceramics			
mean	3.60/3.78	4.69/4.49	2.57/3.65
standard deviation	3.86	2.95	2.06
CV	106.9	62.9	80.2
Nonlocal ceramics			
mean	3.52/3.51	3.26/3.19	2.05/2.94
standard deviation	2.65	3.21	2.44
CV	75.3	98.5	119.0
correlation with elite ceramics			
r	0.43/0.60	0.07/0.15	0.60/0.54
r^2	0.19/0.36	0.01/0.02	0.35/0.29
p values	0.06/0.01	0.40/0.30	0.03/0.04
Nonlocal lithics			
mean	7.57/5.22	2.67/1.93	7.18/5.32
standard deviation	7.83	3.48	3.16
CV	103.4	130.4	44.0
correlation with elite ceramics			
r	0.07/−0.26	−0.62/−0.54	0.44/0.21
r^2	0.01/0.07	0.38/0.30	0.20/0.04
p values	0.40/0.18	0.01/0.02	0.09/0.27
Ceramic diversity index ($\overline{H}$)			
mean	1.46	1.37	1.40
standard deviation	0.30	0.33	0.21
CV	20.3	24.4	14.9
correlation with elite ceramics			
r	0.53/0.64	0.36/0.53	0.39/0.58
r^2	0.28/0.41	0.13/0.28	0.15/0.34
p values	0.02/0.01	0.09/0.02	0.12/0.03

[a]Means and correlation coefficients are expressed as relative frequency/count per cubic meter (density). Standard deviations and CVs are based on frequency data. Because of the closed array effect, the value of r^2 computed over the frequency data is generally slightly less than that computed over the density data when r is positive. The opposite is true when r is negative. Number of proveniences: early, 14; middle, 15; late, 11.

ki Complicated Stamped, and Napier Complicated Stamped. Once again, although some individual pots in this category may have been locally manufactured, the group as a whole certainly contains a high frequency of nonlocally produced vessels. The third test implication, ce-

ramic type diversity, was examined by calculating an index of type diversity ($\overline{H}$) and determining distribution. Lastly, distribution of nonlocal lithic materials (in some instances this included debitage) was determined by plotting distributions of raw materials; silicified coral, quartz, galena, mica, and jasper are all probable non-local raw materials.

Separate SYMAPs of the distributions of each of these variables over the site were obtained for each of the three temporal phases described in the preceding to note changes through time within the hot spots. The resulting four sets of SYMAPs are reproduced here as Figures 4.16–4.19 (the maps have been interpreted in detail in Kohler 1978b:190–205).

Finally for each phase, several statistics including mean, standard deviation, and coefficient of variation CV were computed for each data category. A correlation coefficient for relative frequency and density was computed between elite ceramics and each of the other data categories (nonlocal pottery, nonlocal lithic materials, and ceramic diversity; see Table 4.5).

Elite Pottery

During the early phase, prior to A.D. 300, the highest frequencies of the elite ceramics are found in the area southeast of Mound B (Figure 4.16). Much of the nonlocal bone and the earliest dates also come from this area. Frequencies reach 13%, compared to 3.6% for all proveniences assigned to this phase. During the middle phase (A.D. 300–500), by contrast, there are two distinct peaks in the distribution of elite ceramics. One peak is represented by a group of proveniences that lie in the middle of the southern midden ridge; the relative frequency of these types reaches 9%, compared to 4.7% for the site as a whole. Facing this group across the plaza is the other area, located about 90 m southeast of Mound C, which also contains 9% of these ceramics. During the late phase (A.D. 500–750), the average relative frequency of these types is only 2.6%. Peaks in the distribution are no longer so clear-cut, though two areas in the northeast corner of the site contain 6% of this ceramic group.

Both the mean relative frequency and the mean density of elite types increase from the early to middle phase but fall off noticeably during the final phase. The CV, on the other hand, first increases and then decreases. In this situation the CV can be thought of as measuring whether these ceramics are uniformly distributed or are clustered in their distribution. High values indicate clustering and low values uniformity.

Nonlocal Ceramics

The mean relative frequencies and densities of the nonlocal pottery types (excluding the four types referred to here as Weeden Island elite types) decline steadily through time at the site from the early to the late phase (Figure 4.17). At the same time, their distribution across the site becomes less even, as shown in the rising CVs. In the early phase, one of the two areas having 7% nonlocal pottery (versus 3.5% for the site as a whole during the early phase) coincides with the proveniences southeast of Mound B that had high relative frequencies of elite pottery. During the middle phase, the nonlocal pottery types reach 9 and 10% in two areas on the southern midden ridge; one of these locations also has high percentages of elite pottery during this phase. Finally, during the late phase, only one area, in the eastern midden, has high percentages of nonlocal pottery; this is the same location having high relative frequencies of elite ceramics during the late phase. Our hypothesis predicts positive spatial correlations between elite and nonlocal ceramics. In every case the observed correlations are in the right direction (positive), although the distributions of elite and nonlocal pottery types are significantly correlated in the early and late phases.

Ceramic Diversity Index

Ceramic diversity is measured here using the Shannon–Weiner $\bar{H}$ Index (Odum 1971:144),

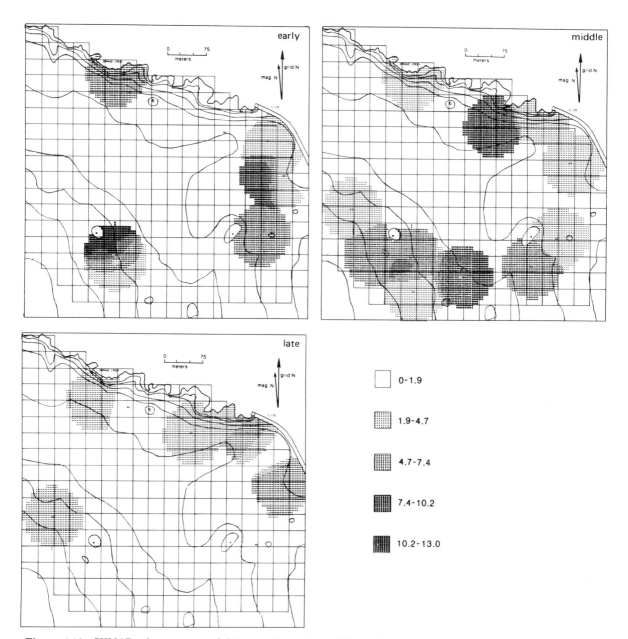

Figure 4.16 SYMAPs of percentages of elite ceramics; early, middle, and late phases. Contour interval is 1.0 m.

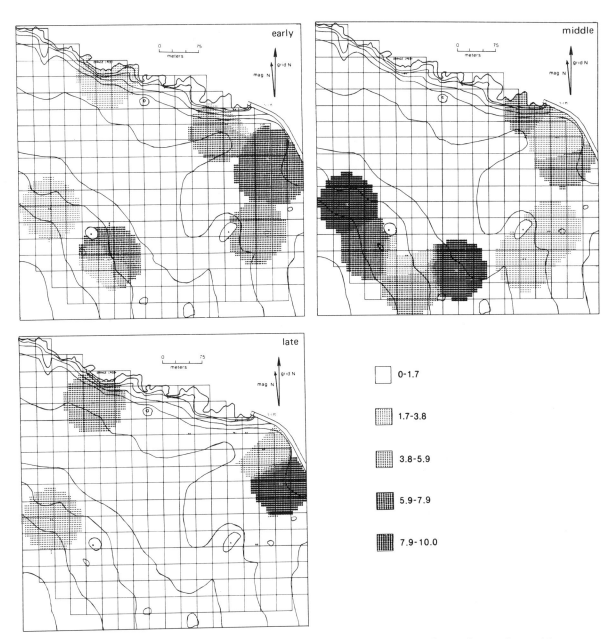

Figure 4.17 SYMAPs of percentages of nonlocal ceramics; early, middle, and late phases. Contour interval is 1.0 m.

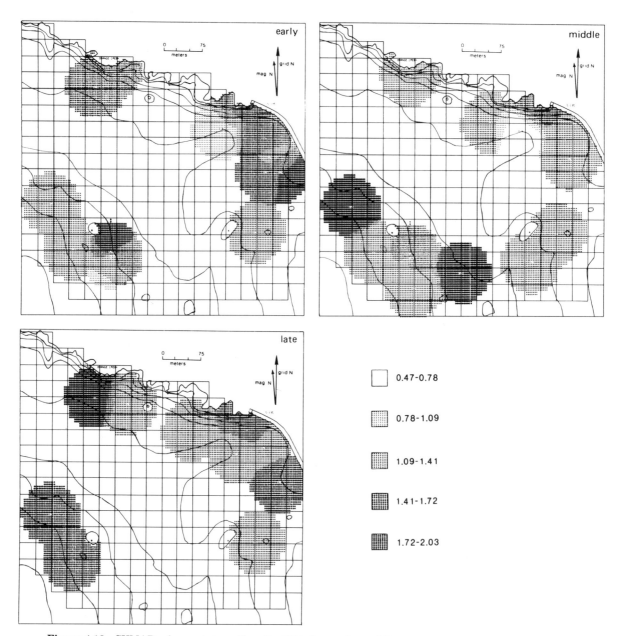

Figure 4.18 SYMAPs of ceramic type diversity (H) index; early, middle, and late phases. Contour is 1.0 m.

which takes into account both the number of categories and the evenness with which the sample is divided among them. Zero indicates minimum diversity. Maximum possible diversity, as predicted by the hypothesis, is the natural logarithm of the number of pottery types in the analysis. As predicted by the hypothesis, proveniences having the most diverse ceramics tend also to have high concentrations of elite and nonlocal ceramics and nonlocal lithics (Figure 4.18). Undoubtedly there is a certain amount of necessary correlation, since nonlocal and elite ceramics contribute to the diversity index, but many other ceramic types not included in these two categories also contribute to the correlation (see Table 4.2). Table 4.5 shows that the mean value for ceramic diversity remains quite stable through time even as the densities and relative frequencies of nonlocal and elite ceramics trail off.

Nonlocal Lithic Materials

There are two peaks of concentration in the distributions of nonlocal lithic materials in the early phase, one of which coincides with the peak southeast of Mound B for the elite and nonlocal ceramics. The other, higher concentration appears in the extreme northeastern corner of the site. During the middle phase there is a dramatic decline in the sitewide frequency of nonlocal lithic materials, but the CV goes up since there is only one area—in the same northeastern corner of the site—having high frequencies of the variable. Finally, in the late phase, the sitewide frequency of nonlocal lithic materials rises, but the materials are spread more evenly across the site (Figure 4.19).

Unlike the nonlocal ceramics, the distributions of nonlocal lithic materials across the site are independent of the distributions of elite ceramics with the exception of the middle phase, during which time there is a strong significant negative correlation between the two categories. The distribution of the nonlocal lithic material does not correspond to the expected pattern. This may be due to the inclusion of silicified coral, which is actually not nonlocal. If there were a specialized production sequence for nonlocal tools, then perhaps only the tools themselves, and not the debitage, would correspond to the expected pattern. Much remains to be learned about lithic production and use at the McKeithen site.

Population Size

Earlier in this chapter it was argued that there are good reasons to expect a general increase in degree of social complexity with increasing residential population size. Groups of less than 100 persons, for example, ordinarily are loosely organized in bands, while groups of between 100 and 500 persons generally benefit from more complex organizational systems (such as those present among tribal societies; the terms *band* and *tribal* society are used here as defined by Service (1962:110–142). A minimum threshold of about 500 for the support of a full-time information specialist, such as a chief, has often been proposed (Birdsell 1968; Flannery 1972; Sanders and Price 1968).

Population estimation at McKeithen cannot depend on floor area of dwellings, spacing of dwellings, counts of house mounds, or volume of surface structure rubble. In the Southeast in general, methods based on high architectural visibility or large-scale excavation are either impractical or very expensive. Workers in other areas have also shown that methods based on site size alone are very poor indicators of habitation floor area and, hence, momentary site population (Cook and Heizer 1965, Table 9; Kohler and Schlanger 1980:31).

One reason for undertaking a probability sampling program at McKeithen was to provide

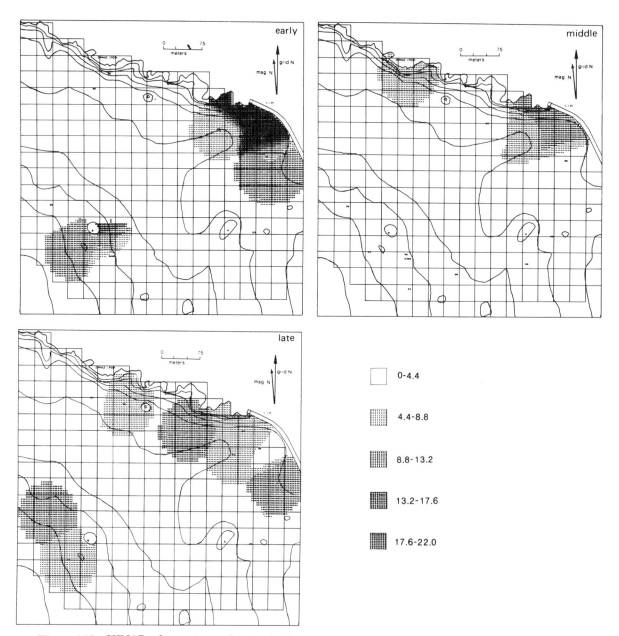

Figure 4.19 SYMAPs of percentages of nonlocal lithics; early, middle, and late phases. Contour interval is 1.0 m.

an alternative to these approaches through time–rate methods using the unbiased estimates of artifact population totals that the probability sample could provide. Using a simulation technique fully explained in Kohler (1978a), estimates of human population levels for the site were obtained through estimates of ceramic population sizes, making assumptions about ceramic breakage rates and household vessel inventories based on ethnographic and ethnoarchaeological work by David (1972), De-Boer (1974), and Foster (1960). Drawing on the results of the ceramic seriation and the mound excavations, a model of population growth during the first two village phases (until A.D. 500) followed by a fairly rapid population decline until abandonment shortly after A.D. 750 seems more plausible than models assuming either a steady population growth or a constant population size. For this population growth–decline model, the best estimate of peak population size at the site is slightly over 100; the maximum estimate, taking into account the standard deviations of the various variables, is about 350 (Kohler 1978a:12). In retrospect, propagation of error techniques (Crandall and Seabloom 1970:139–159) should have been used to deal with the problem of multiplying and dividing variables associated with standard deviations. Had this been done, the difference between the maximum estimate and the best estimate would be narrower. The best estimate would be unchanged.

Despite the many assumptions and uncertainties attached to population estimation using this method, it clearly suggests that the resident population was probably smaller than the population size associated with ethnographically observed chiefdoms. As predicted by the hypothesis (but unfortunately measured only by site size), the resident population at McKeithen considerably exceeded that of the contemporaneous sites in its region.

SUMMARY

It is now known, as it was not when these data were first interpreted and reported (Kohler 1978b), that the three mounds at McKeithen were contemporaneous, fulfilled different functions, and were in use during a portion of the middle occupation phase. In conjunction with the ceramic seriation this suggests that at that time, the site reached its peak population and its greatest internal heterogeneity and inequality as well. It must be concluded that the data presented in the preceding generally support the test implications of the hypothesis.

In addition, the analysis has also provided information on the processes through which increasing social heterogeneity and inequality seem to develop. Elite ceramics are most abundant in the habitation area during the phase of mound construction and use, and are also more evenly spread about the site at this time than during any other phase. Nonlocal lithic materials, on the other hand, are less abundant than during the earlier or later phase and are also less evenly distributed across the site. Moreover, during the middle phase only, there is a strong negative correlation between the abundance of nonlocal lithic materials and elite ceramics in any given provenience. In closing, these and other data suggest the following:

1. The site was occupied both before and after the period of mound construction and use.

2. During the period of mound construction and use, social group interactions within the Weeden Island region are quite high and the four ceramic types called elite reach their maximum popularity.

3. If the use and distribution of these so-called elite types really was controlled by high-status individuals who were also involved in the mortuary ceremonialism and other mound use, then rather than monopolizing these ceramics, they instead distributed elite ceramics more

widely across the site during this phase than they had been before or after. This may also suggest that all of the McKeithen inhabitants were of higher status relative to other local villagers during the period of mound use, a reflection of the increased importance of the site.

4. The other nonlocal ceramics (and it must be remembered that some of the elite ceramics were probably manufactured nonlocally; see Chapter 6) do not respond to this same effect. This may indicate that the networks of production and distribution for the elite ceramics were not the same as those for other nonlocal ceramics. In this case, the suggestion that elites controlled the acquisition and distribution of the so-called elite ceramics, but not of many other nonlocal items, seems reasonable.

5. The negative correlation between nonlocal lithic materials and elite ceramics during the middle phase and the general north–south differentiation between the relative frequencies of ceramic and lithic materials suggest a degree of organization of production or use of nonlocal lithic implements that was not anticipated in a site of this period.

6. Several lithic categories (projectile points, Groups 2 and 6; bifaces, Group 16; microblades, Group 17; side and end scrapers, Group 20; hafted[?] side and end scrapers, Group 22; large, stemmed asymmetrical knives, Group 23; bladelike flakes; and retouched and utilized flakes) are either confined to the northern midden area or are more abundant there than would be expected.

7. Three projectile point types (Groups 3, 4, and 8), small hammerstonelike tools (Group 18), and small quartzite pebbles perhaps involved in ceramic manufacture (Group 26) are the only lithic implements that are more common in the eastern and southern midden areas than in the northern midden. These differential distributions of lithic implements were not anticipated but might indicate more processing of animals for food and hide, more stone tool manufacture, and more expedient use of lithic debitage taking place in the northern midden adjacent to the creek. Perhaps ceramic manufacture and the curation of certain projectile points was concentrated in the eastern and southern midden areas.

5

Charnel Knowledge: McKeithen Mounds

Excavation of the three mounds (A, B, and C) at the McKeithen site began in fall 1977 immediately following the completion of Kohler's investigations in the village midden and plaza. The mound excavations allowed further consideration of the model presented in Chapter 3. We sought information regarding the nature of the village as a center for inter- and intralineage activities. Investigation of the mounds was also expected to provide evidence of inequality in burial patterns, reflecting higher social status for religious specialists. We did not expect to find that the three mounds were a single complex functioning together in time apparently under the control of a single "big man" (or religious specialist or warrior–priest). This unexpected result supports pertinent aspects of the model; the McKeithen site indeed functioned as a center for a period of time. Data from the site relative to social organization and temporal position also lend strong support for our contention that the Kolomoki site was a similar, anomalous center approximately contemporaneous in time.

Kohler's work in the village delineated the nature of the community pattern: a horseshoe-shaped arc of households surrounding a central plaza devoid of midden. During the period of densest village occupation (and greatest population), three low platform mounds were con-

structed on top of older midden deposits along the north, south, and southwest portions of the horseshoe (see Figure 4.3). Our best interpretation of the 11 radiocarbon dates from the mounds—5 from Mound A, not including one data of 1720 ± 80 radiocarbon years: A.D. 230 (UM-1435) from under the mound, and 3 dates each from Mounds B and C—is that mound construction took place at about or after A.D. 350. Activities on the platforms ended at about A.D. 475, at which time all structures on the platforms were burned and removed and the mounds capped. Kohler's (Chapter 4) conclusions regarding the temporal periods of village occupation and the increased complexity and density of occupation during the middle period correlate quite well with the period of mound construction, use, and cessation of use. After the end of mound use (i.e., after A.D. 475), the village continued to be occupied, but its size and importance as a center declined (Kohler's third or late phase of village occupation).

Although Southeast archaeologists generally view as an anathema attempts to relate community plans to astronomical phenomena, we have no such compunction in suggesting that the exact position of the McKeithen mounds was planned to allow the rising sun at the summer solstice to be observed and calculated from Mound B. Together the three mounds form an

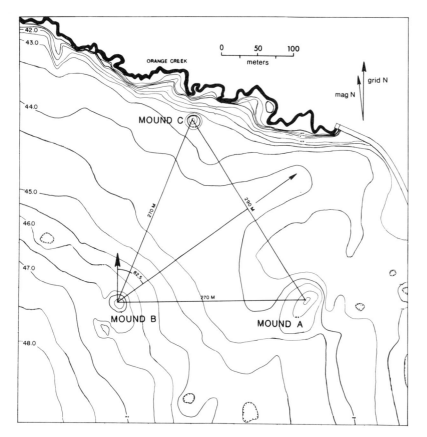

Figure 5.1 Plan of McKeithen mounds. Contour interval is 0.5 m.

isosceles triangle (almost an equilateral), with a line between Mounds A and C as the base and Mound B as the apex (Figure 5.1). The distance along the base (measured from the center of the primary platform mound in Mound A to the same point in Mound C) is 290 m. Length of the sides (measured to the center of the structure erected on the Mound B platform) is 270 m. The perpendicular bisector of the triangle, formed by a line from Mound B to the triangle base, points toward the position of the rising sun at the summer solstice, approximately 62.5° east of magnetic and true north.

As a consequence of its position on the natural ridge paralleling Orange Creek, a ridge further heightened by midden deposits, the top of the Mound B platform was the highest point in

the village, excepting a very small portion of the midden ridge to the southwest of the mound. A portion of that ridge accumulated after the Mound B platform was constructed. Most likely, the Mound B platform was the highest elevation in the village when it was used as the base for a structure. Although the platform itself was only 1 m high, it was 3 m higher than the plaza's center and even higher above the two thirds of the village midden located to the north, northeast, and east of Mound B. The placement of the mound made maximum use of the natural contours of the locale. The mound would have provided a commanding view of the villagers, the plaza, and the line of sight toward the sun at the time of the summer solstice.

The plaza itself was relatively flat. Excavation of the mounds showed that the present ground surface elevations at the site, including the plaza, are almost identical to the elevations at the time the mounds were built. At the time of mound use, the elevation of the plaza was about 44 m AMSL. The surfaces on which Mounds A, B, and C were built were at elevations of approximately 44, 46.5, and 43.5 m AMSL, respectively.

Extending out from the northeast side of the plaza across the village midden and directly between Mounds A and C is an approximately 75-m wide, very low (0.5 m) ridge that follows the 62.5° east-of-north line running from Mound B (see Figures 4.1 and 5.1). The stratigraphy of that ridge is the same as that generally observed throughout the site, and it could not be ascertained that the feature was a deliberate construction of the aborigines.

Figure 5.1 shows the two borrow pits closest to Mound B and the three closest to Mound A. Two other borrow pits, located beyond the coverage of the Figure 5.1 map, are about equidistant to both mounds. There are no borrow pits relatively close to Mound A. That mound seems to have been capped with fine-grained sand taken from the meander belt of Orange Creek. The Mound A primary mound was constructed with humus, old midden, and other soil probably scraped up from the ground surface of the village.

In planning the McKeithen site excavations, sufficient time and money were budgeted for the total excavation of each mound. The use of the bulldozer to move blackdirt and actually to remove a large portion of the cap from Mound A allowed us to complete the planned excavations within schedule. We began investigating each mound with a 3- by 3-m test placed in the eastern side of each mound along its east–west axis. As soon as the edge of the mound cap was clearly delineated, we proceeded toward the center of the mound with several adjacent excavation units totaling 6 or 9 m in width. These units

increased in number as needed to allow a large portion of the mound to be uncovered at the same time.

In all three mounds we found that the construction–use–destruction sequence was the same, although details of platform mound construction differed in Mound A. Each mound began as a low platform, built of soil taken from nearby sources. There was apparently no attempt to get clean soil that did not contain humic inclusions or natural or cultural debris. Only in Mound B was there any attempt to clean the ground surface before depositing the fill for the platform mound. Midden and humic deposits were found on the ground surfaces under Mounds A and C. The platform mounds in Mounds A and B were both rectangular—1 m and 0.5 m high, respectively. The platform mound in C was almost perfectly circular and about 90 cm high.

Structures with walls supported by vertical pine posts were erected on Mounds B and C; the structure on B was a residence or perhaps a temple that was probably inhabited or controlled by the religious specialist who was ultimately interred in it. The Mound C structure probably was a charnel house for the storage of cleaned human burials. No structure was built on Mound A; however, a pine post screen was erected across the platform mound, and the area behind it was evidently used repeatedly to inter and then exhume human burials. Most likely the exhumed bones were cleaned, treated with red ochre, and moved to the Mound C charnel house, where they were stored until they were finally deposited under the Mound C cap.

Together the mounds functioned as a mortuary complex for the disposal of the dead. Presumably the adult male buried in the Mound B structure was the director of the operation. Another duty of this individual was apparently to keep track of a yearly calendar, at least to pinpoint the time of the summer solstice.

At some time, perhaps with the death of the

religious specialist, the mortuary activities ceased. The buildings on Mounds B and C were torn down and burned. Clean white-to-tan sand, the normal leached-out B soil horizon at the site, was then brought in from nearby to cover each platform mound and anything that remained after the structures were burned. The post screen on Mound A was also pulled down and burned in what must have been a giant bonfire. That mound was also capped with white-to-tan sand; but before the soil was brought in, some of the residue of the fire was removed and deposited beyond the western edge of the platform.

By capping or, in effect burying, the three platform mounds, the villagers left nearly permanent monuments. They also afforded the archaeological remains excellent protection and preservation, allowing our interpretations. Detailed descriptions of each mound follow.

PREPARATION OF THE DEAD: MOUND A

Located along the southeast portion of the village midden, Mound A was the largest of the three McKeithen mounds. At the time of excavation the rectangular earthen structure measured 45 by 80 m and reached a height above the old ground surface (the same elevation as the present mound surface) of 1.6 m. The long axis of the mound was oriented approximately 50° east of north.

The highest point of the mound was not the center, but rather a point 25 m inside the northeastern edge. Later it was discovered that this point was at the center of the platform mound; the mound cap had not been centered over the platform mound. Nor was the cap oriented in the same direction as the platform mound the long axis of which was 65.5° east of north, the same heading as the perpendicular bisector of the isosceles triangle formed by the three

mounds (see Figures 5.1 and 5.2). Twentieth-century plowing may account for some of the orientation of the mound cap; however, the asymmetrical position of the cap relative to the center of the platform apparently was deliberate. Extension of the cap toward the southwest was to cover burned material removed from the top of the platform mound prior to capping.

Mound A had been plowed several times in the 1920s for the cultivation of watermelons, and at least two crops of slash pines had been planted on it since then. The second crop was standing at the time we began investigations at the site. During fall 1977, a team of tree harvesters who were thinning out the planted pines were induced to remove all of the pines from Mound A and the immediate area around it. This was easily accomplished with a machine that drove up to each tree, grasped the trunk about 1 m up from the ground with hydraulic arms, and then used giant hydraulic snippers to cut the tree off at ground level. The 10- to 15-m high trees could then be driven away from the mound, still upright and in the clutches of the metal arms. (Those same trees may have been made into the pages of this book.)

We spent 2 weeks during spring 1978 beginning excavation of Mound A. At that time, approximately 6 months after the tree cutting, the pine stumps and their sparse root systems had already begun to rot and could be removed easily. By the time we completed excavations in winter 1979, the stumps and roots were so rotten that we could wait until our excavations had totally exposed the 15 to 20-cm thick trunks and about 1 m of the taproot and then simply kick the stump over. Kicking the stump became standard operating procedure; and by the time each excavation unit reached the level of the platform mound under the mound cap, all evidence of the pine forest had disappeared. The pines had little effect on our excavations and did little damage to the mound features and stratigraphy. (One reason that the trees rotted so

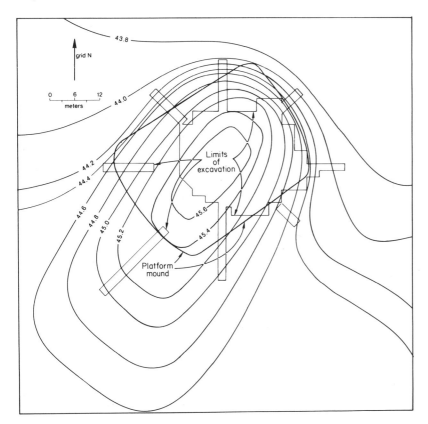

Figure 5.2 Contour map of Mound A and plan of platform mound, cap, and excavations.

rapidly was that the pines were infested with a beetle that crawled under the bark, made most of the trees look sickly, stunted their growth, and even killed some of them. In moderate gusts of wind, even 25 mph, the more brittle, living trees would break off with a large snap about 2 m above ground level. This was nerve shattering enough when we were working on the mound, but was even more disconcerting if one of us happened to be answering a call of nature in the pines when the wind picked up.)

Once hand excavations in Mound A had determined that a mound cap about 1.1 m deep (at its thickest part) had been placed over a platform mound, and once the edges of the platform mound were located by hand- and bulldozer-excavated trenches, the bulldozer was then used to strip off a large portion of the cap. The hand

excavations produced no evidence to indicate that any structure had ever been placed atop the stratum that we interpreted as a cap. After delineating the platform mound's location, hand excavations centered on the eastern three quarters of the platform mound where the burial cleaning activities had taken place (Figure 5.2).

The Mound A rectangular platform mound measured 31 by 42 m. Its top was flat; but because the underlying ground surface sloped upward toward the south (away from the lower elevation of the plaza), more soil was needed on the northern side. Consequently, the thickness of the platform varied from 0.2 to 0.5 m. The top of the rectangular platform would have been about 3 m above the elevation of the surface of the midden along the creek. By positioning the mound on the natural ridge, the builders made

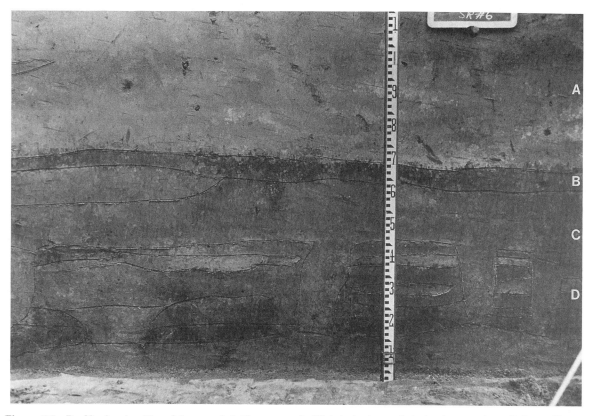

Figure 5.3 Profile showing Mound A cap and platform mound with interior layered strata: A, mound cap; B, burned layer; C, platform mound; D, layers of grey and tan sand.

it appear from the plaza and most of the village that the mound was 2–3 m high; when in fact only 0.5 m of soil (maximum) had been deposited. We were to learn that this was not the only labor-saving ploy that Mound A's builders utilized.

A profile through the mound (Figure 5.3) clearly shows the mound strata that resulted from construction, use, burning, and capping. A 15-cm-thick zone of plowed humus, the result of watermelon and pine cultivation on the top of the mound cap overlies the light, yellowish sand of the remainder of the mound cap. These strata were almost totally devoid of artifacts. Probably the sand came from the borrow pits

placed outside or at the edge of the village midden. The soft mound cap sand provided easy digging for pocket gophers, gopher tortoises, and archaeologists.

Under the mound cap and lying on top of the platform mound was a layer of very distinctive scorched sand. This stratum, a lurid orange to pink in color, also contained charred wood and decomposed, partially burned organic matter. Replicative experiments with fires and sand showed that this stratum could be reproduced exactly, though on a much smaller scale, at the bottom of a camp fire.

Under the fire zone was the distinctive dark grey sand of the platform mound that overlaid the submound humus and midden on which the platform mound was constructed. A radiocarbon date of A.D. 230 came from a charred pine post in the submound midden.

The various major strata within the mound were rather easy to distinguish and excavate in discrete units. Consequently, the history of major mound construction activities was not difficult to determine. The platform mound, however, presented some interesting puzzles, especially early on in its investigation. Our discussion of the mound, including the peculiar interior platform mound and the evidence for the activities carried out on the platform, follows. We will reverse the sequence of our description of the mound presented thus far by beginning at the mound bottom and working our way from the ground up.

Platform Construction

The "construction foreman" for the mound had three tasks to complete before any soil was brought in for the platform. First (not necessarily in temporal sequence), the humic matter and most of the humic zone was scraped off an approximately 1-m-wide line 23 m long and curving in the middle so that the two 11.5-m legs formed a 120° angle. This arching clean line marked the eventual location of the pine post screen across the surface of the platform mound (Figure 5.4). Secondly, a rectangular pit 2 by 4.5 m was excavated to a depth of about 1.7 m below the ground surface. The yellow-to-tan sand from this aboriginal excavation was spread on the ground surface a few meters to the north near the line cleared to mark the eventual post screen. Location of the large, almost straight-sided and flat-bottomed pit was behind the curving screen. A fire was kindled on the pit spoil and the ashes and burned sand were left in place after the fire went out (Figure 5.4).

The third and last task preliminary to constructing the platform was not evident archae-

ologically but must have been carried out. A 12-by 14-m rectangular area was marked off behind the planned screen's location (on the side encompassed by its angle). This rectangle was marked off immediately beside the deep rectangular pit and the remains of the fire. No effort was made to remove any humus or midden within the 12- by 14-m area, nor was any other part of the ground surface under the planned platform mound cleaned, except as noted for the screen.

The actual construction of the mound then began. Dark grey soil with a high humic content was brought in, apparently in baskets; some basket loading of the mound fill stratum was apparent. Occasional pockets of tan-to-white sand were mixed in. In the area marked for the screen, no soil was deposited. As the height of the platform gradually increased, a trench less than 1 m wide at the bottom with sloping walls was formed. This saved the aboriginal dirt carriers from having to move the same dirt—that intended to anchor the posts of the screen in the trench—three times: once to carry it in, once to dig it out to form the trench, and a third time to put it back in the trench to anchor the posts and fill the trench. Instead, they simply moved it once, bringing in the soil to anchor the posts and fill the cleverly formed trench. (Archaeologists should be so lucky with their spoil.)

After the trench was formed but before the posts were put in place, a rain shower (summer in Florida?) occurred and washed some soil down the sloping sides of the trench into the bottom. This distinctive water-deposited varve extended under the portion of the platform mound fill on the outside of the screen, indicating that only the inside portion of the trench (and platform mound) had been deposited at that point. In some places it was impossible to separate the outside edge of the trench from the rest of the mound, indicating that the "filling" of the screen trench and the deposition of some of the platform mound were one construction

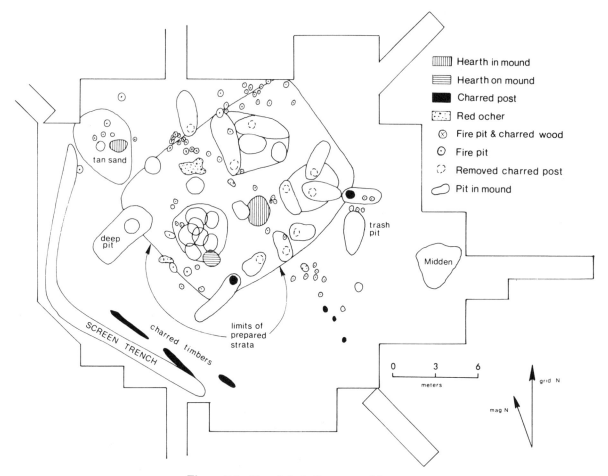

Figure 5.4 Mound A platform mound features.

operation; that is, the posts were held erect and mound fill was deposited around them and continued to be deposited to form the front edge of the platform.

Before any fill was deposited in the 12- by 14-m rectangular area, a peculiar operation took place, one perhaps intended to sanctify or cleanse the 168 m² of the platform mound that would eventually be used for cleaning human bodies. (This probably took place before the screen was built.) First a layer of organic matter (perhaps matting or similar material) was laid down exactly over the 12- by 14-m area. When excavated, this stratum was 2–4 cm thick. Then an approximately 3-cm-thick layer of grey sand identical in texture and color to that brought in to form other portions of the platform mound was spread over the organic matter. This was in turn followed by a thin layer of yellowish tan sand of similar thickness and then another layer of grey. A second layer of the yellowish tan sand was added exactly like the first, and a third layer of the grey sand followed. This was covered by another layer of organic matter, again 2–4 cm thick. The result of this activity was an approximately 25-cm-thick zone of seven distinct strata (see Figure 5.3).

After the middle (second) grey zone was deposited, a small fire was kindled just south of the center of the rectangular area. Some potsherds were also found on that same grey layer, probably deposited at the same time the fire was built. Like the hearth under the mound and beside the rectangular pit, this hearth was left undisturbed and covered with subsequent soil strata. A radiocarbon age of 1690 ± 90 years: A.D. 260 (UM-1644) was obtained from charred wood gathered from the small hearth.

On top of this multilayered sandwich, about 25 cm of the same grey sand used elsewhere for the platform was deposited. From the surface of the completed platform mound, which reached a height of about 50 cm, the buried strata could not be seen and there was nothing to distinguish that portion of the platform from the rest of the mound, except that the buried strata were behind the pole screen and beside the deep rectangular pit. The people who carried out activities on the mound certainly knew where the buried, multilayered construction was, since all of the presumed charnel-related activities took place exactly over that 12- by 14-m portion of the mound (see Figure 5.4).

Platform Use

Imagine the following taking place on the platform mound in the charnel area behind the pine post screen. The body of a dead individual is carried to Mound A for cleaning by or under the direction of the religious specialist. Much in the same fashion that a deer is cleaned, the body is dismembered and the head is removed, at times with some of the cervical vertebrae still attached. The head, limbs, and hands are carefully wrapped and buried together in almost circular pits measuring about 1 m across that are dug into the floor of the platform mound down into the buried multilayered deposit. Viscera (including ribs, lumbar and thoracic vertebrae, and pelvis) are discarded; perhaps they are placed in the deep (still-open) rectangular pit and covered with soil.

Over a period of time, several interments of skulls and limbs are made, often in adjacent pits. Eventually, each bundle of bones is exhumed. The skull and hands, perhaps wrapped together, are not further cleaned; perhaps they are rewrapped. The long bones are further cleaned and rewrapped. These bundles—skulls, hands, and long bones—are moved to the Mound C charnel house where they are stored and made accessible to lineage members for viewing or handling. Through time, more pits are added to the Mound A platform; some of the pits from which the body parts have been removed are reused.

From the view of the McKeithen villagers, the process of burial preparation is polluting. It required the involvement of specialists, and care had to be taken to purify such individuals along with the objects they used, including the mound. Such purification returned people and objects to a normal state within society.

Purifying rituals included kindling fires in small pits and the use of red ochre, perhaps to place on the bundles of cleaned bones or some of the bones themselves at the time they were removed to the Mound C charnel house. Small fires were also kindled for the burning of special substances, which helped to purify the area.

Medicines were prepared, served, and drunk from special ceramic vessels as a part of a purification ritual(s). Other ceramic vessels—pedestaled animal effigies with triangular cutout sections and hollow bases, were placed on the carved peg tops of large pine posts raised in specially prepared anchoring trenches among the burial pits. The posts were occasionally moved. Perhaps they marked the location of certain pits containing bones and were moved when the bones were removed.

Debris associated with the body preparation activities was polluted as a result of association with the charnel area and required special deposition. Consequently, it could not be tossed on the usual village middens; instead, the debris had to be discarded around the edges of the platform mound and in dumps on the fringes of the mound, away from the special charnel area.

When the time arrived to close down the mortuary activities at the village, all pits still containing body parts were emptied. Two individuals, either stored at Mound A or elsewhere, had not yet been cleaned, but they were moved to Mound C with the other bones and the ceramic effigies, as well as the ceramic vessels used for preparing and drinking medicines. A layer of clean white sand was strewn over the charnel area on the mound. The wooden posts from the screen were pulled out of their anchoring trench and placed on top of the cleaned sand around some of the still upright peg-top posts on which the effigies had been placed. All of this wood was then ignited and a large bonfire ensued.

Once the fire had cooled, most of the remnants, including some scorched sand and a great deal of charcoal, was dumped just off of the western edge of the platform mound. Portions of three charred pine posts were moved near the edge of the platform. One was intact, 3.5 m long. (A radiocarbon age of 1445 ± 90 years: A.D. 505 [UM-1643] was obtained from this long post.) The entire platform mound and the remnants of the fire previously deposited off the western edge of the mound were then buried under a layer of clean sand taken from the borrow pits located just beyond the village midden. Through time, that cap eroded down to its central height of just over 1 m when excavated. The cap served to bury the platform mound and the polluted materials associated with it, including the burned screen and other posts. Because the cap had to extend over the debris beside the platform, it was not round in shape, as were the caps of Mounds B and C, but it was much more rectangular. Its thickest point, however, was over the center of the platform.

This somewhat fanciful reconstruction is undoubtedly incorrect in some details, especially when it attributes to the McKeithen peoples behavior and beliefs that cannot be directly proven on the basis of the archaeological evidence. As a model, however, it does explain in a general fashion many of the archaeologically observable features, and it is not inconsistent with activities historic period Timucuan and other Southeast peoples are known to have carried out (e.g., Hudson 1976; Milanich and Sturtevant 1972). The explanation also fits with the archaeological evidence and reconstructions for Mounds B and C.

Figure 5.4 shows many of the archaeological features related to the Mound A charnel activities. Circular burial and maceration pits were very much in evidence. Seven such pits in a cluster near the western end of the charnel area were only the latest seven of many to have been dug and redug in that same spot. Two other repeatedly used pits were also found, both toward the eastern end of the platform. Both evidently had also been used as the locations for large posts, each of which were placed in the deep end of a long, sloping trench. (The sloping trenches and the posts in Figure 5.4 resemble the outlines of golf fairways and greens.) The upper portion of the deep rectangular pit just west of the charnel area had also been redug several times.

All of the presumed grave pits were intrusive down into the banded deposits directly below the charnel area within the platform mound. A few scraps of acid-eaten bone were taken from some of the pits, but none could be positively identified as human. High phosphorous levels were present in the fill of each pit and also in the deposits on the surface of the platform mound. Identification of the pits for body maceration is not absolute, but highly likely.

Almost the entire floor of the rectangular charnel area had some red ochre on it; the mineral appears to have been strewn about quite liberally. Three very dense deposits are noted in Figure 5.4. The smallest in extent, 0.3 by 0.5 m, was pure ochre to a depth of 10 cm. Perhaps it was a stored supply.

Three kinds of fires were evident on the platform. One was a central hearth approximately 1.1 m in diameter near the western end of the charnel area. It was cleaned and reused several times at least. Near the northern side of the charnel area were 11 very small, circular hearths, all containing wood charcoal and all measuring roughly 15 cm in diameter. Each appears to have been used only once; the ash and charcoal deposits were only 1–3 cm thick. Each appeared to have been kindled in a small depression. When a new fire was lit, the spoil was used to cover up an old one. All of the 11 fires were hot enough to turn the soil for 2 cm around them an orange color. Charcoal taken from one of these small fires yielded a radiocarbon age of 1530 ± 80 years: A.D. 420 (UM-1645).

The third type of fire was a series of at least 50 small pits. Each fire was kindled in a round depression or pit 10–30 cm in diameter (most about 15 cm) and 10–30 cm deep (most 15–20 cm). All contained a great deal of ash and only flecks of charred wood. Ashy deposits generally filled each pit. Unlike the small depressions containing charcoal, these fires were not hot enough to turn the surrounding soil matrix orange. Care was taken to try to identify what was burned in the pits, but we met with no success. The ash was not resinous.

One of the most puzzling types of features found on the surface of the platform mound in the charnel area are the long, sloping trenches, all of which anchored posts and some of which were intrusive into older sloping trenches or grave pits. Each trench was 2–3.5 m long and about 1 m wide. They all sloped downward at about a 10° angle for three fourths of their length, then plunged straight downward, forming a straight-walled, large posthole the bottom of which was about 60 cm deeper than the adjacent section of trench (1 m below the surface of the platform). Presumably, the post was laid in the sloping trench, the top end was then lifted up, allowing the butt end to slide down into the deep posthole.

At the time that the charnel activities ceased and the large fire took place there were probably 11 such posts standing. In each case the actual post and its posthole were intrusive into the banded strata within the platform. In a few instances the upper, shallow end of the sloping trench extended off the charnel area. All of the upright posts burned in place when the bonfire was lit. Nine either fell over or were pulled out of their trenches after burning, leaving molds and some charcoal and burned sand. The vertical bedding resulting from subsequent filling in of the mold when the mound was capped was apparent in several cases.

Two of the post butts, burned *in situ,* were still present when the mound was excavated (Figure 5.4, at the southwest and southeast corners of the charnel area). Perhaps the tops had broken off in the fire. Both posts were pine and were quite large. One measured 42 cm in diameter and had a flat bottom. A date of 1770 ± 70 radiocarbon years: A.D. 180 (UM-1642) was obtained from a large sample of the charred wood. This date seems too early when compared to the others from Mound A. The second *in situ* charred post butt was 50 cm in diameter. Its bottom curved in on all sides to a round central core 10 cm in diameter. Presumably the peculiar shape of the post butt resulted from the chopping that felled the tree from which the post was taken. Or, perhaps what we observed was the actual peg top of a post placed upside down. A radiocarbon age of 1515 ± 70 years: A.D. 435 (UM-1646) was assigned this charred post.

Our reconstruction of the posts as bases for

the pedestaled ceramic animal effigies is highly speculative. The effigies, however, did indeed fit mortise and tenon fashion on something, since their round sleeve bases were battered and worn (the vessels are described in Chapter 7).

After the screen was pulled up and burned, much of the charred wood and some scorched soil was taken and deposited off of the southwestern edge of the platform mound. A hand-excavated trench cut through these deposits, which were covered with the same mound cap that was placed over the platform mound (Figure 5.2).

As a result of activity on the platform mound, some debris accumulated. Artifacts were found scattered about the platform and in two dumps, one just on the eastern edge of the platform mound and the other immediately adjacent to the eastern edge of the rectangular charnel area (see Figure 5.4). Most of this debris consisted of deer bone and potsherds, many from partially reconstructable vessels. The acidic nature of the soils probably destroyed small animal bones; many acid-eroded fragments were found.

Unlike Mounds B and C described later in this chapter, the reconstructed vessels from the Mound A platform were the same types found in the village middens; utilitarian vessels with the same designs and shapes were found by Kohler. The Mound A vessels were also smoke-clouded and many had carbon deposits on them, suggesting that they were used for cooking. Either food was brought to the mound in such vessels, or it was cooked on the mound in vessels placed above the small fire pits, which seems unlikely. Another possibility is that the vessels were used in the bone maceration process.

Cordell (Chapter 7) carried out a ceramic analysis of the 1836 potsherds that were collected on the platform mound. Analysis of the zooarchaeological remains from the mound was performed by Arlene Fradkin using the comparative collections of the Florida State Museum's Zooarchaeology Range. The complementary results of these two analyses show that debris was concentrated in the two dumps; however, some sherds and animal bones matching with vessels and bones found in the dump were scattered about the mound.

The dump on the edge of the platform included the following identifiable pieces of deer bone: 3 humeri, 7 scapulae, 6 femora, 15 tibiae, 1 astragalus, and 1 calcaneus. Fradkin's analysis shows that these bones came from a minimum of 7 deer. The other, smaller dump produced bones from a minimum of 2 additional deer and included 4 humeri, 2 scapulae, 1 femur, 1 tibia, 2 sternum fragments, and 3 rib fragments. All of the other deer bone recovered from the platform could have come from any of these 9 deer. The total of all deer elements from the platform mound is 8 humeri, 10 scapulae, 10 femora, 20 tibiae, 1 astragalus, 1 calcaneus, 2 sterna fragments, and 3 rib fragments.

The elements are overwhelmingly from the haunches of deer, as we might expect. Whoever was eating deer on the Mound A platform mound was receiving almost solely the haunches. Presumably the deer were butchered elsewhere. The only other identifiable faunal elements were a mallard duck (*Anas platyrhynchus*) humerus and a fish vertebra from the large dump, a ring-necked duck (*Aythya collaris*) tarsometatarsus from the small dump, and a rabbit (*Sylvilagus floridana*) pelvis fragment from one of the small fire pits dug down into the surface of the platform mound.

The potsherds from the platform mound were analyzed in five separate groups. The groups correspond to five spatial contexts on the platform mound: (1) the rectangular charnel area, (2) adjacent portions of the platform behind the post screen, (3) the larger dump, (4) the platform mound outside of the post screen, and (5) the smaller dump.

A minimum of 27 pottery vessels were identi-

Table 5.1
Vessels from Mound A Platform

Vessel type	Form	Diameter of mouth at rim[a] (cm)	n
Undecorated	Collared bowl	17	1
	Bowl	13	1
Undecorated, red-washed	Bowl	—	2
Carrabelle Punctated	Bowl	17, 17, 17, 20	4
Carrabelle Incised	Bowl	13, —	2
	Collared bowl	14, 15	2
Keith Incised	Collared bowl	24	1
Tucker Ridge-pinched	Dish or shallow bowl	23	1
Weeden Island Plain	Bowl	26, 30, 32, 36	4
	Dish or shallow bowl	17	1
Weeden Island Incised	Bowl or beaker	13	1
Weeden Island Red	Shallow bowl	33	1
Papys Bayou Incised	Dish	—	1
Crooked River Complicated Stamped	Pot or bowl	26, —	2
Napier Complicated Stamped	Pot or bowl	32, 34	2
New River Complicated Stamped	Pot or bowl	34	1

[a]A dash indicates that the mouth diameter could not be determined.

fied from among the 1836 potsherds (Table 5.1). Size and frequency of potsherds were used as the criteria for distinguishing between sherds fortuitously deposited during construction of the platform and those that were deposited when vessels were broken during activities on the mound. Sherds representing 4 vessels were found almost exclusively in the larger dump on the eastern edge of the mound. Three additional vessels came from adjacent excavations units and were probably on the fringes of the dump. Four sherds from other parts of the platform matched 4 of these latter vessels. These 7 vessels included (vessel shape terminology from Willey 1949:496–506) 2 Carrabelle Punctated bowls, 1 Carrabelle Incised collared bowl, 1 Weeden Island Plain shallow bowl or dish, 1 Weeden Island Incised bowl or beaker, 1 New River Complicated Stamped bowl or pot, 1 undecorated bowl. All of the vessels except the complicated stamped one are relatively small

and all probably were bowls, although some may have been pots; they were not complete enough to determine the vessel height relative to diameter.

Two vessels were reconstructed from sherds found just inside the post screen but off the charnel area. One is a Carrabelle Incised collared bowl and the other a Crooked River Complicated Stamped bowl or pot, another example of a relatively larger complicated stamped vessel.

Sherds representing two Weeden Island Plain bowls were found on the southern edge of the charnel area, and sherds from an undecorated collared bowl or pot were excavated from the charnel area and the smaller trash pit just to the east. Two Carrabelle Punctated bowls were partially reconstructed from sherds found on the western edge of the smaller dump.

Seven vessels were identified from sherds recovered almost exclusively from the charnel

Table 5.2
Vessels from Mound B Platform

Vessel type	Form	Diameter of mouth at rim[a] (cm)	n
Weeden Island Plain	Large shallow bowl	32	1
Weeden Island Incised	Globular bowl	19	1
Weeden Island Red	Large shallow bowl or dish	30	1
Weeden Island Zoned Red	Plate	ca. 15 × 26	6
	Dish	14	1
Papys Bayou Plain	Large shallow bowl	45 (?)	1
Papys Bayou Punctated	Bowl or beaker	—	1
Check stamped	Unknown	—	1

[a]A dash indicates that the mouth diameter could not be determined. The measurement for the Weeden Island Zoned Red plates indicates the minimum lengths and widths of the oblong plates.

area: 2 undecorated residual red bowls (each with a fugitive red substance on their interiors, 1 Crooked River Complicated Stamped bowl or pot, 1 Papys Bayou Incised dish, 1 Tucker Ridge-pinched dish or shallow bowl, 1 Weeden Island Plain bowl, and 1 Carrabelle Incised bowl.

An additional 6 vessels were partially reconstructed from sherds scattered over the entire platform mound. A Carrabelle Incised bowl and a Weeden Island Red bowl were found mainly on the fringes of the mound and up against the inside of the post screen. The other 4 vessels are 1 Weeden Island Plain bowl, 1 Keith Incised collared bowl, and 2 Napier Complicated Stamped bowls or pots.

Table 5.1 summarizes the 27 vessels by type (they are described in detail in Chapter 7). It is interesting to compare this table with Tables 5.2 and 5.3, which list the vessels from Mounds B and C. Clearly each mound is associated with a specific complex of vessels and shapes. Those from Mound A are most like the vessels found in the village, although the percentage of decorated vessels is higher in the mound.

Few other artifacts were found on the platform mound. Two small pits, 10 and 20 cm in

diameter and about 10 cm deep, were located south of the charnel area on the platform mound. Both contain about a double handful of freshwater mussel shells (*Eliptio* sp.). Mica bits, ranging in size from mere flecks to pieces 2 cm across, were scattered over the charnel area floor and elsewhere on the mound. Likewise, chert and silicified coral debitage was found on the platform mound as well as in the mound fill. Several lithic tools—small triangular points or knives like those found by Kohler (Chapter 4) in the village—also were found in both the fill and on the activity floor. One notable artifact is a flat, well-worn slab of Appalachian quartz sandstone (containing feldspar and garnets) measuring 9 by 11 cm and 6 mm thick that was found just inside the post screen. The only other item not duplicated in the mound fill were pea-to kumquat-size lumps of clay found scattered about the top of the platform. None of these materials appear to offer much evidence for mound activities.

The five radiocarbon dates from Mound A contexts—A.D. 180 ± 70, 260 ± 90, 420 ± 80, 435 ± 70, 505 ± 90—average A.D. 354 ± 35 (Long and Rippeteau 1974). This is the same

Table 5.3
Mound C Pottery Cache Vessels

Type	Form	Diameter of mouth at rim[a] (cm)	n
Undecorated	Derived bird effigies	12, 15	2
	Bowl (with lugs)	11	1
	Globular bowl	10	1
Weeden Island Plain	Derived 4-headed effigy (dogs and bird)	10	1
Weeden Island Incised	Squared globular bowl (with wood ibises)	17	1
	Unique "wing nut" (with spoonbills)	13 × 15	1
Weeden Island Red	Pedestaled bird effigies	8, 11 × 16	2
	Derived bird effigies	12, 17	2
	Bowl	15	1
	Square, shallow dish (bird head adorno?)	19 × 19	1
Weeden Island Zoned Red	Derived bird effigy	13 × 17	1
Indian Pass Incised	Bowl	14	1
Papys Bayou Plain	Bowl	20, 22	2
Papys Bayou Punctated	Bowl	36	1

[a]Some vessel mouths were oval or squared.

average as the dates from Mound B, reported in the next section of this chapter. Thus, it seems likely that the mound was built, utilized, and capped following A.D. 350; perhaps the actual period lasted only a decade or less. As an archaeological challenge, Mound A was one of the most interesting pre-Mississippian period mounds that its excavators have ever encountered.

RESIDENCE AND TOMB OF THE
RELIGIOUS SPECIALIST: MOUND B

At the time of excavation Mound B was a circular sand mound about 1 m high and 27 m in diameter. Like Mound A, Mound B began as a low, rectangular, 14- by 10.5-m platform mound. The platform had been erected on the natural and midden ridge that paralleled Orange Creek. When it was built, the top of the 40-cm high platform was about 3 m above the center of the plaza. Thus, like Mound A, judicious location selection allowed the mound's builders to give the illusion of great height relative to the plaza and most of the village without actually having to move much soil.

The mound had never been plowed; however, timbering in that portion of the site had taken place. Dragging logs across the mound and some clearing activities undoubtedly helped to cause erosion of the mound. Our excavations showed that the present configuration was the result of this erosion. When capped, the mound was greater in height and its circumference was smaller.

Excavation of Mound B was hampered by sev-

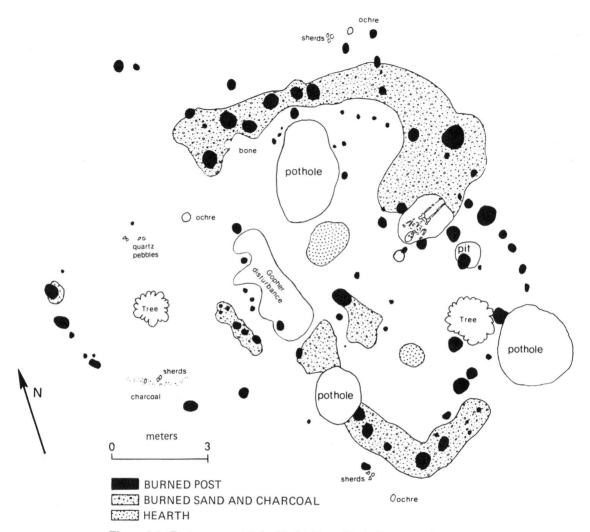

Figure 5.5 Features associated with the Mound B platform mound structure.

eral large shade-producing trees, one of which was surreptitiously removed after working hours, much to the chagrin of the field crew. Four potholes had been dug into the mound; all but one were shallow. The one deep one obliterated the southeastern corner of the aboriginal structure built on the platform mound. An equally destructive disturbance was a pocket gopher "condominium" placed along the western edge of the same structure. This series of

interlocking burrows and tunnels, which extended downward from about the level of the platform mound to the premound ground surface, was discovered when an excavator standing above them suddenly dropped almost 0.4 m. The potholes and gopher disturbances are shown in Figure 5.5.

A previous archaeological test pit, excavated and backfilled by David Phelps, was intercepted at the north edge of the mound cap. It did not

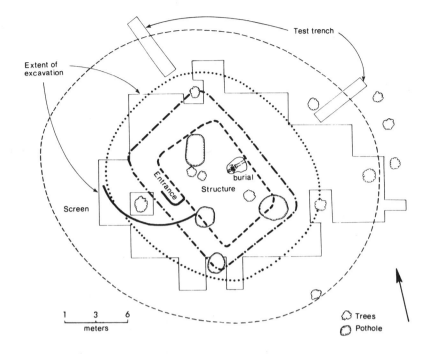

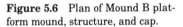

Figure 5.6 Plan of Mound B platform mound, structure, and cap.

intersect the actual platform and posed no interpretive problems.

The Mound B platform was composed of humus and midden deposits probably taken from a borrow pit to the south that had intersected a portion of older village midden. Some basket loading was apparent, especially along the fringes of the platform. Before the soil for the platform was deposited, the humus on the old ground surface was apparently removed. The old humus stratum was very apparent beside the platform and under the edges of the overlapping mound cap, but was not present under the platform.

Once the platform was built, a rectangular structure was erected on it. It was oriented so that its long axis was oriented 62.5° east of north, the same heading as the line between Mounds A and C (i.e., the base of the triangle formed by the three mounds). Possibly the structure was rebuilt or repaired at least once. It measured 6.9 by 10.2 m (Figure 5.6). The pine

wall-support posts, 10–15 cm in diameter, were placed about 50 cm apart. Most likely the walls were thatched. Later this structure was burned to the ground.

Radiocarbon ages of 1590 ± 70 years: A.D. 360 (UM-1234) and 1550 ± 75 years: A.D. 400 (UM-1235) were obtained from two charred wall posts from the easterly side of the structure. Both samples were from the butts of the posts that were still *in situ* in the platform mound.

A doorway or entrance into the structure was on the western side toward the village midden and away from the plaza. That entrance appears to have had a small pole or post screen jutting out and turning at a right angle to shield the entrance. Possibly the screen was thatched; the posts were not spaced right beside one another. A second post screen was also present on the eastern side of the structure. It apparently connected with the front of the structure and curved outward along the edge of the platform, shielding the entrance. Like Mound A, the screen was on the village side of the mound, not the plaza side.

Sherds and other debris were found on and beside the northwest side of the structure (Figure 5.5). This material might have been swept out of the entrance of the structure. At various places beside the platform, thin, bedded deposits of grey, white, and tan sand were apparent; perhaps the result of occasional cleaning of the platform and the deposition of clean sand. Between the curving screen and the front of the structure there was a definite thin stratum of clean tan sand.

Inside the structure a number of burned posts and postmolds were encountered. Benches or sleeping platforms may have been present at both interior ends. Two hearths were found, one just inside the entrance and the other toward the south end of the structure.

Bones of deer were found both inside the structure, evidently thrown under the presumed benches, and outside it. Like Mound A, the bones were from deer haunches. A minimum of two deer was present, one mature and one immature. Red ochre and fragments of mica were found on the interior floor of the structure and outside the entrance on the surface of the platform. One large deposit of ochre came from just outside the southwest corner. Several small quartz cobbles also came from just outside of the entrance.

As a whole, the artifact assemblage from the Mound B platform was quite different from Mounds A and C. Presumably, the artifacts found in the structure were associated with the individual who resided there. They probably reflect his special status. Most notable is the collection of 1747 potsherds associated with the platform. During analysis, five contexts were treated separately: (1) inside the structure, (2) along the inside and outside walls of the structure, (3) outside the structure in adjacent excavation units, (4) near the curving screen by the structure entrance, and (5) the east side

of the structure. The greatest percentage of elite ceramics came from inside the structure and from against the walls, where one might expect debris to be discarded.

Analysis of the ceramic collection was undertaken by Cordell. Her detailed comparative findings are presented in Chapter 7. From the sherd collection, she was able to reconstruct partially 13 vessels, all presumed to have been used in the structure and discarded there. Seven of the vessels were Weeden Island Zoned Red; 6 were plates and 1 was a shallow dish. Five of the plates were decorated with what appears to be a bird motif. All of the sherds from these 5 plates were found mainly outside the north end of the structure, both on and just off the platform. A few sherds were found within the structure.

The two other Weeden Island Zoned Red vessels were decorated with a column motif (described more fully in Chapter 7). One was reconstructed from sherds that were found mainly on the north outside end of the structure as well as sherds from inside the structure and outside the east and west sides. Sherds from the seventh vessel were well scattered outside the east, north, and west sides of the structure.

A Weeden Island Red shallow bowl and a Weeden Island Incised globular bowl were also reconstructed from sherds distributed mainly outside the structure on the north end. The remaining 4 vessels—Weeden Island Plain, check stamped, Papys Bayou Plain, and Papys Bayou Punctated—had a different distribution than most of the zoned red, red, and incised vessels. Their sherds were found mainly on the west side of the structure and occasionally inside it.

Apparently the Weeden Island Zoned Red plates and dishes were reserved for use by the structure's occupant(s). The bird motif is intriguing, especially in light of the ceramic bird head placed near the feet of the burial in the structure, discussed below (see Knight's interpretation in Chapter 8).

Other artifacts on the Mound B platform included chert debitage and several chert cores. The cores and most of the debitage appear to have been heat treated. Other debitage was silicified coral and quartz. Broken tips and bases from small triangular projectile points and several intact specimens, some of which are typologically Pinellas points, also came from the platform, both inside and outside the structure. Several were thermally altered and appear to have been made from the heat-treated chert. They are thought to have been deposited on the platform and are not accidental intrusions in the mound fill.

Within the structure near the right rear wall and adjacent to the grave pit or tomb of the individual believed to have been the resident religious specialist was a relatively large (for Mound B) post. The pine post, charred *in situ* like many other of the structure's post, measured 33 cm in diameter and was placed in a posthole 75 cm in diameter. When dug by the aborigines the pit would have extended 40 cm below the surface of the platform. The charred post went almost to the bottom of the posthole and was solid charcoal for about 25 cm of its length. An intial radiocarbon age of 1980 ± 70 years: 30 B.C. (UM-1233) came from a portion of the charcoal. This date seemed much too early and another sample was later analyzed. That sample produced a radiocarbon date of 1660 ± 80 years: A.D. 290 (UM-1564), a much more satisfactory date. Together the three satisfactory Mound B dates of A.D. 290, 360, 400 yield an average of A.D. 354 ± 43 radiocarbon years, the same average as the five dates from Mound A.

The ritual of burning the Mound B structure and then capping the mound was quite like the closing ceremony from Mound A. Perhaps it was the death of the individual buried in the structure that provided the impetus for the abandonment of the mortuary activities and the destruction of all the mound structures and the capping.

The excavated skeleton from Mound B was examined *in situ* by William R. Maples, a phys-ical anthropologist at the Florida State Museum. Later the remains were removed to the museum for additional analysis, including a detailed osteometric analysis. Those data are on file at the Florida State Museum. Maples concluded that the person was a gracile adult male in the mid to late 30s, whose stature was probably between 164 and 170 cm. Some possible cranial cradle board deformation was present.

Sticking at a slightly downward angle into the left illium of the individual was a small triangular projectile point. From the tip to the midpoint of the base, the point measured 3.16 cm; width of the base was 1.19 cm. Almost the entire length of the point penetrated the bone. The point had very slight basal ears, and the base between the ears was thinned and ground (Figure 5.7). Manufactured from a local opaline chert, it is very similar to the Pinellas-like points found elsewhere at the site and could have been hafted on an arrowshaft.

Maples' analysis concluded that the point had been in place at least several months before death, perhaps much longer. Bone had grown over a small portion of the base. An infection, encapsulated and localized by the time of death, had occurred as a result of the wound. The infection was in the area where the point would have been hafted, suggesting that some of the hafting material (perhaps sinew or resin) had stayed in the wound when the shaft was removed. Spongy bone of the illium had grown tightly around the upper two thirds of the point (Figure 5.7).

This presumed religious specialist was buried extended and on his back in a shallow grave about 25 cm deep cut into the floor of the structure (see Figures 5.6 and 5.8). Spoil from this shallow grave was spread over the floor of the structure to the southeast of the grave.

The body was exposed for a period of time before being covered. This period could have been only several days; it is not certain that the body was actually in the grave when exposed. Marks from rodent gnawing were present on many of the bones that are covered with only a

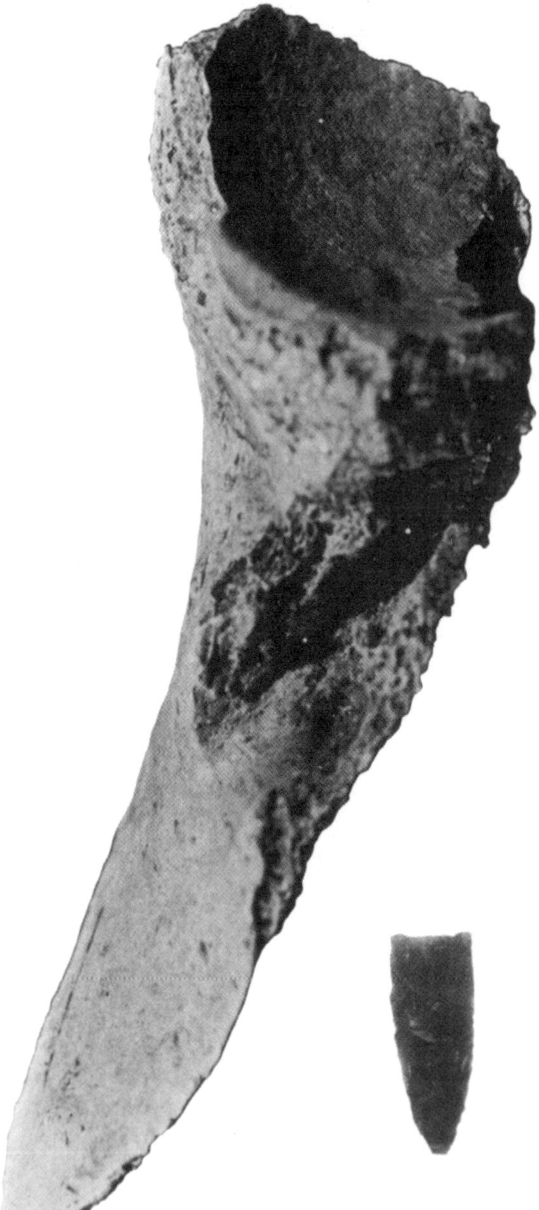

Figure 5.7 Arrow point in left ilium and removed; length of point is 3.16 cm.

little flesh, including one clavicle, one humerus, both tibias, one fibula, and possibly the frontal bone just above the left orbit. Some of the tooth marks were quite broad and may have come from a dog.

After being exposed long enough for animals to chew on the body a bit, some type of tomb was erected over the individual. Apparently the tomb was built of pine posts and soil. Two parallel lines of postholes were found down each side of the grave pit in the floor of the structure. These posts possibly supported a tomb roof. Soil was later (after exposure of the body) placed over the tomb, covering the body. This mound or tomb within the structure was about 0.5 m high. After the structure was burned, the tomb posts were removed leaving some charcoal and burned sand as well as the postmolds to mark their former locations. Burned sand also was found on the top of the tomb. Because the burial was covered with earth at the time the structure was burned, the body was not cremated. The ash from the fire may have helped counteract the acid nature of the soil and preserved the bones.

The individual's arms were both bent at the elbow and his palms were open and facing up near his shoulders. Under his head was a deposit of red ochre that had probably been in his hair. Also under his head was an approximately 5- by 5-cm piece of human occipital bone from another individual, probably an adult. Perhaps that bone had been part of a headdress. Another bone, an anhinga (*Anhinga anhinga*) lower-leg bone (tibiotarsus) was found under the individual's neck and was also probably a portion of a headress. (The anhinga, also called the water turkey or snake bird, is an anomalous-behaving bird; see Knight's discussion of other such birds and their relation to Weeden Island symbolism in Chapter 8.)

The long axis of the burial was the same as the perpendicular bisector of the isosceles triangle formed by the three mounds. The burial is also centered relative to the structure's back wall. It is easy to speculate that in life the indi-

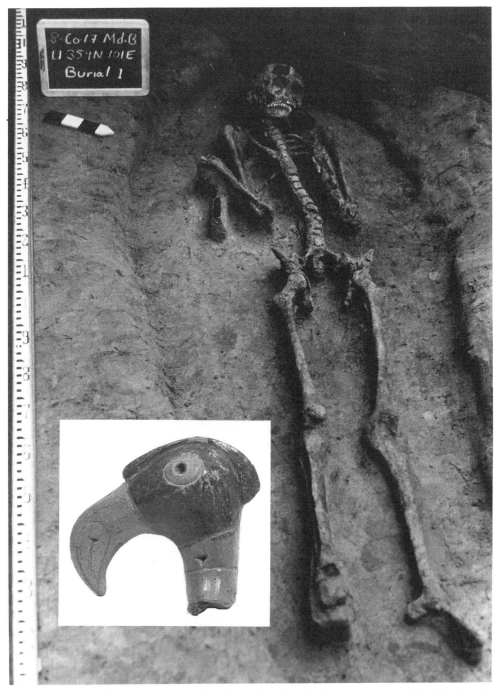

Figure 5.8   Mound B burial with ceramic bird head effigy found at feet; maximum height of bird head is 5.7 cm.

vidual may have made his sightings of the summer solstice from this same position.

It is also easy to speculate on the importance of the arrow wound. Was surviving this wound in the hip instrumental in giving the individual his exalted status? Were all three mounds built and used during a portion of this individual's lifetime? Have the generalities of radiocarbon analysis given us a broadened temporal perception of a mortuary cult perhaps operated by one individual for only a few years, perhaps even only the several years between his suffering the arrow wound and his death?

One artifact not yet described, and which gives us additional evidence for the status of this person, is a Weeden Island Zoned Red ceramic bird's head buried in the top of the platform mound just outside the back of the structure on a line with the long axis of the burial. Buried about 10 cm down in the platform, the head was less than 1 m from the individual's feet. The exquisite head, shown in Figure 5.8, is broken off at the neck and was apparently an adorno on a vessel; the remainder of the vessel was not present.

This head (representing a turkey vulture), the anhinga bone, and the stylized birds on the Weeden Island Zoned Red plates and dishes suggest an association between the priest and bird symbols. Was there an ideological link between vultures and bone cleaning and the priest, his bird symbols, and his charnel duties?

Once the individual was interred in his tomb, the structure and the screen were burned to the ground. The fire scorched large portions of the earthen platform, especially along the walls (see Figure 5.5). Some soil was scorched an orange to reddish color, as in Mound A. Burned debris from the structure was scattered over much of the platform, and many of the wall-support posts and some interior posts were charred *in situ*. Some of the charred posts, perhaps any still standing, were pulled up and removed. Those that had burned to ground level were left.

Some cleaning of burned debris was carried out, especially in the interior of the structure where the tomb was placed. Charcoal and burned sand were moved to the edges of the platform. Then tan sand probably from the nearby borrow pits was brought in to cap the platform and burned structure, burying both. At the time of excavation the round cap was only about 0.9 m thick at the center, directly above the platform.

FINAL INTERMENT: MOUND C

When we first saw Mound C, the initial reaction was not to bother to excavate it. Pothunters had dug the eastern quarter of the mound, uncovering and breaking a number of vessels from a pottery cache in the southeast quadrant of the mound. Most of the rest of the mound had also been potholed, and ugly gouges and spoil were apparent everywhere. About 40% of the mound's surface was disturbed. The exact center of the mound, however, appeared to be undisturbed, and we decided to excavate to determine if a central tomb, such as Kolomoki Mounds D and E, was present. In hindsight, this proved to be a wise decision, even if the reasoning was wrong. Important information was gathered, despite the severity of the disturbances, which turned out to be worse than expected.

We eventually determined that closer to 70% of the mound had been disturbed; tunnels, not visible from the surface, crisscrossed much of the inside of the mound, making the gopher disturbances in Mound B seem mild by comparison (Figure 5.9). While excavating we often discussed the possibility of finding a would-be archaeologist smothered in his or her caved-in tunnel. None were found; but on the other hand, later pothunters probably would have already dug right through them.

The mound had a number of trees on it, both large and small oaks and pines. Their distribu-

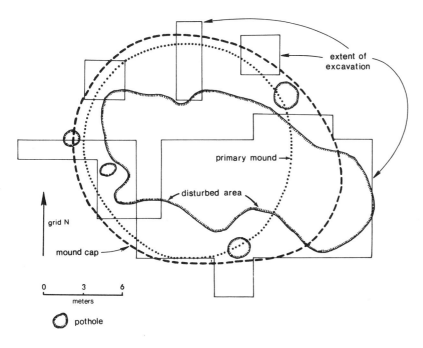

extent of
excavation

primary mound →

disturbed area

grid N

mound cap ─

0   3   6
    meters

⬭ pothole

Figure 5.9 Plan of Mound C with platform mound, cap, and extent of previous disturbance.

tion had hindered the vandals' earlier attempts to totally demolish the mound, just as they hindered our investigations.

When work began on the mound in fall 1977, northern Florida was in the midst of a severe drought and the sand of all strata in Mound C seemed like dry sugar. This made recognition of stratigraphy and features nearly impossible. Because the mound was within 100 m of our field camp, we were able to hook a garden hose from our well to a lawn sprinkler on the mound and soak the mound during the night. This was very successful in producing uniform wetness (and color) throughout the mound (and the trees enjoyed it too).

The height of the mound, about 2 m above the surrounding ground surface on its south side, also mitigated against the pothunters, since they rarely dug deep enough to reach the sub-mound surface. In several instances their explorations did not reach the surface of the platform mound; in others they actually cut through burials lying on or beside the platform mound, evidently failing to notice them.

Eventually most of this pottery cache was recovered, including a burnished bowl that appeared in Milanich's office with almost no questions asked. During our excavations we recovered sherds from all of these vessels, including a bottom sherd from the *kill hole* (a round hole knocked in the center of the vessel base; possible explanations for this practice are discussed in Chapter 8) of the burnished bowl, proving that all had indeed come from Mound C.

Lex McKeithen, just home from the war in Southeast Asia, had found the mound badly disturbed and immediately sought to bring the pot-hunting activities to a halt (by establishing some ingenious boobytraps at the entrances to the site). He recorded information on where large portions of pots were in the spoil as well as noting other mound features. He was also able to recover some of the pots that had come from the pottery cache. These data were important in helping us to interpret the mound.

Like the other two mounds, Mound C began as a platform. Unlike the other two mounds, however, this platform (or primary mound) was

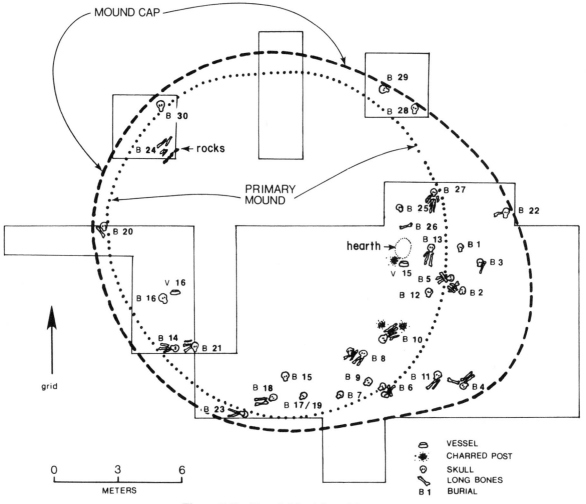

Figure 5.10 Mound C burials and features.

circular, 15.7 m in diameter and 95 cm high at its center (Figure 5.10). The soil used in the platform was very mottled and contained a large number of artifacts. Apparently, it was soil scraped up from the nearby midden that ran along the southern edge of the creek bank. In places under the platform, the premound humus was apparent. It had not been scraped away before the mound was constructed.

Before the fill of the platform was deposited,

someone placed an intact, unused, small Tucker Ridge-pinched bowl upright on a small portion of cleared ground under what was to be the southwest quadrant of the round platform. No reason for this was apparent.

A structure had been built on top of the mound; probably it was a charnel house for the storage of bundles of cleaned human bones. Several charred pine posts marking the eastern edge of this structure were found *in situ* on a portion of undisturbed platform mound. One post with a sharpened (beveled) bottom yielded a radiocarbon age of 1455 ± 70 years: A.D. 495 (UM-1434). On most of the undisturbed portions of the platform mound (which were small in area), a layer of combusted organic matter was deposited. This was thick (10 cm) on the east and south parts of the mound. The material probably represents the burned remains of the charnel structure. On the western side of the platform mound, several pieces of charred pine posts had rolled down or been pulled off the platform (they were lying horizontally against the edge of the platform). One sample was divided into two parts and the radiocarbon analyzed. The samples yielded ages of 1470 ± 70 radiocarbon years: A.D. 480 (UM-1436) and 1500 ± 70 radiocarbon years: A.D. 450 (UM-1565). The two ages are statistically the same.

Several square meters of the platform were intact at the center of the mound as was the submound surface. No central burial or tomb was present, either in the platform mound or under the platform.

After the structure was burned, the remains were apparently not removed to the extent that they were in Mounds A and B. The burned material was much thicker in Mound C. Prior to the capping of the platform, some type of closing ceremony took place, during which burials and ceramic vessels and effigies were deposited (Figure 5.10). Apparently as a part of this same ritual, a fire was kindled on the platform near its eastern side on top of the burned material. The consumption of food (perhaps a feast) took place around this fire, and the bones of animals eaten (many calcined) were recovered from the fire's remains and the area immediately around it. Included on the menu were 1 fish, 1 mud turtle (*Kinosternon* sp.), and 1 unidentified rodent. No deer bone was found in the deposit.

Medicines might also have been taken as a part of the ritual. On the south side of the hearth, positioned on top of the burned material on a portion of the platform was a Weeden Island Plain globular bowl with four effigy head adornos attached to the thickened rim. A kill hole is present in the bottom. Two of the heads, situated opposite one another, are probably dogs. One of the other heads is a vulture. All three face inward. The fourth head appears to be a beakless bird, which faces outward and is hollowed out so that it can function like a spout.

At least 17 other ceramic vessels (some being pedestaled effigies better described as hollow figurines) were placed on the southeastern portion of the circular platform or immediately beside the platform on a cleaned ground surface. This cache of 18 total vessels has been carefully studied by Cordell, whose findings are presented in Chapter 6. A total of 2569 potsherds was excavated from Mound C, including the mound cap, the platform mound, the submound surface, and the pothunters spoil (which includes sherds from all of these contexts). Of that total, 494 sherds, all from the spoil and the platform, fit with the pottery cache pottery vessels. These vessels also form an important data set for Knight's analysis presented in Chapter 8. Table 5.3 lists the 18 vessels of the pottery cache by type and vessel shape.

Overall, the assemblage of vessels in the cache correspond quite well to the types that Kohler referred to as elite types in his village analysis (Chapter 4). Comparison of Tables 5.1, 5.2, and 5.3 clearly shows the correlation of elite types—although two distinct assemblages—with types represented at Mounds B and C versus the more utilitarian types from Mound A. Just as important as the differences in decoration are the differences in vessel forms among the three mounds.

Along with the ceramic vessels, the bones of at least 36 people were deposited on and beside the Mound C platform. All of the burials were probably bundles of bone when interred. Most consisted of a skull and long bones. Several included more than 1 skull and long bones from

Table 5.4
Excavated Burial Population from Mound C

Field number	Age and sex data	Comments
1	1 adult, 30s–40s	Skull, 1 femur; occipital flattening
2	1 child, ca. 12	Cranimum, long-bone fragments
3	1 child	Cranium, 1 long bone
4	1 adult, 50s–60s	Skull fragments
5	1 male, 40s–50s	Skull, both femora, tibia, humerus, radius, vertebrae fragments, bony growth in auditory canals; occipital flattening
6	1 male, 30–40 1 male, 40+	2 skulls, 2 femora, humerus, ulna, some cervical vertebrae; both robust; 1 has healed fracture of left parietal
7	1 female(?), 60s+	Skull, 3 cervical vertebrae, atlas
8	1 male, 45–55	Skull, fragments of long bones; occipital flattening
9	1 adult, 60+	Fragments of skull and 2 long bones
10	1 female(?), 60+	Skull, fragments of hand and 2 long bones; bony growth in auditory canal
11	1 female, 30s–40s	Skull, 3 cervical vertebrae, 2 long bones
12	1 male, late 20s	Skull, 5 cervical vertebrae, fragments of long bones, phalanges, some ribs, clavicle, scapula; robust
13	1 adult	Fragments of skull, long bones, 3 phalanges
14	1 male, 40s	Skull, 6 long bones, clavicle, vertebrae, shell beads on neck area
15	1 adult, 30s	Cranium
16	1 child	Cranium fragments
17	1 child, 8–9	Mandible
18	1 female, 50s	Fragments of skull, hand, and humerus
19	2 adults 1 child	Teeth and child skull fragments
20	1 adult, 20s 1 child, 5–8	Skull, clavicle, scapula, humerus
21	1 female, 50s–60s	Skull, 5 long bones, 7 shell beads
22	1 female, 40s	Skull, radius, humerus
23	1 male, 50+	Skull, fragments of long bones, atlas
24	1 child	Femur, humerus, 3 long-bone fragments
25 and 26	1 male, 30s–40s	Skull, fragments of long bones; red ochre
27	1 male, early 20s 1 child, 2–4	Skull, long-bone fragments
28	1 female, 50s	Fragments of skull and long bones
29	1 female, 20s–30s	Cranium, femur
30	1 teenager	Cranium
31	1 child	Fragments of skull and long bones from pothunters' spoil; frontal and occipital flattening

more than 1 person. One burial was a deposit of teeth from at least 3 individuals. Burials 12 and 14 (see Table 5.4) were most complete in terms of bones present. Both also contained such bones as vertebrae and clavicles, which were not found with the other bundles. Burial 12 also contained some ribs and a scapula. When excavated, Burial 12 appeared at first to be a primary, flexed burial, as did Burial 14. However, close examination of 12 showed that not all of the bones were present and those bones present in 14 were not arranged in anatomical order.

Burials were deposited on the southeastern fringe of the platform as well as beside the mound on that side. This is the same distribution as in the pottery cache. Burials were also placed around the edge of the circular platform mound spaced about 1.5 m apart (Figure 5.10).

In every instance burials recovered were on a layer of clean sand, even in the southern and eastern portions of the mound where the burned material was most dense. These sand deposits were deliberately laid down before each respective bundle was arranged.

Table 5.4 lists the burials by age and sex and includes other pertinent comments. More detailed information is on file at the Florida State Museum where analysis was carried out by William R. Maples. The total of 36 individuals includes 26 adults and 10 children (72% and 28%). These percentages in this small burial population compare favorably with those from other nonstratified societies (see Brothwell 1972:66). The male–female ratio (10:9) also is normal, suggesting that the burial population represents a cross-section of the McKeithen population; that is, all members of the village (or of a lineage within the village) had equal access to burial preparation and deposition.

The degree of preservation of the bones varied considerably from one pile to the next. Some had the consistency of wet cardboard, others were relatively well preserved, and still others were very eroded due to ground acids.

We suspect that the 36 individuals are only one half or less of the number of people originally interred in Mound C. The entire fringe of the mound was not excavated and we estimate that another 10 burials may still be present. Also, the pothunters' spoil contained numerous fragments of skull and long bones. We estimate that at least 15 burials in the southeast quadrant (and beside the platform at that point) were destroyed.

After the structure was burned and the ceramic vessels and bones deposited, a mound cap was placed over the entire platform mound. The tan-mottled-with-grey sand cap just covered the circular platform, extending outward only about 1 m, except on the southeast side where it extended out from the mound about 3 m in order to cover the bones and part of the pottery cache placed beside the platform at that point. About 1.1 m thick in the center, the cap was at least half again as high originally. Considerable erosion, aided by the pothunting, greatly reduced the height.

Included in the cap and placed directly on the platform mound were about 40 sandstone and limestone rocks ranging in size from that of a grapefruit to that of a 12-inch television set. Similar rocks were found at Kolomoki in Mound E (Sears 1956:12). At McKeithen, none of the rocks was scorched, but several were excavated *in situ* on the burned material atop the platform mound. This suggests that they were placed on the mound after the fire, perhaps with the ceramics and burials. Their purpose is unknown. Did they have special status, perhaps serving as some sort of marker associated with mortuary activities?

GOOD NEWS–BAD NEWS ARCHAEOLOGY

As noted in Chapter 1, what we found at the McKeithen site, especially in the mounds, was not what we had suspected prior to excavation when our initial project was being designed. The prefield supposition, supported most strongly by Milanich, was that the three mounds were all burial mounds, each a tomb for a chiefly individual whose burial would contain sumptuary goods (ceramic vessels) and retainer sacrifices—a sort of down-home version of Mounds D and E at the Kolomoki site. After Kohler completed his investigations in the McKeithen village, it seemed possible that each mound would date to one of his three village phases; allowing us to record the changes in chiefly burial form through time, which would reflect the growth of an increasingly complex society. The bad news is that this was not to be.

Instead our results strongly suggest that the three McKeithen platform mounds were jointly constructed, used, and capped (ending their use) during the period A.D. 350–475. Probably this temporal range is much too broad. The mortuary activities of which we have evidence, and the rise and death of the priestly "big man" might all have taken place within one generation or even a small portion of a generation (i.e., only several years). During the period of mound use, the McKeithen site was an anomaly in North Florida (but a predictable one), a three-mound mortuary center with some societal ranking—a protochieftainship, if you will. At that same time, the most common Weeden Island village in North Florida, as well as those elsewhere within the greater Weeden Island region, had only one or no mounds and did not function as a major religious or intergroup center. Other exceptions to this pattern, anomalies like McKeithen, are the Aspalaga site in Northwest Florida (Moore 1918:481–488) and Kolomoki in southwestern Georgia (Sears 1956).

These latter two sites along with McKeithen all represent blips in an imaginary line graph charting increasing cultural and societal complexity against time in the Weeden Island region (and the remainder of the Southeast). Aspalaga was probably very similar in terms of scale of complexity and duration of occupation as McKeithen. But Aspalaga and McKeithen only warrant a very small blip compared to the larger Kolomoki site, which was probably a more important site for a longer period of time.

In retrospect, the archaeological remains from the three mounds are quite close to what a knowledgeable Southeast archaeologist, one in the mainstream of thought regarding culture history and evolutionary process, might predict for a culture that preceded Mississippian developments by 500 years. It is gratifying that this result fits well with Kohler's (Chapter 4) village data and conclusions regarding the growth, peak, and decline of the McKeithen village and Sigler-Lavelle's (Chapter 3) predictive model concerning the appearance of interlineage centers and their leaders in early Weeden Island societies.

Kohler's village work also demonstrated differential, nonrandom distribution of certain artifacts in the McKeithen village, a reflection of some ranking of kin groups. Within the Mound C burial mound, however, there is no evidence for social differentiation based on status; unless shell beads associated with two burials can be construed as indicating higher status. We doubt it. Perhaps this implies that the individuals in Mound C were all from one lineage, or, at least, all from the more important lineages.

Special status does surround the adult male who apparently lived in the Mound B structure and was buried in it. Presumably he was a priest, or "big man," or head warrior, or combination of all of these statuses. Archaeological evidence for his status includes the following: a special structure on a platform mound; almost exclusive association with a ceramic assemblage; association with bird symbolism; extended burial in a special tomb; and association with other special paraphernalia, that is, the red ochre in his hair and the human occipital bone and anhinga bone under his head and neck (all perhaps part of a head decoration or headdress). We could also add that he is the only person at the site who had been shot in the buttocks with an arrow.

This list is modest, especially when compared to status indicators found at Mississippian mound centers. It is, however, of the same order of magnitude as the archaeological evidence found in the earliest manifestation of the early Mississippian center of Cemochechobee on the Chattahochee River, dating about A.D. 950 (Schnell et al. 1981:31–36). Again, this is what one might expect.

Certain Mississippian traits do appear in nascent form at McKeithen, supporting the present widely accepted view that Mississippian developments in the Southeast were autochthonic and not the result of introduction from Mesoamerica or migrations of populations out of one area of the Southeast into another. At McKeithen we find platform mounds (predecessors of temple mounds), a special residence or structure on a mound (a temple), mounds organized around a plaza, a horseshoe-shaped village around a plaza, the plaza itself, a religious specialist or priest, bird symbolism associated with the specialist, and sacred ceramics. Such a list is certainly not a revelation; but it does emphasize that like other Southeast cultures of the 200 B.C.–A.D. 900 period, McKeithen Weeden Island fits well along the evolutionary continuum between early Woodland and Mississippian cultures. The good news is that Weeden Island is no surprise.

6

Technological Analysis of the Ceramics

Although potsherds are not people, they can convey a great deal of information about human societies. Archaeologists routinely use numeric data derived from counts of pottery types to reflect the distributions of archaeological cultures through time and space. The Weeden Island culture is one such example of a prehistoric culture whose presence is indicated by a ceramic complex. But ceramic analysis has moved well beyond simply counting pottery types. We now use the methods of ceramic technology and ceramic ecology (e.g., Arnold 1975; Matson 1965; Rice 1976, 1981; Shepard 1976) to investigate a host of other questions about prehistoric peoples, including questions regarding social stratification and the production and distribution of pottery.

The excavations at the McKeithen site provided a well-documented collection of Weeden Island pottery from mound and village contexts. By employing the methodologies of ceramic technology and ceramic ecology, we can address issues pertinent to the model of Weeden Island societal organization as well as other questions. Specifically, analysis of the McKeithen ceramic collections allows us to examine (1) origin(s) of ceramic vessels (e.g., were all pedestaled effigies manufactured at a central site such as Kolomoki and distributed?), (2) evidence for specialized use of ceramic types and vessel forms (e.g., what is the nature of the sacred–secular dicotomy within the Weeden Island ceramic complex? [Sears 1973]), and (3) craft specialization, (e.g., are the Weeden Island elite ceramics produced by either full- or part-time specialists or artisans).

In order to investigate these questions, Cordell followed a research design that employed the facilities of the Ceramic Technology Laboratory of the Florida State Museum. Initially the study collection used in her research included the 13 vessels recovered from Mound B along with the ceramic bird head (see Chapter 5), the 19 vessels from Mound C, and 26 clay samples collected from the immediate vicinity of the McKeithen site and from other locales in Columbia and Suwannee counties. Also included were 212 sherds selected from a total of 1122 sherds recovered by Kohler from the village. These latter sherds were taken from contexts contemporary with the site's middle occupation phase when the mounds were constructed and used. The vessels from Mound A were not included in this initial analysis; however, the Mound A vessels were later analyzed using the same techniques, and all of the vessels from the three mounds are described in Chapter 7. A detailed discussion of the methods of ceramic technology and ceramic ecology used in her analysis can be found in Cordell (1984).

ORIGIN OF MANUFACTURE

One goal of Cordell's analysis was to determine if certain pottery types or individual vessels were manufactured locally at the McKeithen site using clays taken from adjacent locales or if they were made elsewhere. The importance of such information to the interpretation of Weeden Island social and political organization has long been recognized. As early as 1961, Sears stated "If analysis demonstrates that some of these artifacts [including Weeden Island pottery] were distributed from a single source, then the evidence for the existence of full-time specialists in certain communities becomes more certain, and the existence of a network of regional social relationships is indicated" (1961:228). Evidence for a single source for Weeden Island elite ceramics (i.e., the Kolomoki site) would lend strong support to the contention that Kolomoki "served as the ceremonial center for a culture marked by a ceramic complex composed of members of the Weeden Island . . . ceramic series" and that such a settlement hierarchy is "demonstrative of the existence of a state cult, serving as the sub-organization for transmission of social policy" (Sears 1962a:118, 119). Such evidence—that the elite pottery from the McKeithen site was not made locally—would be in conflict with our model of Weeden Island social and political organization.

Cordell's analysis was carried out in five steps:

1. The physical properties of the potsherd and clay samples were measured and described.
2. A statistical grouping (cluster analysis) of the potsherd and vessel samples was carried out to define paste categories believed to represent separate clay resources.
3. Properties of these respective cluster groups were compared with similar data

from the clay samples to determine origins of manufacture for the groups.
4. Results were then applied to the separate pottery types and to specific vessels from Mounds B and C to determine their origins of manufacture.

Variables selected for measurement were ones that permitted definition of the kinds and numbers of clays used in the manufacture of the potsherd collection under study. These were also variables that could be measured on both the sherd and the 26 clay samples. Such variables included fundamental physical properties of aplastic paste composition (usually referred to as *temper*), color, and porosity.

In order to identify the probable number of clay sources represented in the potsherd sample, a *multivariate cluster analysis* (a computerized statistical technique used to create classifications) called CLUSTAN HIERARCHY (Wishart 1978) was used to sort the sherds into relatively homogenous groups on the basis of similarity between sherds in terms of the values of the variables measured. The potsherd sample was first divided into three subsamples based on gross paste composition—micaceous paste, sponge spicule paste, and quartz sand–grit paste—and a separate cluster analysis was run on each subsample.

Results of these statistical procedures demonstrated that at least 13 distinctive clays were used consistently in the manufacture of the pottery sample, that is, each potsherd came from one of the 13 clay sources. Four of the 13 are micaceous clays, 3 are sponge spicule clays, and the remaining 6 are sand–grit clays (lacking both mica and sponge spicules). Brief descriptions of the cluster results are presented in Table 6.1 (a more detailed narrative can be found in Cordell 1984:Chapter 5).

Origin of manufacture for each of the clay–paste clusters was hypothesized by comparing cluster results with data collected on the 26 clay

Table 6.1

Descriptions and Origins of Paste Clusters

Cluster	Origin	Description
Micaceous paste		
1 and 3	Nonlocal	Abundant mica, very fine texture, variable refired colors
2	Local	Rare mica, fine to medium-fine texture, very pale brown paste
4	Uncertain[a]	Occasional mica, fine texture, reddish–brownish paste
5	Local	Rare mica, medium-fine texture, red paste
Sponge spicule paste		
1	Nonlocal	Abundant spicules, fine texture, light yellowish-brown paste
2	Nonlocal	Abundant spicules, fine texture, yellowish-red paste
3	Nonlocal	Abundant spicules, fine texture, retention of grey coring
Quartz sand–grit paste		
1	Uncertain	Medium-fine texture, retention of grey coring
2	Local	Medium-fine texture, light yellowish-brown paste
3	Local	Medium-fine texture, reddish yellow-brown paste
4	Local	Coarse to medium texture, reddish yellow-brown paste
5	Local	Coarse texture, light yellowish-brown paste
6	Local	Coarse texture, red to reddish-brown paste

[a]Probably nonlocal.

samples while also taking into account information on the distribution of particular kinds of clays in Florida. Archaeological "oral tradition" suggests Northwest Florida and southern Georgia as sources for micaceous paste ceramics recovered at Florida Weeden Island sites (e.g., Goggin 1962:19; Sears 1973:33). Clays with variable but relatively high mica contents are indeed known to occur in Northwest Florida and southern Georgia (see White 1981a:602), however, the geological literature mentions the presence of micaceous clays in Central Florida as well (Bell 1924:73; Calver 1949:2, 1957:57; Pirkle 1960:1398). Also rare amounts of mica were found in 5 of the 26 North Florida clay samples. Despite the presence of some mica in North Florida clays, it seems likely that oral tradition is correct: Potsherds containing conspicuously large amounts of mica in the paste are nonlocal to North Florida, at least to the McKeithen site vicinity. Northwest Florida or southwestern Georgia may indeed be the source of most such clays, although, as discussed in the following, at least two of the micaceous paste clusters may be from North Florida.

The source of clays containing freshwater sponge spicules (which appear under the microscope as tiny glassy needles) is traditionally thought to be East Florida, the region of the St. Johns ceramic complex. The characteristic chalky feel of this ware comes from the silty paste texture. A study by Thanz and Shaak (1977) suggests that the distribution of such clays in the state may be much wider than East Florida. The presence in the Central Peninsular Gulf Coast region (Tampa Bay and vicinity) of a spiculite paste ware in relatively large frequencies (Willey 1948:241) suggests that region as an additional source of such clays (Mitchem and Welch 1983:149). No sponge spicules were observed in any of the 26 North Florida clay samples, indicating that sherds with spiculite paste are probably nonlocal to the McKeithen region, perhaps coming from East Florida or the Central Peninsular Gulf Coast region.

Comparison of paste clusters with the 26 clay samples within the context of the information on clay source distributions suggests the following origins for the pottery in the study collection (see Table 6.1): (1) Two of the micaceous paste clusters and 5 of the 6 quartz sand–grit clusters are clays that were probably acquired locally; (2) the other 2 micaceous paste clusters, both of which contain conspicuous amounts of mica, are nonlocal and probably came from Northwest Florida or Southwest Georgia; (3) the sixth

Table 6.2
Origins of Pottery Types

Type	Local (%)	Uncertain (%)	Nonlocal (%)	n
Weeden Island Red	82	12	6	17
Weeden Island Zoned Red	50	40[b]	10	10
Weeden Island Incised	63	5	32	19
Weeden Island Punctated	100			11
Weeden Island Plain[a]	75	12	12	16
Carrabelle Incised[a]	70		30	10
Complicated stamped[a]	58	33	8	12
Undecorated micaceous paste	64	28	8	25
Undecorated sand–grit paste	77	23		52
Sponge spicule			100	36

[a]Percentages listed are biased in favor of uncertain and nonlocal origins because the samples of these types were not representative in terms of the proportions of micaceous versus spiculite versus sand–grit paste classes observed in the sampling population.

[b]30% probably nonlocal.

sand–grit cluster paste may not be local, but no source can be suggested; (4) all 3 of the spiculite paste clusters are nonlocal, their sources being probably eastern or western peninsular Florida.

When these results are examined (see Table 6.2) with respect to pottery types represented in the study collection, several conclusions can be drawn.[1] First, the majority of all of the nonspiculite sherds were manufactured locally (all of the spiculite paste sherds are nonlocal). Two nonspiculite types, Weeden Island Incised and Weeden Island Zoned Red, are the only types in which a significant percentage of the sherds (32 and 40%, respectively) are not made from local clays and can be presumed to have been brought to the site from elsewhere. We suspect that much of the Weeden Island Incised pottery is from Northwest Florida or southwestern Georgia; this may also be the same general source for

[1]Because of rounding off, the percentage totals in this and subsequent tables may not equal 100.

the majority of the Weeden Island Zoned Red sherds. The same conclusion was reached by Rice in a trace-element analysis of Weeden Island pottery (Rice 1980). In both Cordell's (1984) and Rice's studies, a local origin is suggested for most of the other pottery types, including Weeden Island Red, Weeden Island Punctated, Weeden Island Plain, Carrabelle Incised, complicated stamped, and undecorated ware.

For elite pottery (pottery found in sacred contexts), Rice (1980) proposed the existence of multiple centers of manufacture, rather than a single source, such as Kolomoki. The following results were obtained when origin of manufacture of the 33 vessels from McKeithen Mounds B and C was determined (see Table 6.3). We find that 10 of the 33 vessels (this total includes the Mound B bird head) are made of micaceous clays from probable nonlocal sources. Weeden Island Incised, Weeden Island Zoned Red, Weeden Island Plain, and an undecorated vessel are represented among the nonlocal mound vessels. Also from nonlocal sources are 6 vessels manufactured of spiculite clays. Represented in this category are Papys Bayou Punctated, Papys Bayou Plain, and the Weeden Island Zoned Red Mound B bird head effigy. Two Weeden Island Red vessels, including one of the Mound C pedestaled effigies, are made from the sand–grit paste that may be nonlocal but for which the origin is unknown.

The remaining 15 vessels all appear to have been made from locally available clays. Those 15 include vessels of the types Weeden Island Red, Weeden Island Zoned Red, undecorated, Indian Pass Incised, Tucker Ridge-pinched, and check stamped. Three of the 4 Kolomoki-style effigies with cutouts and 3 of the 4 derived effigies (lacking cutouts) are from the paste groups that match local clays, and we can conclude that they were manufactured locally at the McKeithen site. The fourth Kolomoki-style effigy (a pedestaled vessel) is the one made from the possible nonlocal sand–grit cluster clay and

Table 6.3

Origins of Manufacture for Mounds B and C Pottery[a]

Local	Uncertain	Nonlocal
Micaceous paste		
Cluster 2	Cluster 4[e]	Cluster 1 and 3
Weeden Island Red 4[b]	Weeden Island Zoned Red 20	Weeden Island Incised 1
Weeden Island Red 9[b]	Weeden Island Zoned Red 22	Weeden Island Incised 12
Weeden Island Zoned Red 19[c]	Weeden Island Zoned Red 23	Weeden Island Plain 15[c]
Weeden Island Zoned Red 24	Outlier:	undecorated 17
Weeden Island Zoned Red 25	Weeden Island Zoned Red 21	Weeden Island Plain 28
Weeden Island Zoned Red 26		Weeden Island Incised 29
Cluster 5		
undecorated 5[c]		
undecorated 6[c]		
undecorated 7		
Sand–grit paste		
Cluster 2	Cluster 1	
Tucker Ridge-pinched 16	Weeden Island Red 2[d]	
Cluster 3	Weeden Island Red 13	
Weeden Island Red 3[d]		
Weeden Island Red 8		
Indian Pass Incised 14		
check stamped 30		
Cluster 4		
Weeden Island Red 27		
		Spiculite paste
		Cluster 1 and 4
		Papys Bayou Plain 10
		Papys Bayou Punctated 11
		Papys Bayou Plain 18
		Papys Bayou Plain 32
		Outliers
		Papys Bayou Punctated 31
		Weeden Island Zoned Red 33

[a]Vessel numbers are indicated for each sherd:
   Vessels 1–19 are from Mound C;
   Vessels 20–33 are from Mound B.
   Outliers are sherds which did not cluster with any of the main groups (clusters).
[b]Derived effigy vessels with cutouts.
[c]Derived effigy vessels lacking cutouts.
[d]Pedestaled effigy vessels with cutouts.
[e]Probably nonlocal.

the four-headed Mound C derived effigy (a Weeden Island Plain bowl) contains large amounts of mica and is one of the vessels thought to be from Northwest Florida or southwestern Georgia.

Our observations on the Mound B and C vessels support Rice's multiple-center model for the manufacture of such Weeden Island elite pottery. The results refute any notion that Weeden Island ceremonial wares, including

Kolomoki-style effigies with cutouts, were manufactured at a single site. Indeed, there is little doubt that some such vessels were made, used, and disposed of at the McKeithen site. Such a conclusion also calls into question the contention that the Weeden Island culture was a single, interacting society with Kolomoki as its major town and the source of religious paraphernalia. Rather, the conclusions support our model of Weeden Island society, which interprets the McKeithen site as a relatively short-term center with political, social, and religious influence over a relatively small region within the Weeden Island culture area.

SPECIALIZED USE: SACRED–SECULAR CERAMIC VARIABILITY

In Chapter 2 we introduced the concept of the sacred–secular, or dual nature, of Weeden Island archaeological assemblages. Sears in his important paper "The Sacred and the Secular in Prehistoric Ceramics" first formally presented the concept and used the Weeden Island ceramic series as an example of a ceramic complex that contained vessels from burial mounds that were quite different from "secular 'cook-pot' assemblages . . . recovered from midden deposits" (1973:31). Sears suggests that the pottery from mound or sacred contexts and midden or secular contexts differ qualitatively, reflecting the functional differences of the assemblages. Qualitative differences consist of one or all of the following: decoration, vessel form, and quality, or degree of craftsmanship. Referring to the sacred Weeden Island pottery assemblage from Mound D at the Kolomoki site, Sears (1973:39) concludes:

> These pots are not then the products of potters whose training and experience is limited to occasional production of cookpots for their own use, whether these be male or female. The mastery of medium and of technique call for complex training processes which must involve social support. It is then reasonable . . . to suggest that in this community there

were artisans as well as priests, or priests who were artisans, whose ceramic efforts were primarily devoted to service of the supernatural.

At the time Sears was writing, as he noted, methods were not readily available to measure qualitative differences in ceramic assemblages. Today such methods exist, and the McKeithen ceramic collection offered an excellent opportunity to examine sacred–secular differences in a Weeden Island ceramic complex.

In order to test Sears' ideas on the differences between sacred and secular pottery, Cordell examined the relations between (1) surface decoration and depositional context, (2) vessel form and depositional context, and (3) degree of craftsmanship and depositional context. Collection of data for testing the hypotheses about surface decoration and vessel form used the decorative and formal ceramic typologies, respectively, established by Willey (1949), Sears (1956), and Sabloff (1975). Collection of data to examine degree of craftsmanship initially involved identification of ways to measure objectively such a subjective concept. Many researchers have stated that a higher degree of craftsmanship characterizes pottery recovered from mound contexts. This supposition implies that sacred or mound ware is in some way better than secular ware, perhaps in terms of greater time or effort spent in manufacture and greater control in the manipulation of the clays used. Specifically, there could be observable differences in methods of vessel construction, finishing, and firing. Such differences might also, however, reflect the use of different kinds of clays for manufacture of sacred versus secular pottery. Thus, in order to examine these implications, degree of craftsmanship was operationally defined by measurement of physical properties and other variables that reflect resource selection and manufacturing technology, including processes of vessel construction, finishing, and firing.

General comparisons in terms of the measured attributes were carried out for subsamples of pottery from mound versus midden contexts. In addition, further comparisons were made to determine whether observed sacred–secular differences or similarities persisted when the samples were controlled for decoration. Ideally, this comparison should have been carried out for individual pottery types occurring in both contexts. Extremely small sample sizes for individual types in the study collection made such comparisons prohibitive. A compromise was reached by subdividing the mound and midden samples into four subsamples for comparison. These four categories were (1) decorated mound pottery, (2) *matching* midden pottery, consisting of the same decorated types as were observed in the mounds, (3) *nonmatching* midden pottery, consisting of all other decorated types, and (4) undecorated midden pottery. These comparisons examine the relationships between a given variable (e.g., vessel form) while controlling, at least in some small measure, for decoration.

Surface Decoration

Comparisons of surface decorations on pottery from sacred versus secular contexts were made by considering the entire sample (1122) of midden sherds (i.e., that group from which the study sample of 212 was chosen). The sampling population was used here because the smaller study sample was not representative in terms of decorative variability. All sherds were classified with reference to established typologies (Kohler 1978b; Sears 1956; Willey 1949).

A sacred–secular dichotomy in decoration is readily apparent when the frequencies of decorated versus undecorated cases are compared (see Table 6.4A). Seventy-six percent of the midden ceramics are undecorated, contrasting with only 12% in the mound sample. The significance of this difference must be viewed cautiously, however, because whole or nearly whole vessels are being compared with pot-

Table 6.4

Sacred–Secular Variability in Surface Decoration[a]

	Mound (%)	Midden (%)	n
A. Decorated versus undecorated			
undecorated	12	76	854
decorated	88	24	301
B. Variability among decorated types			
Weeden Island Red	24	4	19
Weeden Island Zoned Red	31	0.4	10
Weeden Island Incised	10	6	20
Weeden Island Punctated	—	5	14
Weeden Island Plain	7	18	51
Carrabelle Punctated	—	8	23
Carrabelle Incised	—	8	23
Keith Incised	—	4	10
Tucker Ridge-pinched	3	1	3
Indian Pass Incised	3	1	5
check stamped	3	2	7
complicated stamped	—	8	23
miscellaneous stamped	—	4	11
miscellaneous incised	—	14	37
Papys Bayou Punctated	7	3	11
Papys Bayou Plain	10	3	10
St. Johns stamped	—	9	24
C. Variability among elite types			
Weeden Island Red	37	27	19
Weeden Island Zoned Red	47	2	10
Weeden Island Incised	16	39	20
Weeden Island Punctated	—	32	14
D. Variability among matching pottery types			
Weeden Island Red	24	11	19
Weeden Island Zoned Red	31	1	10
Weeden Island Incised	10	16	20
Weeden Island Plain	7	46	51
Papys Bayou Punctated	7	8	16
Papys Bayou Plain	10	6	10
Indian Pass Incised	3	4	5
Tucker Ridge-pinched	3	2	3
check stamped	3	6	7

[a]Chi-square tests show that these mound–midden differences are significant at an alpha level of .001.

sherds. Caution is due because the field of decoration on many Weeden Island vessels is only a small portion of the total vessel surface area; breakage may result in inflated proportions of undecorated sherds.

When undecorated categories are excluded

Table 6.5
Sacred–Secular Variability in Vessel Form[a]

Visual form	Form versus context			Form versus context, controlling for decoration				
	Mound (%)	Midden (%)	n	Decorated mound	Matching midden	Nonmatching midden	Undecorated midden	n
Plate	19	2	7	21	6	—	—	7
Dish	6	2	3	7	6	—	—	3
Outslanting bowl	9	30	13	11	41	16	36	17
Vertical bowl	6	4	2	7	—	—	18	4
Incurving bowl	28	19	18	25	24	26	—	16
Vase–bowl[b]	3	28	9	4	18	26	45	14
Jar–bowl[b]	—	15	7	—	6	31	—	7
Effigy	28	—	8	25	—	—	—	7

[a]Plate and dish categories were combined for calculation of corrected chi-square values; alpha level for uncontrolled variability is .001 and for controlled variability is .01. Vessel wall orientation for plate and dish forms is outslanting; for vase–bowls, it is predominantly vertical; and for jar–bowls, it is compound–independent restricted.

[b]Vessel height relative to diameter could not be estimated.

from comparisons, a distinction based on context still persists (see Table 6.4B). Conspicuously absent from the mound assemblage are Carrabelle Punctated, Carrabelle Incised, and complicated stamped types. These and other types make up over 50% of the decorated pottery from the midden (Table 6.4C). Sixty-four percent of the decorated mound ceramics consist of elite, Weeden Island types, as defined by Kohler (1978b), versus only 16% for the midden context. Conspicuously absent from the mound assemblage is Weeden Island Punctated, an elite type that is modal in the midden subsample.

Decorated types occurring in both contexts include: Weeden Island Plain, Red, Zoned Red, and Incised; Papys Bayou Punctated and Plain; Indian Pass Incised; Tucker Ridge-pinched; and check stamped. Comparison of relative frequencies in this subsample show contextual differences for Weeden Island Plain, Red, and Zoned Red (Table 6.4D). Weeden Island Plain is the predominant midden type, making up almost half of the subsample of the decorated pottery (46%), contrasting with 9% in the mound contexts. Weeden Island Red and Zoned Red make up 24 and 31%, respectively, of mound decorated pottery as opposed to 11 and 1%, re-

spectively, in the midden subsample. Relative frequencies of the other pottery types occurring in both contexts are similar.

Vessel Form

Trends observed for vessel form include unusual forms such as effigy vessels found in the mounds; plate forms, another unusual vessel form, occurring primarily in the mound contexts but also present in the matching midden subsample; vase–bowl and jar–bowl forms were observed primarily in the nonmatching and undecorated midden subsample; and bowls were present in all contexts and decorative categories (Table 6.5). These data indicate that while there are still differences in vessel form between sacred and secular contexts, regardless of category of decoration, the differences are less pronounced for subsamples having the same decorations.

Manufacturing Technology

Presence or absence of appliquéd or modeled features, vessel wall thickness, method of surface finishing, and presence and degree of luster

Table 6.6
Sacred–Secular Variability in Vessel Manufacture[a]

Feature	Mound (%)	Midden (%)	n
Appliquéd or modeled features			
present	55	2	18
absent	45	98	66
Wall thickness (mm)[b]			
≤5	13	23	52
6	59	30	83
7	16	25	59
≥8	13	22	50
Exterior surface finishing			
wiped wet (plastic)	—	15	28
scraped wet (plastic)	—	3	4
rubbed wet (plastic)	—	14	26
wiped leather-hard	—	3	4
scraped leather-hard	—	0.5	1
burnished leather-hard	100	66	157
Interior surface finishing			
wiped wet (plastic)	9	9	22
scraped wet (plastic)	6	7	17
rubbed wet (plastic)	6	14	31
wiped leather-hard	—	0.5	1
scraped leather-hard	—	1	2
burnished leather-hard	78	69	170
Degree of luster			
none	18	39	90
low	36	41	99
moderate to high	45	19	56

[a]Chi-square tests were run for mound–midden differences for each set of attributes. Alpha level is .001 for appliquéd features and exterior surface finishing, .02 for thickness, .3 for interior surface finishing, and .01 for luster.

[b]Mound mean and range are 6.2 and 4.4–8.0 mm; midden mean and range are 6.6 and 3.5–10.2 mm.

were among the variables used to document sacred–secular context differences in manufacturing technology (see Tables 6.6 and 6.7). Of these four, only presence or absence of modeled or appliquéd features exhibits a strict contextual pattern that persists when samples are divided according to decoration. Only one potsherd from the midden had such features; although from the nonmatching category, it is perhaps significant that it is a Weeden Island

Punctated sherd, an elite type. When vessel wall thickness, surface finishing, and degree of luster are considered, there is a division on the basis of decoration and not context: Mound plus matching midden ceramics are somewhat thinner than nonmatching and undecorated midden samples, regardless of depositional context; and the mound subsamples exhibit a greater proportion of burnished and lustrous surfaces than nonmatching and undecorated midden subsamples.

To test for sacred–secular differences in terms of clays selected and used for manufacture, variability in general class of paste and the results of the cluster analysis of sherds were examined (Tables 6.8A and 6.9A). In terms of general class of paste (or resource) type, there is a marked division between mound pottery in general plus the matching midden subsample, versus nonmatching and undecorated midden subsamples. The former were made principally of micaceous clays. Other midden subsamples were made primarily of quartz sand–grit pastes. This contrast suggests that at the site, particular clays were used for the manufacture of certain decorative types; and those clays are distinct from those used for manufacture of most midden pottery. Nonlocal pottery acquisition may, of course, account for some of the contrast between subsamples.

For a closer look at sacred–secular variability in specific paste groups, the cluster analysis results were used (Tables 6.8B and C, and 6.9B and C). Within the micaceous paste subsample, variability in paste indicated that the matching midden category is more similar to the mound assemblage than to nonmatching and undecorated midden categories. For sponge spicule paste ceramics at McKeithen, there is a sacred–secular context division only in terms of range of paste groups represented, which is wider in the midden subsample. There are no significant differences in cluster affiliation for the sand–grit subsample of pottery.

Table 6.7
Sacred–Secular Variability in Vessel Manufacture, Controlling for Decoration[a]

Feature	Decorated mound (%)	Matching midden (%)	Nonmatching midden (%)	Undecorated midden (%)	n
Appliquéd or modeled features					
present	52	—	5	—	15
absent	48	100	95	100	65
Wall thickness (mm)					
≤5	14	38	21	14	52
6	64	31	28	31	82
7	18	14	26	32	59
≥8	4	17	24	23	47
Exterior surface finishing					
wiped wet (plastic)	—	4	20	19	28
scraped wet (plastic)	—	2	—	3	4
rubbed wet (plastic)	—	13	14	14	26
wiped leather-hard	—	4	—	2	4
scraped leather-hard	—	—	—	1	1
burnished leather-hard	100	77	66	60	153
Interior surface finishing					
wiped wet (plastic)	—	5	10	11	19
scraped wet (plastic)	—	12	7	4	17
rubbed wet (plastic)	—	3	18	17	31
wiped leather-hard	—	—	2	—	1
scraped leather-hard	—	—	—	2	2
burnished leather-hard	100	79	64	65	92
Degree of luster					
none	10	19	62	47	96
low	41	38	28	43	91
moderate to high	48	43	10	10	54

[a]Chi-square tests were run to determine significance of differences; alpha level is .001 appliquéd features, thickness, exterior surface finishing, and luster, and .01 for interior surface finishing.

Sacred–secular variability in original firing conditions were evaluated by considering original surface and core colors, Moh's scratch hardness, and porosity and from refiring experiments carried out to measure weight loss and color change with increasing temperature. (Tables presenting these variables can be found in Cordell 1984.) For the micaceous paste subsample the matching midden sherds are once again more similar to the mound assemblages than to nonmatching and undecorated midden categories. The mound subsample appears to be the highest fired (i.e., fired at the greatest temperature or for the longest duration), while undecorated midden sherds are the *lowest fired* (i.e., fired at the lowest temperature or for the shortest duration). For surface color alone, there is a distinction on the basis of decoration (mound plus matching midden versus nonmatching and undecorated midden subsamples) regardless of context. No differences between contexts were observed for variables describing original firing conditions for either the spiculite or sand–grit paste subsamples. In general, sub-

Table 6.8

Sacred–Secular Variability in Paste[a]

Paste	Mound (%)	Midden (%)	n
General class			
micaceous	58	20	249
sponge spicule	18	14	168
sand–grit	24	65	738
Micaceous subsample			
Clusters 1 and 3	32	10	13
Cluster 2	32	56	46
Cluster 4	16	15	14
Cluster 5	16	7	8
outliers	5	11	9
Sponge spicule subsample			
Clusters 1 and 4	67	45	21
Cluster 2	—	24	9
Cluster 3	—	16	6
outliers	33	16	8
Quartz sand–grit subsample			
Cluster 1	25	16	17
Cluster 2	12	12	12
Cluster 3	50	37	38
Clusters 4 and 6	12	18	17
Cluster 5	—	6	6
outliers	—	10	9

[a]Chi-square tests showed significance at the alpha level of .001 for general-class mound–midden differences. Alpha levels for subsamples are .2, .9, and .99, respectively.

samples appear to have been relatively low fired relative to the micaceous paste group. Hardness varied according to decoration (mound plus matching midden versus non-matching and undecorated midden) and is believed to reflect differences in surface finishing rather than firing.

Summary

Differences in degree of craftsmanship, as identified through variables measuring manufacturing technology, indicate that greater time and effort was spent in making, finishing, and firing certain categories of decorated pottery, regardless of depositional context at the site. The observed trends are summarized in

Table 6.10. It also appears that greater time and effort was spent making elite pottery in general. The special purpose or ceremonial function conferred on mound ceramics on the basis of depositional context, unusual forms, and the like might also be extended to matching midden ceramics on the basis of qualitative similarities. The degree to which matching midden pottery can be called sacred varies, however. The context variability in vessel forms and decorations just discussed suggests functional differences within the sacred category. Rather than a sacred–secular dichotomy, the context differences in forms and decorations, and similarities in manufacturing technology for overlapping decorative categories (pottery occuring in both mound and village contexts) seem to support a tripartite functional division for Weeden Island pottery. Interestingly, this tripartite scheme is the same arrived at independently by Knight, using a very different analytical paradigm (see Chapter 8). That scheme posits the existence of *cult pottery* (effigy vessels or mortuary ware in its strictest sense, Sears 1956:22–23); *prestige ware* (corresponding to Kohler's Chapter 4 definition of elite pottery); and *utilitarian ware* (that thought to have been used for everyday activities, such as storage and cooking). The latter two represent a continuum rather than discrete classes. With respect to the McKeithen site, cult ware is found only in mound contexts; prestige ware is found in mound and, to a lesser extent, in midden contexts; and utilitarian ware is found in both midden and mound contexts but primarily in the midden.

Those characteristics or traits indicative of relatively great expenditure of time and effort in manufacture—such as modeled or appliquéd features, higher surface luster, thin vessel walls, and higher temperature or longer duration of firing—were probably not necessary features of utilitarian ceramics, which dominate the collections from the McKeithen midden. Indeed, such characteristics may not have been

Table 6.9
Sacred–Secular Variability in Paste, Controlling for Decoration[a]

Paste	Decorated mound (%)	Matching midden (%)	Nonmatching midden (%)	Undecorated midden (%)	n
General class					
micaceous	52	38	24	18	245
sponge spicule	21	16	21	13	168
sand–grit	28	46	54	70	738
Micaceous subsample					
Clusters 1 and 3	33	17	5	5	12
Cluster 2	40	63	65	38	46
Cluster 4	20	7	10	33	14
Cluster 5	—	7	5	10	5
outliers	7	7	15	14	9
Sponge spicule subsample					
Clusters 1 and 4	67	33	33	55	21
Cluster 2	—	33	25	20	9
Cluster 3	—	17	17	15	6
outliers	33	17	25	10	8
Quartz sand–grit subsample					
Cluster 1	25	7	20	17	17
Cluster 2	12	14	8	13	12
Cluster 3	50	43	36	36	38
Clusters 4 and 6	12	14	20	17	17
Cluster 5	—	—	4	10	6
outliers	—	21	12	6	9

[a]Chi-square tests were run on these data. For the general-class difference, alpha level is .001. For the subsamples, negative correlations were indicated: alpha levels are .70, .99, and .99, respectively.

desirable for a sound storage or cooking vessel. The relatively low firing conditions observed for the utilitarian ceramics, particularly those ceramics made of quartz sand–grit pastes, may, in fact, have been optimal, given the nature of the clays used. Relatively low porosity values are exhibited by the quartz sand–grit paste pottery, a probable result of low firing conditions and perhaps high organic content of the paste. Such characteristics would be advantageous, exerting a binding effect that would enhance the strength or durability (and perhaps water-tightness) of vessels. Complete oxidation of organic materials through higher-temperature firing or longer firing time would reduce those

desired characteristics given the coarser paste textures. This judgment is supported by observed changes in physical properties of the pottery after refiring at 700° C. Nearly all of the refired specimens, regardless of paste, decoration, or context, exhibited a decrease in scratch hardness and an increase in percentage of apparent porosity. Many potsherds, particularly in the quartz sand–grit paste subsample, also became extremely friable after refiring (Cordell 1984:150, 235). The observed differences in degree of craftsmanship in terms of manufacture, finishing, and firing appear, therefore, to represent differences that are appropriate if not optimal given the resources used in the manufac-

Table 6.10

Trends in Sacred–Secular Variability[a]

Vessel form	D
Degree of craftsmanship	
General paste	D
Cluster affiliation	
micaceous paste	D
sponge spiculite paste	A
sand–grit paste	A
Technology	
presence or absence of appliqués	B
thickness	C
surface finish	C
degree of luster	C

Technology	Micaceous paste	Spiculite paste	Sand–grit paste
surface color	C	A	B
coring	E	A to B	A
hardness	B	C	C
porosity	A	B	B
% firing weight loss	E	F	B
color change	E	A	A

[a]A, no differences between subsamples regardless of context or decoration; B, differences exist based on secular versus sacred contexts; C, differences exist based on decoration (decorated mound and matching midden pottery versus nonmatching and undecorated midden pottery); D, differences exist between mound pottery versus nonmatching and undecorated midden pottery (matching midden pottery is intermediate between these two groups, with more similarities to the mound pottery); E, differences exist between mound pottery versus undecorated midden pottery (decorated midden pottery is intermediate between these two groups); and F, differences exist between decorated versus undecorated pottery.

ture of utilitarian pottery and the intended uses of the products.

CRAFT SPECIALIZATION IN THE MANUFACTURE OF POTTERY

As pointed out in the beginning of this chapter, some specialization has long been inferred for certain kinds of Weeden Island pottery. In the past, efforts to identify and describe objectively the nature of this specialization have been hindered by a lack of appropriate quantifiable criteria. Rice (1981) has outlined a methodology for the archaeological recognition and description of pottery specialization. She suggests that assessment of *standardization* (reduction in variety) and *elaboration* (increase in variety) of ceramic traits (e.g., forms, pastes, decorations) provide objective indicators of relative specialization or nonspecialization (1981:220).

As specialization develops over time, Rice proposes that standardization and elaboration in ceramic traits will increase with increasing social complexity. Her model for pottery specialization arbitrarily divides an evolutionary continuum into four stages of increasing social complexity ranging from egalitarian (Step 1) to stratified (Step 4) social systems. Each step is described with a series of archaeologically testable expectations (1981:222–224). She suggests that the processes of standardization and elaboration will be evident initially in certain kinds of pottery designated (for interpretive convenience) as elite ceramics, defined by Rice as high-value luxury or prestige commodities with ceremonial or special function and restricted distribution. Utilitarian pottery, according to Rice, exhibits the converse of the just-mentioned characteristics, but she cautions that overlap is likely between the two categories in terms of patterns of production and usage.

Following Rice's methods, Cordell compared pottery types in terms of variability in formal and technological attributes. This allows identification of trends toward standardization in the manufacture of pottery types. Variables examined include vessel form, general class of paste, cluster (paste) affiliation, and four variables describing manufacturing technology. Context of deposition is ignored in these comparisons, and no a priori assumptions concerning the eliteness of certain pottery types are

Table 6.11
Vessel Form Variability According to Pottery Type[a]

Type	Plate	Dish	Effigy	Outslanting bowl	Vertical bowl	Incurving bowl	Vase–bowl	Jar–bowl	n
Weeden Island Red	—	8	16	48	12	8	4	4	25
Weeden Island Zoned Red	77	8	15	—	—	—	—	—	13
Weeden Island Incised	—	—	—	12	12	71	6	—	17
Weeden Island Punctated	—	9	—	45	—	27	9	9	11
Weeden Island Plain	1	6	1	58	8	11	14	2	103
Carrabelle Punctated	—	—	—	7	—	43	39	11	28
Carrabelle Incised	—	—	—	6	6	25	12	50	16
Keith Incised	—	—	—	17	—	17	50	17	6
Indian Pass Incised	—	—	—	—	—	100	—	—	4
Check stamped	—	—	—	—	—	—	—	—	0
Complicated stamped	—	—	—	—	—	33	17	33	12
Miscellaneous incised	—	—	—	17	—	33	17	33	12
Papys Bayou Punctated	—	—	—	20	40	—	40	—	5
Papys Bayou Plain	—	11	—	44	11	33	—	—	9
St. Johns Check Stamped	—	—	—	—	—	—	100	—	3
Undecorated micaceous	—	7	14	29	21	21	7	—	14
Undecorated spicule	—	—	—	50	—	50	—	—	2
Undecorated sand–grit	—	2	—	35	18	13	27	5	62

[a]Percentages are based on totals that include 275 cases from Mound A platform.

made. From the McKeithen Weeden Island study collection (representing both mound and midden deposits), 18 pottery types were chosen for comparisons of the variables. Results are summarized in the sections that follow. Particulars of data collection and analysis can be found in Cordell (1983:Chapter 7).

Vessel Form

Thirteen of the 18 types or decorative categories were hand sorted into 8 categories of vessel form, defined on the basis of modal form categories and range of forms. These groupings are listed in Tables 6.11 and 6.12.

Some degree of correlation of forms with types is evident. Weeden Island Zoned Red (characterized by plate forms), Weeden Island Incised and Indian Pass Incised (characterized by incurving bowl forms), and complicated stamped categories (characterized by vertical vase or bowl forms) all exhibit narrow ranges of

vessel forms. The remaining types exhibit relatively wide ranges of forms or less peaked or more even distributions.

The narrow range of forms and more peaked distributions characterizing some of the decorative types in these groupings is indicative of restricted manufacture or some degree of specialization. This may mean that fewer individuals were involved in the manufacture of these types or that the types may have been intended for a more restricted range of functions. The wider range of forms and less peaked distributions of the types in the latter vessel form categories just listed might indicate a greater number of producers or a wider variety of functions.

General Class of Paste

Most of the pottery types can be sorted into four groupings in terms of the general kinds of

Table 6.12

Pottery Type Based on Patterns of Form Variability

Form variability	Types
Plates predominate	Weeden Island Zoned Red
Outslanting bowls predominate	Weeden Island Red
	Weeden Island Punctated
	Weeden Island Plain
	Papys Bayou Plain
Variable vessel form, with incurving bowls, vase–bowls, and jar–bowls modal	Carrabelle Punctated
	Carrabelle Incised
	Keith Incised
	Miscellaneous incised
Incurving bowls predominate	Weeden Island Incised
	Indian Pass Incised
Vase–bowls predominate	Complicated stamped
	St. Johns complicated stamped
Variable vessel form, with outslanting bowls and vase–bowls modal	Papys Bayou Punctated
Variable vessel form, with outslanting bowls, vertical bowls, and vase–bowls modal	Undecorated sand–grit paste
Variable vessel form, with outslanting bowls, vertical bowls, and incurving bowls modal	Undecorated micaceous paste

clays selected or used in manufacture (see Table 6.13). The first group, consisting of types that were made almost exclusively of micaceous clays, is made up of the two types Weeden Island Zoned Red and Indian Pass Incised.

The second group is made up of types in which a micaceous paste is still predominant, but in which quartz sand clays constitute close to one third of the cases. Weeden Island Incised, Weeden Island Punctated, and Weeden Island Red all fall into this group. A third group consists of those types in which sand–grit paste is predominant, and it is made up of the largest number of types, including Weeden Island Plain, Carrabelle Punctated, Carrabelle Incised, miscellaneous incised, complicated stamped, check stamped, and miscellaneous

stamped types. Significantly smaller proportions were made of micaceous (primarily) and spiculite clays. The complicated stamped category, however, includes a variety of motifs that have been given status as separate types. Larger samples for individual types or motifs may yield different patterns of paste variability.

The fourth and last group of types consists of Papys Bayou Plain, Papys Bayou Punctated, St. Johns Check Stamped, and St. Johns complicated stamped, all of which, by definition, are made exclusively of spiculite clays. Keith Incised pottery, the remaining type, is intermediate between the second and third categories. Micaceous and sand–grit pastes were observed in equal proportions (40%) of the sample sherds of that type.

Relations between paste and decoration described in the preceding paragraphs would seem to indicate standardization in manufacture of Weeden Island pottery in terms of the selection of general classes of clay resources used. Nonlocal pottery acquisition is believed to account for some of the contrasts among types, however. Spiculite clays, for example, must be considered to be foreign to the McKeithen region and pottery made from such clays must be nonlocal. Excluding spiculite pottery, the relations between pottery type and general class of paste may represent a combination of conscious selection of particular local clays and nonlocal acquisition. Whether or not the observed general relations do provide positive evidence for standardization or specialization of manufacture at the McKeithen site can be clarified by considering paste-cluster affiliation.

Cluster Affiliation

The results of the cluster analysis carried out on the potsherd and vessel samples in the study collection (see Cordell 1984:175) were reviewed to examine more closely the relations between

Table 6.13
Pottery Type According to General Class of Paste

Type	Mica (%)	Sponge spicule (%)	Sand–grit (%)	n
Weeden Island Red[a]	58	—	42	19
Weeden Island Zoned Red[b]	90	10	—	10
Weeden Island Incised[a]	65	—	35	20
Weeden Island Punctated[a]	71	—	29	14
Weeden Island Plain[c]	31	—	69	51
Carrabelle Punctated[c]	22	9	70	23
Carrabelle Incised[c]	17	17	65	23
Keith Incised[e]	40	20	40	10
Tucker Ridge-pinched[c]	33	—	67	3
Indian Pass Incised[b]	80	—	20	5
Check stamped[c]	29	—	71	7
Complicated stamped[c]	26	—	74	23
Miscellaneous incised[c]	27	11	62	37
Miscellaneous stamped[c]	7	21	71	14
Papys Bayou Punctated[d]	—	100	—	11
Papys Bayou Plain[d]	—	100	—	10
St. Johns complicated stamped[d]	—	100	—	11
St. Johns Check Stamped[d]	—	100	—	10

Paste groupings defined via variability in the general class of paste. Percentages are based on the entire sampling population.
[a]50% micaceous paste ($n = 3$, where n is number of types).
[b]80% micaceous paste ($n = 2$).
[c]60% sand–grit paste ($n = 8$).
[d]Sponge spicule paste ($n = 4$).
[e]Micaceous and sand–grit paste modal ($n = 1$).

clay resources and pottery types. These relations can be summarized as follows. A variety of clays was used in the manufacture of the McKeithen site pottery; however, one cluster of micaceous clay (Cluster 2) and one of quartz sand–grit clay (Cluster 3) were widespread and consistently used almost across the range of pottery types at the site. That same micaceous paste cluster was used almost exclusively in the manufacture of two pottery types—Weeden Island Punctated and Weeden Island Red. Most other types exhibit relatively wide and evenly distributed ranges of pastes.

Although micaceous paste 2 was at least a significant minority paste in all other pottery types (excluding, of course, undecorated sand–grit and spiculite categories), it was hypothesized, on the basis of the relative proportions of micaceous versus sand–grit paste within the sampling population, that Cluster 2 occurs in less frequency in the types Carrabelle Incised, Weeden Island Plain, and complicated stamped ware (i.e., types that are made predominantly from clays lacking mica). On the basis of the sampling population, it can also be hypothesized that these three types plus the undecorated quartz sand–grit category will be characterized by a variety of pastes, but with consistent use of the Cluster 3 sand–grit clays. Sand–grit clays were used less frequently for manufacture of Weeden Island Red, Incised, Punctated, and Zoned Red types. These observed and hypothesized relations have implications for some degree of specialization in terms of certain kinds of clays being restricted for manufacture of particular types of pottery.

Although sample sizes are relatively small, very pale brown-firing clays (micaceous paste Cluster 2) appear to have been used most frequently, although not exclusively, for manufacture of Weeden Island Red and Punctated types. This paste cluster matches locally available clays, specifically ones from Orange Creek, which forms the northern boundary of the McKeithen village. When nonlocal cases are excluded, Weeden Island Incised and Zoned Red types can also be grouped with the Weeden Island Red and Punctated types because most local cases are made from the same Cluster 2 local micaceous clay. It is significant that these four types have been separated out as a class of elite wares. Close proximity to the site may be one reason for restricting use of creek clays to the manufacture of pottery having special uses or functions.

The buff or almost white fired color of the Cluster 2 clays may also have significance for explaining the relations between decoration and paste. On the basis of the sample of 26 clays, very pale, brown-firing clays appear to be somewhat rare; only 4 of the 26 could be characterized as having a very pale brown or buff color. Such clays may have been valued as a scarce resource and were therefore restricted for special production. Possible explanations might also draw on analogy to color symbolism among the Southeastern aborigines. In the Southeast belief system, the color white symbolized purity, happiness, peace, and social harmony (Hudson 1976:132, 226, 235; also see Chapter 8 in this volume). This color often is found in association with its opposite, red, which symbolizes conflict, disunity, fear, and danger (1976:235). It is tempting to cite Weeden

Island Red and Zoned Red types as examples of the articulation between these opposites. (Most examples of these types were also buff in color before refiring.)

The apparent relations between particular pottery types and pastes constitutes good evidence for some degree of specialization in local manufacture of types traditionally considered sumptuary goods. Typological variation in manufacturing technology is examined next to ascertain if the present sample of elite types can also be distinguished from other pottery in terms of this criterion.

Manufacturing Technology

Four attributes were considered in the investigation of typological variability in manufacturing technology. These variables are vessel wall thickness, exterior and interior surface finishing, degree of luster, and degree of firing. A cluster analysis was used to sort 18 pottery types into groupings on the basis of similarities among these attributes (see Cordell 1984:178–183).

Three clusters of pottery types were defined from this procedure. The first cluster consists of 6 types: Weeden Island Zoned Red, Weeden Island Red, Weeden Island Incised, Weeden Island Punctated, Papys Bayou Punctated, and Indian Pass Incised. These types are characterized in general by thin vessel walls (most often ≤6 mm), moderate to high luster, and exterior and interior surface burnishing. Types in this cluster also appear to have been the highest fired, as inferred from the degree of color change at different temperatures of refiring (Cordell 1984:187).

A second cluster is made up of 7 of the 18 types: Weeden Island Plain, Carrabelle Incised, Papys Bayou Plain, miscellaneous incised, undecorated micaceous and spiculite paste pottery, and Keith Incised. These 7 types exhibit variable thickness, but the majority of cases are greater than or equal to 6 mm in thickness. The 7 types are also characterized by low luster and by surface burnishing. Percentage of sherds with surface burnishing in this group is not as high, however, as the percentage in the first group of 6 types. Sherds in this second cluster varied in degree of firing, but most appear to have been moderately well fired.

The third cluster produced by the cluster analysis contains the remaining five types: Carrabelle Punctated, complicated stamped (nonspiculite pastes), St. Johns complicated stamped, undecorated sand–grit pottery, and check stamped. This group is characterized by variable thickness, with most cases thicker than 6 mm and no surface luster present. Surface finishing is variable, but these types exhibit the highest frequency of finishes that were carried out on surfaces that were still relatively plastic. This group is also fairly homogenous in degree of firing; most cases appear to have been moderately fired.

On the basis of these findings, three patterns of manufacture were identified. Rather than being discrete groups, these units appear to represent a continuum with the first and third clusters at the two extremes and the second being intermediate.

Comparisons indicate that the first group tends to be less variable in many of the measured attributes (e.g., thickness and surface finishing). When earlier findings are considered, it is observed, for example, that three of the pottery types in the first group (Weeden Island Zoned Red, Weeden Island Incised, and Indian Pass Incised) exhibit the greatest standardization of vessel forms (see Tables 6.11, 6.12). This standardization in manufacturing technology and vessel form is also accompanied by standardization or a narrow range of variability in general class of paste (see Cordell 1984:189), a reflection of resource selection. Five of the six pottery types in this first cluster are made pre-dominately of micaceous clays. Papys Bayou Punctated is the exception, being made of spiculite clays (by definition). Sand–grit and spiculite clays characterize the third cluster of types. The middle cluster is intermediate in that it has a wider range of paste types, with some type categories being made pre-dominately of sand–grit clays, some made exclusively of spiculite clays, and two types in which micaceous clays were predominate or modal. Although earlier findings show that the first group exhibits standardization in terms of vessel forms, when viewed from a different perspective—as a group relative to the other two clusters of types—the six types in this category have the widest range of vessel forms, including nearly the only occurrences of unusual effigies and plate forms (Cordell 1984:189). Cluster 2 also occurs in a wide range of forms, but the distribution is less even, with fewer uncommon plate and effigy forms. This group also exhibits the widest range of decorations. The painted, slipped, incised, and punctated designs contrast with the incised and undecorated types in the second cluster and the punctated, stamped, and undecorated types in the third cluster. The numbers and kinds of forms and decorations in the first cluster can be considered as evidence for elaboration of manufacture, which is also said to be an indicator of specialization versus nonspecialization (Rice 1981:220).

This cluster pattern of two extremes and an intermediate grouping in terms of manufacture and general paste is, as might be expected, also reflected in physical properties such as color and hardness. For example, the first group of pottery types has the highest incidence of well-oxidized cores and surface colors. The other two groups, which are more variable in general paste and degree of firing or exhibit somewhat lower degrees of firing, are more variable in surface color, with greater percentages of poorly and moderately oxidized colors. Dark cores are predominant in the middle or intermediate cluster of pottery types and are almost exclusive in the third cluster (Cordell 1984:191).

These three groups of types represent points along a continuum in terms of function as well as pattern of manufacture. An elite designation for the six types in the first cluster is suggested on the basis of standardization or consistency of manufacture, which is said to be visible initially in elite goods (Rice 1981:223). An elite designation, conferring ceremonial or prestige functions, is also indicated by the restricted distribution of these types at the McKeithen site. These types occur more frequently in mound or ceremonial contexts than the other types. The wide range of vessel forms and decorations in this cluster indicate some degree of elaboration in manufacture, an indicator of specialization of manufacture of elite goods (Rice 1981:220). This group of elite types would subsume both prestige wares and cult objects, according to Knight's terminology (see Chapter 8). Using the village collections, four of these types were designated as elite or prestige commodities by Kohler (Chapter 4) on the basis of apparent proficiency or time and effort expended in manufacture. The present results extend the elite designation to Papys Bayou Punctated and Indian Pass Incised types. That these types were not included as elite by Kohler is due to their low representation in his attribute sample.

Pottery types in the third cluster may represent types with more strictly utilitarian functions. Almost all of these types were recovered exclusively from midden contexts; only one member of one of the types was recovered from a ceremonial context. A utilitarian ware classification is also supported by the fact that three of the five types are paddle stamped. It is generally acknowledged that the increased surface area produced by the raised design of a stamped vessel has functional significance for heat transfer in cooking and for gripping the vessel during use.

The second or middle group of seven types

may be intermediate or overlapping in terms of function as well as in manufacturing technology. Three of these types have members that were recovered from ceremonial contexts (Weeden Island Plain, undecorated micaceous paste, Papys Bayou Plain); and three cases in the group are effigy vessels, having either head or tail adornos or both at or just below the vessel rim.

When local manufacture of Weeden Island pottery is considered, the picture that emerges bears similarities to the description of Step 2 in Rice's model for development of pottery specialization (1981:223). Specifically, there is evidence for standardization of paste composition for certain categories of pottery, and great skill or consistency in manufacture and firing (Implications 1 and 2 in Rice 1981:222). There is evidence for the beginning of differentiation of elite or status-reinforcing goods in terms of decoration and forms, manufacturing technology, standardization of paste, and nonrandom spatial distribution at the site (Implications 2, 3, and 4 in Step 3 in Rice 1981:223). The relationship between four elite types and a paste cluster that matches a clay source with immediate proximity to the site suggests restricted access to that deposit. Perhaps manufacture of elite pottery was undertaken by a restricted number of individuals at the site. Of the locally made items, some appear to have been made specifically for mortuary-related ritual. Others may represent tangible prestige items that may or may not have had special ceremonial functions.

When integrated with our model of the level of sociopolitical organization for the McKeithen region (see Chapter 3), some understanding of the degree of specialization of pottery production at the McKeithen site is obtained. We expect that within the McKeithen culture, all households were capable of pottery manufacture (units of production and consumption of goods are the same) and probably manufactured pottery for their own utilitarian uses such as cooking and storage. Manufacture of special-purpose pottery appears to have been for use in ritual or trade. Perhaps some local elite pottery was made to exchange for nonlocal pottery, such as some Weeden Island Incised and Zoned Red vessels, Papys Bayou series pottery, or other nonlocal materials. Given the hypothesized so-cioeconomic level of McKeithen society, however, specialized pottery making as an occupation for gaining, or contributing significantly to, subsistence or livelihood is doubtful. Overall, the results obtained from the ceramic technological analysis are compatible with our model.

7

Description of the Pottery Vessels from the McKeithen Mounds

This chapter describes in detail the pottery recovered from the three mounds at the McKeithen site. Archaeological contexts for these vessels were discussed in Chapter 5. The mound ceramics are described here in terms of decoration, vessel form, manufacturing technology (construction, finishing, and firing methods), and origin of manufacture. Methods of ceramic technological analysis are the same as those employed in the study of the site ceramic collection presented in Chapter 6 (see also Cordell 1984).

In the cataloging process, all sherds less than or equal to $\frac{1}{2}$ in.^{2} were counted or weighed and discarded. All other specimens were catalogued according to surface decoration (or lack of it) and general class of paste. Decoration classifications were taken from Willey (1949), Sears (1956), and Kohler's (1978b) observations based on the McKeithen village collection. A binocular microscope ($\times$ 70) was used to classify the sherds into the four general paste categories: (1) mica, (2) sponge spicules, (3) very fine to medium quartz inclusions, exclusive of mica and sponge spicules, and (4) coarse to very coarse quartz inclusions, exclusive of mica and sponge spicules but not exclusive of smaller quartz inclusions. Results of the analysis are presented separately for each mound.

MOUND A

A total of 1836 potsherds were recovered from the top of the Mound A platform mound. It is assumed that these sherds were discarded as a result of activities associated with the cleaning and preparation of bodies for final deposition in Mound C. As noted in Chapter 5, 27 pottery vessels were identified among the Mound A platform mound collection. A list of pottery types represented by these vessels can be found in Table 5.1. Table 7.1 lists each individual Mound A vessel, providing information on form, paste, and origin, as well as giving the vessel numbers that were used for analysis and are used here for reference. Many individual vessels from the mounds are illustrated in Figures 7.1–7.8 and 7.10–7.23 in this chapter.

Decoration

Four different shapes of punctations are present on the four Carrabelle Punctated bowls. One bowl, Vessel 39 (Figure 7.2), has two rows of lunate-shaped fingernail punctations that encircle the vessel just below the rim. Another, Vessel 49 (Figure 7.5), has numerous randomly placed punctations that are linear-to-triangular in shape. These are found within an incised band 7 cm in width that begins ca. 2.5 cm below the rim. Vessel 51, the third bowl, has fingernail punctations that are eliptical in shape (size and angle of impression differ from Vessel 39). The decorated field consists of four rows contained within an incised band (3.5 cm in width) just below the rim. Decoration of the fourth Carrabelle Punctated bowl, Vessel 55, consists of four rows of rectangular punctations encircling the vessel 2.5 cm below the rim; the punctation shape was made by impressing a sharp but concave-edged tool, 5 mm in length, to the surface at a 90° angle and then dragging the tool to the right for a distance of about 3–4 mm at a lesser angle.

Two of the four Carrabelle Incised vessels do not have the characteristic herringbone design. The decoration on the first, a bowl (Vessel 43, Figure 7.4), consists of an incised zigzag band 1 cm in width contained within an incised band 4 cm in width that encircles the bowl below the collared rim. The triangular spaces created by the zigzag pattern are filled with 7–12 parallel, horizontal incised lines. Decoration on the second vessel (Vessel 50; Figure 7.1), a collared bowl, is composed of closely spaced (2 to 4-mm) vertical incised lines that start at an incised line just below the collared rim. These lines are crisscrossed by at least 4 parallel incised lines.

Vessel 41, a Keith Incised collared jar–bowl, is unusual in having relatively large (1.5- by 2-cm) diamond or parallelogram shapes created by the hatched incised lines (Figure 7.3). The Tucker Ridge-pinched dish or shallow bowl (Vessel 45) has V-shaped columns of pinching, creating an unidentified geometric pattern, an unusual decorative motif for this type. Vessel 48, New River Complicated Stamped, departs from Willey's original definition (1949:386) in having a check stamped pattern within concentric circles, as well as in part of its background decorative field (Figure 7.6).

The Weeden Island Incised design on Vessel 52 is incomplete but includes parallel incised and punctated meanders, unidentified appli-

qued elements, occasional bold circular punctations, and hatched fillers. Red ochre appears to have been rubbed into the incised and punctated areas. The Papys Bayou Incised dish, Vessel 42, does not have the typical complex Weeden Island–like design (see Willey 1949: 443). Instead, the decoration consists of three medium-width and one bold parallel incised lines that encircle the interior of the vessel. Each of the three medium-width incised lines have small triangular punctations spaced equidistantly at about 1-cm intervals. Another bold incised line is located on the exterior surface about 2.5 cm below the rim.

Observations relating to the condition of vessel surface (plastic versus leather-hard) at the time it was being decorated were also made for each decorated vessel from the mounds. For Mound A, most of the vessels appear to have been decorated while the surfaces were still relatively plastic (12 out of 17). Surfaces were leather-hard or drier on the other 5.

Form

Eight vessel forms, defined on the basis of general form, wall orientation, and mouth diameter, were identified for the 27 Mound A vessels. These included 4 collared bowls, 6 large pots or bowls, 3 medium-sized vertical bowls, 3 incurving globular bowls, 2 large open bowls, 3 medium-shallow open bowls, 2 large shallow open bowls, and 1 beaker–vase (see Table 7.1). Vessels from Mound A are shown in Figures 7.1–7.6, pages 142–145. In addition, 1 Carrabelle Incised vessel (Vessel 57) and the 2 undecorated red vessels (Vessels 36 and 60) are probably unrestricted open bowls, but this is not certain because rim sherds were not recovered.

Eleven of the vessels have the Weeden Island rims, which are folded or thickened and underscored by an incised line. Nine vessels have rounded rims and 3 have thinned or tapered rims.

Figure 7.1 Portions of Vessel 50, Mound A, Carrabelle Incised collared bowl with compound walls: rare mica in paste, local manufacture, and mouth diameter of 15 cm.

Table 7.1
Type, Form, Paste, and Origin of the Mound A Vessels

Vessel	Type	Form	Paste	Origin
34	Undecorated	Bowl–jar, collared	Rare mica	Local
35	Weeden Island Plain	Bowl, large	Sand–grit	Local
36	Undecorated (residual) red	Bowl	Rare mica	Local
37	Crooked River Complicated Stamped	Bowl–pot, large	Sand–grit	Local
38	Undecorated	Bowl, globular	Rare mica	Local
39	Carrabelle Punctated	Bowl–vase	Sand–grit	Unknown
40	Carrabelle Incised	Bowl, globular	Occasional mica	Nonlocal(?)
41	Keith Incised	Bowl–jar, collared	Sand–grit	Local
42	Papys Bayou Incised	Dish	Spicules	Nonlocal
43	Carrabelle Incised	Bowl, collared	Sand–grit	Local
44	Weeden Island Red	Bowl, shallow	Rare mica	Local
45	Tucker Ridge-pinched	Dish–bowl, shallow	Sand–grit	Local
46	Napier Complicated Stamped	Bowl–pot	Rare mica	Local
47	Weeden Island Plain	Dish–bowl, shallow	Rare mica	Local
48	New River Complicated Stamped	Bowl–pot	Rare mica	Local
49	Carrabelle Punctated	Bowl–vase	Rare mica	Local
50	Carrabelle Incised	Bowl, collared	Rare mica	Local
51	Carrabelle Punctated	Bowl, globular	Rare mica	Local
52	Weeden Island Incised	Bowl–vase–beaker	Abundant mica	Nonlocal
53	Weeden Island Plain	Bowl, large	Rare mica	Local
54	Crooked River Complicated Stamped	Bowl–pot	Spicules	Nonlocal
55	Carrabelle Punctated	Bowl–vase	Rare mica	Local
56	Weeden Island Plain	Bowl, large and shallow	Abundant mica	Nonlocal
57	Carrabelle Incised	Bowl–vase	Sand–grit	Local
58	Weeden Island Plain	Bowl–pot	Rare mica	Local
59	Napier Complicated Stamped	Bowl–pot	Rare mica	Local
60	Undecorated (residual) red	Bowl	Rare mica	Unknown

Figure 7.2 Vessel 39, Mound A, Carrabelle Punctated (fingernail) bowl–vase with vertical walls: sand–grit paste, uncertain origin, and mouth diameter of 17 cm.

Figure 7.3 Vessel 41, Mound A, Keith Incised collared bowl–jar with compound walls: sand–grit paste, local manufacture, and mouth diameter of 24 cm.

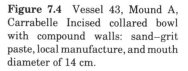

Figure 7.4 Vessel 43, Mound A, Carrabelle Incised collared bowl with compound walls: sand–grit paste, local manufacture, and mouth diameter of 14 cm.

Figure 7.5 Vessel 49, Mound A, Carrabelle Punctated (triangular) bowl–vase with vertical walls: rare mica in paste, local manufacture, and mouth diameter of 17 cm.

Figure 7.6   Vessel 48, Mound A, New River Complicated Stamped bowl–pot with vertical walls: rare mica in paste, local manufacture and mouth diameter of 34 cm.

Manufacturing Technology

All of the Mound A vessels exhibit evidence of coiled construction. The Weeden Island Incised bowl–beaker (Vessel 52) also has modeled or appliquéd elements near the rim. The modal type of surface finishing is *burnishing* (finishing a leather-hard surface by rubbing a smooth unyielding surface against it); only 8 vessels exhibited luster resulting from burnishing. A close second in terms of surface finish is the use of a smooth, unyielding tool (e.g., waterworn pebble) to finish or rub surfaces that are not quite leather-hard. Another surface finish method observed is the use of a yielding tool (e.g., fingers or a cloth) to wipe surfaces. Condition of the surfaces (e.g., plasticity) was difficult to determine in these latter cases, but it is probable that the leather-hard surfaces were dampened when this technique was applied. No luster was observed on the vessels on which either of these latter two finishing methods was applied.

Surface colors of the Mound A vessels are predominantly grey to dark grey. Core colors are also dark; most can be described as having heavy dark coring (see Cordell 1984:Figure 9). Such colors are indicative of a smoky atmosphere in firing, relatively low firing temperatures, short duration of firing, high organic content in the clays used, or a combination of all of these factors (Shepard 1976:102–107).

Origin of Manufacture

A limited technological analysis was carried out to determine origin of manufacture for the Mound A vessels. Relative texture (fine, coarse, etc.), distinctive paste constituents, and color were recorded for each vessel; color was measured on fragments refired to 700° C. These data provided the basis for comparison with cluster characteristics described for the study collection of McKeithen pottery selected from the site as a whole.

Comparisons suggest that the 27 Mound A vessels were made of at least 13 different clays. Twenty of the vessels appear to have been made locally (see Table 7.1). Half of these are from a single clay group characterized by fine to medium paste texture and reddish firing colors. They appear to match a sand–grit cluster (#3) that was found to be fairly similar to many locally available clays. This large group contains Vessels 35–37, 41, 43–45, 48, 55, and 57.

Four of the 27 vessels, each representing a separate clay source, are probably all nonlocal. Two of those have micaceous paste: a Weeden Island Incised bowl–beaker with abundant mica, very fine paste structure, and buff refired color (Vessel 52); and a Weeden Island Plain vessel with abundant mica, coarse texture, and buff refired color (Vessel 56). The other 2 vessels were both manufactured from spiculite clays. The first, a Papys Bayou Incised dish, has buff refired color, fine texture, and abundant sponge spicules (Vessel 42). The second is a Crooked River Complicated Stamped pot with occasional spicules, fine to medium paste texture, and reddish refired color (Vessel 54).

Origins of the remaining 3 Mound A vessels are uncertain. These are a Carrabelle Incised globular bowl with a micaceous paste that may be nonlocal, a sand–grit paste Carrabelle Punctated bowl, and a residual red bowl with a sand–grit paste.

MOUND B

Thirteen vessels were partially reconstructed from the 2024 potsherds excavated from the Mound B platform surface, including the floor of the structure built on that platform (Table 5.2, Table 7.2, and Figures 7.7, 7.8, and 7.10). These vessels presumably were associated with activities that took place in and around the structure. The ceramic bird head found buried in the top of the platform near the feet of the human burial is also included in the analysis.

Decoration

Distinctive or unusual features of decoration include possible stylized bird motifs on five of the eight Weeden Island Zoned Red vessels (Vessels 21, 22, 24, 25, and 26; Figure 7.8). Most of these vessels were too fragmentary, however, to reconstruct the design completely. The elements of the design appear similar to the design on the vessel shown in Figure 7.9, a Weeden Island Zoned Red plate from the Florida State Museum's Simpson Collection recovered from an unknown mound in North Florida. Two other of the zoned red vessels are decorated with a column motif (Vessels 20 and 23; Figure 7.8, top). The Weeden Island Zoned Red bird head effigy portrays a crested turkey vulture (Figure 5.8). In each case, a red-firing paint was applied to the vessel surface (interiors for all the vessels except the bird head) within incised areas prior to firing.

The design on the Weeden Island Incised vessel (Vessel 29, Figure 7.10) is characterized by curving double meanders with a punctated background or filler. A geometric arrangement of linear, parallel rows of stab-and-drag punctations (triangular in shape as in the type Ruskin Linear Punctated) was present on the Papys Bayou Punctated vessel. Larger, bolder triangular punctations occur occasionally in empty spaces. Most of the decorating on the Mound B vessels was carried out on surfaces that had dried to the leather-hard state; two were decorated while the clay was still in a relatively plastic state.

Vessel Form

Six different vessel forms were identified from the Mound B assemblage, as defined by form and vessel wall orientation. Included are 6 plates, 1 dish (Figure 7.7), 3 large shallow bowls, 1 incurving globular bowl, 1 bowl–vase, and 1 effigy (the fourteenth vessel, which was check stamped, was not complete enough to determine the form).

Rims were present for 10 of the 14 vessels. All but one of the 10 have Weeden Island rims,

Figure 7.7 Vessel 27, Mound B, Weeden Island Red dish–shallow bowl: sand–grit paste, local manufacture, and diameter of 30 cm.

Table 7.2
Type, Form, Paste, and Origin of the Mound B Vessels

Vessel	Type	Form	Paste[a]	Origin
20	Weeden Island Zoned Red	Plate	Occasional mica	Nonlocal(?)
21	Weeden Island Zoned Red	Plate	Rare mica	Unknown
22	Weeden Island Zoned Red	Plate	Occasional mica	Nonlocal(?)
23	Weeden Island Zoned Red	Plate	Occasional mica	Nonlocal(?)
24	Weeden Island Zoned Red	Plate	Rare mica	Local
25	Weeden Island Zoned Red	Dish	Rare mica	Local
26	Weeden Island Zoned Red	Plate	Rare mica	Local
27	Weeden Island Red	Dish–bowl, shallow	Sand–grit	Local
28	Weeden Island Plain	Bowl, shallow	Abundant mica	Nonlocal
29	Weeden Island Incised	Bowl, globular	Abundant mica	Nonlocal
30	Check stamped	Unknown	Sand–grit	Local
31	Papys Bayou Punctated	Bowl–vase	Spicules	Nonlocal
32	Papys Bayou Plain	Bowl, shallow	Spicules	Nonlocal
33	Weeden Island Zoned Red	Effigy head	Spicules	Nonlocal

[a]All rare mica pastes also contain sand–grit clays.

Figure 7.8 Portions of Vessels 20, 21, 22, and 25 (top to bottom), Mound B, Weeden Island Zoned Red plates (20–22) and a dish (25): Origins of plates is uncertain but may be nonlocal; dish has rare mica in paste and is local; and size of all four is about 15 by 26 cm or larger.

Figure 7.9 Portions of a Weeden Island Zoned Red plate from unknown site in northern Florida (Florida State Museum Simpson Collection). It is very similar to the Mound B Weeden Island Zoned Red plates. Note the rim adorno and the possible bird motif. Size is about 15 by 26 cm.

Figure 7.10 Portions of Vessel 29, Mound B, Weeden Island Incised globular bowl: micaceous paste, non-local manufacture, and diameter at mouth of 19 cm.

which are folded or thickened and underscored by an incised line. One Weeden Island Zoned Red vessel has a tapered or thinned rim.

Manufacturing Technology

Thirteen of the Mound B vessels (excluding the bird head effigy) were constructed by coiling. Two Zoned Red plates (Vessels 22 and 25) also have modeled or appliquéd features at the rim; 1 has a rounded projection identical to the one on the Simpson Collection plate (see Figure 7.9), and the other is not identifiable.

With the exception of the check stamped vessel, both exterior and interior surfaces of all of the vessels were burnished. As a consequence, those vessels exhibit luster ranging from low to moderate to high. Relative degree of luster is higher on the exterior surface of the restricted vessels and also higher on the interiors of the plates and most unrestricted vessels. Finishing streaks appear to exhibit some degree of plastic flow on the interiors of restricted vessels and on the exteriors of most unrestricted vessels. These observations indicate that the interiors of the restricted vessels appear to have been finished before the exteriors; on most unrestricted vessels the opposite was true—exteriors were finished before the interiors. The interior surface of the check stamped vessel appears to have been rubbed or smoothed before reaching the leather-hard state and exhibits no luster.

Surfaces of most of the vessels exhibit well-oxidized colors (e.g., very pale brown, light yellowish brown). This indicates that conditions of the original firing were predominantly oxidizing, or of sufficient temperature or duration to oxidize naturally present organic matter, at least on the surfaces. On the basis of changes in core colors with refirings at 500 and 700° C (for 30 minutes each), it is believed that at least half of the vessels were fired originally under conditions (in terms of atmosphere, temperature, and

duration) that achieved or exceeded the 30-minute oxidizing firing at a temperature of 500° C.

Origin of Manufacture

The 13 reconstructed vessels and the bird head effigy from Mound B were found to have been made from at least 7 different and distinct clays (see Table 7.2). Five of the 14 specimens were made locally: 2 Weeden Island Zoned Red plates (Vessels 24 and 26), 1 Weeden Island Zoned Red dish (Vessel 25), the Weeden Island Red dish–shallow bowl (Vessel 27), and the check stamped vessel.

Five other vessels all are nonlocal and are made from either micaceous or spiculite clays: 1 Weeden Island Plain bowl (Vessel 28), 1 Weeden Island Incised bowl (Vessel 29), 1 Papys Bayou Plain bowl (Vessel 32), 1 Papys Bayou Punctated bowl–beaker (Vessel 31), and the bird head effigy (Vessel 33). The origin of the remaining 4 Weeden Island Zoned Red plates (Vessels 20–23) is not certain, but they are probably nonlocal.

MOUND C

The sample of pottery selected for analysis from Mound C consists of 19 whole and fragmented vessels, including 4 Kolomoki-style effigies (Table 5.3, Table 7.3, and Figures 7.11–7.23). Eighteen of these had been placed together on the southeastern quadrant of the primary mound (or immediately beside it) in a separate pottery cache and covered with the mound cap. The nineteenth vessel, a single Tucker Ridge-pinched bowl (Vessel 16, Figure 7.21) was found on the west side of Mound C just under the edge of the primary mound. Potsherds remaining after reconstruction of the pottery cache vessels indicate that another pedestaled crested bird effigy was originally included in the pottery cache. That vessel was probably very similar in size and shape to Vessel 2; however, the parts from this ephemeral effigy were not included in this analysis.

Decoration

The 18 vessels in the cache can be divided into 6 Weeden Island pottery types and an undecorated micaceous paste type: 6 Weeden Island Red, 2 Weeden Island Incised, 1 Weeden Island Plain, 1 Weeden Island Zoned Red, 1 Indian Pass Incised, 2 Papys Bayou Plain, 1 Papys Bayou Punctated, and 4 undecorated micaceous paste vessels. Notable decorative motifs include stylized bird designs on the two Weeden Island Incised vessels (Vessels 1 and 12). Each also has appliquéd bird heads on opposite sides of the vessel at the shoulder (Vessel 1; the bird is a wood ibis; Figure 7.11) or rim (Vessel 12; roseate spoonbill; Figure 7.17).

Four of the 6 Weeden Island Red vessels are distinctive in having incised designs on the exterior surface that were carried out before the vessel surface was slipped. All 4 are effigy forms (birds) with triangular cutouts; incisions outline body contours and bulbous wing areas. A red-firing slip covers the entire exterior surface of each. This slip was applied after the incisions were made, but before firing. Wing areas on one vessel (Vessel 2, Figure 7.12) are darker in color than the rest of the vessel. These areas may have been intentionally discolored or fire-clouded in firing to make them more conspicuous. An alternative explanation is that the discoloration could have resulted from some organic substance or object (e.g., cloth, leaf, or leather) used simply as an aid in removing the hot vessel from the fire. The other two Weeden Island Red vessels were slipped on both interior and exterior surfaces prior to firing.

Painted areas on the 1 Weeden Island Zoned Red vessel are separated from the unpainted areas by incised lines; these elements occur on the exterior surface. The punctated design on the Papys Bayou Punctated vessel is very intricate, but occurs only on a folded, thickened rim that has rounded lateral projections. Seven of the vessels were decorated when they had achieved the leather-hard state of dryness; three others were decorated while the clay was still plastic.

Form

The 19 Mound C vessels can be grouped into only 4 forms: 8 effigies (both pedestaled and derived), 8 incurving globular bowls, 2 vertical bowls, and 1 dish (see Table 7.3). Most of the unusual characteristics of vessel form occur on the 8 effigy vessels. Any vessel having a modeled adorno or appendage was categorized as an effigy. Two of the effigies are Weeden Island Red (incised and slipped) pedestaled birds (Vessels 2 and 3, Figures 7.12 and 7.14). Both have triangular cutouts, prefired basal perforation, and a flat base. One (Vessel 2) has a crested bird head with bulging or "pop" eyes, and a downward pointing tail on the opposite side of the vessel; both appendages are attached below the rim. The bird may be a quail. Complete reconstruction of the other vessel was not possible. Several "facial" pieces, suggestive of an owl, may belong to this vessel because they are identical in paste.

The 6 other effigies are derived effigy forms. Two are incised-and-slipped vessels with triangular cutouts and prefired basal perforation. One of these (Vessel 4, Figure 7.16) is a turkey vulture with the incised head attached at the lip, and a tail attached to the opposite side below the rim. An unusual feature of this vessel is its flattened and squared base. Head and tail portions for the other incised-and-slipped effigy (Vessel 9) were not recovered, but there is a definite wing area; the form of the base is round. Both effigies are derived from vase or beaker forms.

Three other of the 6 derived effigies are de-

Figure 7.11 Vessel 1, Mound C, Weeden Island Incised squared globular bowl with two stylized bird motifs and two appliquéd wood ibis heads: micaceous paste, nonlocal manufacture, and height to shoulder of 25 cm. (Light portions are reconstructions.)

Table 7.3
Type, Form, Paste, and Origin of the Mound C Vessels

Vessel	Type	Form	Paste	Origin
1	Weeden Island Incised	Bowl, squared globular	Abundant mica	Nonlocal
2	Weeden Island Red	Pedestaled effigy	Sand–grit	Unknown
3	Weeden Island Red	Pedestaled effigy	Sand–grit	Local
4	Weeden Island Red	Derived effigy	Rare mica	Local
5	Undecorated	Derived effigy	Rare mica	Local
6	Undecorated	Derived effigy	Rare mica	Local
7	Undecorated	Bowl, globular	Rare mica	Local
8	Weeden Island Red	Bowl, shallow	Sand–grit	Local
9	Weeden Island Red	Derived effigy	Rare mica	Local
10	Papys Bayou Plain	Bowl, globular	Spicules	Nonlocal
11	Papys Bayou Punctated	Bowl	Spicules	Nonlocal
12	Weeden Island Incised	Bowl, unique globular (wing nut shape)	Abundant mica	Nonlocal
13	Weeden Island Red	Dish, squared	Sand–grit	Unknown
14	Indian Pass Incised	Bowl, globular	Sand–grit	Local
15	Weeden Island Plain	Derived effigy	Abundant mica	Nonlocal
16	Tucker Ridge-pinched	Bowl, globular	Sand–grit	Local
17	Undecorated	Bowl, globular	Abundant mica	Nonlocal
18	Papys Bayou Punctated	Bowl, globular	Spicules	Nonlocal
19	Weeden Island Red	Derived effigy	Rare mica	Local

Figure 7.12 Vessel 2, Mound C, Weeden Island Red pedestaled effigy (probably a quail): sand–grit paste, uncertain origin, and maximum height of 21.5 cm. (Light portions are reconstructions.)

Figure 7.13 Vessel 8, Mound C, Weeden Island Red shallow bowl with vertical walls and rounded bottom: sand–grit paste, local manufacture, and mouth diameter of 15 cm.

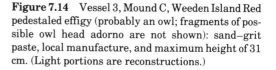

Figure 7.14   Vessel 3, Mound C, Weeden Island Red pedestaled effigy (probably an owl; fragments of possible owl head adorno are not shown): sand–grit paste, local manufacture, and maximum height of 31 cm. (Light portions are reconstructions.)

Figure 7.15   Vessel 14, Mound C, Indian Pass Incised globular bowl: sand–grit paste, local manufacture, and mouth diameter of 14 cm.

Figure 7.16   Vessel 4, Mound C, Weeden Island Red derived effigy, turkey vulture: rare mica in paste, local manufacture, and height to top of the head of 26 cm.

Figure 7.17   Vessel 12, Mound C, Weeden Island Incised globular bowl with unique wing nut shape and two stylized bird motifs with two appliquéd spoonbill heads: micaceous paste, nonlocal manufacture, and mouth diameter of 13 by 15 cm. (Light portions are reconstructions.)

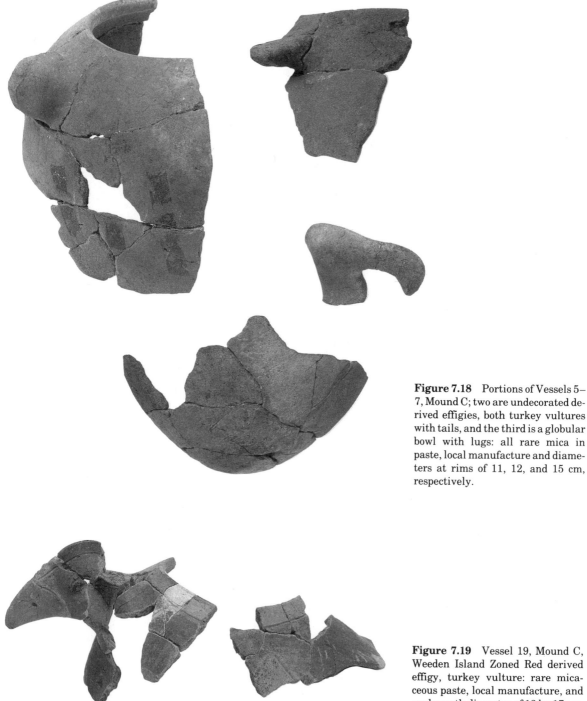

Figure 7.18 Portions of Vessels 5–7, Mound C; two are undecorated derived effigies, both turkey vultures with tails, and the third is a globular bowl with lugs: all rare mica in paste, local manufacture and diameters at rims of 11, 12, and 15 cm, respectively.

Figure 7.19 Vessel 19, Mound C, Weeden Island Zoned Red derived effigy, turkey vulture: rare micaceous paste, local manufacture, and oval mouth diameter of 13 by 17 cm.

Figure 7.20 Vessel 13, Mound C, Weeden Island Red squared dish (may have had a small bird head adorno): sand–grit paste, uncertain origin, and measures 18 by 20 cm.

Figure 7.21 Vessel 16, Mound C, Tucker Ridge-pinched globular bowl: sand–grit paste, local manufacture, and mouth diameter of 14 cm.

Figure 7.22 Vessel 15, Mound C, Weeden Island Plain derived effigy with one turkey vulture head, two dog heads, and a spout or bird head with beak missing, all of which are adornos: micaceous paste, nonlocal manufacture, and mouth diameter of 10 cm.

Figure 7.23 Vessel 17, Mound C, undecorated globular bowl: micaceous paste, nonlocal manufacture, and mouth diameter of 10 cm.

rived from incurving, restricted globular bowl forms. Two of these, Vessels 5 and 6, are undecorated and are identical in size and shape (Figure 7.18). Both have vulture head and tail appendages on opposite sides of the vessel; heads are attached at the lip, and the tails are attached below the rim. The third (Vessel 15) is a Weeden Island Plain vessel with 3 effigy adornos (1 bird and 2 dog heads) and spout (a beakless bird head?) affixed to the thickened rim (Figure 7.22).

The sixth derived effigy vessel, Weeden Island Zoned Red Vessel 19, appears to be derived from an incurving bowl; basal and lower-body portions were not recovered (Figure 7.19). A vulture head and tail are attached below the rim on opposite sides. No cutouts were present on the portions of this vessel, nor on any of the 3 effigies derived from incurving, restricted globular bowls just described.

The 2 Weeden Island Incised vessels each have a pair of bird heads appliquéd on opposite rim-shoulder areas, and both have unusual shapes. One, Vessel 1, is square and the other, Vessel 12, has a unique wing nut shape.

Vessel 7, an undecorated bowl, has two rounded lugs on opposite sides below the rim (Figure 7.18). This bowl is identical in basic form, size, and paste to the undecorated derived effigies just described (Vessels 5 and 6). The Weeden Island Red dish (Vessel 15) has a square shape. There is evidence at one corner of the dish indicating that a small crested bird head (approximately 2 cm tall, recovered from the pothunters' spoil) may have originally fitted onto this vessel. Connecting pieces, however, are lacking.

The 2 pedestaled effigies (Vessels 2 and 3) and the 2 derived effigies with cutouts (Vessels 4 and 9) also have prefired cut killholes. All of the effigy vessels and most of the other 10 vessels from the pottery cache all have battered and eroded bases, indicating a relatively long use-life. Five of the vessels have postfiring killholes (Vessels 1, 12, 13, 15, and 17); evidence for such holes on 5 other vessels (5, 6, 7, 8, and 10) is ambiguous. Bottoms of 4 vessels (11, 14, 18, and 19) were not recovered. The Tucker Ridge-pinched bowl, not a part of the pottery cache, was broken *in situ,* probably after deposition.

Ten of the 19 Mound C vessels have Weeden Island rims. Round, flattened, and beveled rims were also present.

Manufacturing Technology

Most of the 19 vessels, including the incised-and-slipped effigies, exhibit definite evidence of coiled construction. Evidence is ambiguous on the squared globular Weeden Island Incised bowl (Vessel 1). On this bowl, flattened slabs of clay, rather than ropes or coils may have been used. The wing nut vessel was coiled, but fracture patterns indicate that the lobes, or wings, were constructed separately and welded to the cut sides of the vessel.

The wing areas on the incised-and-slipped effigies are bulbous and are thinner than other portions of the vessel walls. This indicates that a tool such as a pebble or fingers may have been used as an anvil to force the wing areas outward, thus thinning the walls at the same time.

Twelve of the pottery cache vessels have modeled or appliquéd features. The heads and spout of the Weeden Island Plain derived effigy bowl (Vessel 15) and the heads on 2 other derived effigies (Vessels 4 and 19) are hollow. Vessel 15 has holes extending underneath the rim up through the adornos, indicating that they may have been constructed around some object, perhaps a wooden dowel, that would have burned away during firing. It is not certain whether the effigy heads on the other 2 vessels were manufactured around a template. That the turkey vulture head of Vessel 4, a derived effigy, was hollow would not have been obvious had the head not been broken. The tail area on one Weeden Island Red pedestaled effigy (Vessel 2) is also hollow and was accretionally modeled, a technique somewhat similar to coiled construction.

The tail associated with the hollow turkey vulture head (Vessel 4) and the round lugs on Vessel 7 are not hollow and were also accretionally modeled. Bird heads from Vessels 2, 5, and 6 and the small bird head that may be from the squared dish (Vessel 13, Figure 7.20) are not hollow and all apparently were shaped from solid lumps of clay.

That same square dish shows evidence of drying shrinkage—cracks 1–3 cm in length. In order to correct the problem, the potter applied an extra layer of clay over the cracks to hide them before the vessel was fired.

The exterior surfaces on one of the Papys Bayou Plain bowls (Vessel 10) and on the Papys Bayou Punctated vessel (Vessel 11) appear to have been paddle malleated (perhaps with a check stamped paddle) during construction. Evidence of the paddle motif has been almost completely obliterated by subsequent smoothing and burnishing; only very faint, closely spaced ripples remain.

Both exterior and interior surfaces of most of the pottery cache vessels were burnished. Interior surfaces of Vessels 2 and 3 were scraped with an edged tool and wiped with a yielding tool such as a cloth or the hand while not quite leather-hard. Interiors of Vessels 5, 6, and 7 were wiped.

Most vessels exhibit some degree of luster, ranging from low to moderate to high. Relative degree of luster (higher on vessel exteriors) and the flowing appearance of finishing streaks, indicate that interiors were finished before exteriors; that is, the exterior surface was drier than the interior when finished. Vessels 5, 6, 7, and Vessel 17 (Figure 7.23) appear to have *self-slips,* by-products of the finishing method. Most of the vessels have well-oxidized interior and exterior surface colors. On the basis of core color changes at refiring temperatures of 500 and 700° C, it is believed that over one half of the pots were fired under conditions that achieved or exceeded a 500° C 30-minute oxidizing firing.

Origin of Manufacture

The 19 vessels from Mound C were found to have been made of at least 8 distinct clay sources. Ten of the vessels, representing 2 micaceous and 2 sand–grit clays, were locally made (see Table 7.3). Local vessels include 1 incised-and-slipped pedestaled effigy (Vessel 3); 2 incised-and-slipped derived effigies (Vessels 4 and 9); 2 undecorated derived effigies (Vessels 5 and 6); the undecorated bowl with round lugs (Vessel 7, which is very similar in size and shape to Vessels 5 and 6); the Weeden Island Red (Figure 7.13), Indian Pass Incised (Figure 7.15), and Tucker Ridge-pinched bowls (Vessels 8, 14, and 16, respectively); and the Weeden Island Zoned Red derived effigy (Vessel 19).

Seven of the remaining 9 Mound C vessels are considered to have been made nonlocally. The nonlocal clays are micaceous (Vessels 1, 12, 15, and 17) and spiculite (Vessels 10, 11, and 18—the Papys Bayou ware). Vessels 2 and 13, made of a sand–grit clay, are of uncertain origin.

COMPARISON OF THE MOUND CERAMIC ASSEMBLAGES

From the preceding descriptions, differences between the three pottery assemblages are readily apparent (Table 7.4). On the general level of types, based largely on surface decoration, a dichotomy exists between pottery from Mounds B and C and the pottery from Mound A. The types from Mounds B and C are predominantly elite types. Mound A pottery, on the other hand, is characterized overwhelmingly by utilitarian types, principally Carrabelle Punctated, Carrabelle Incised, and complicated stamped types.

On a more particularistic level, there are dec-

Table 7.4

Comparison of Vessel Types, Forms, and Origins from Mounds A, B, and C

	Mound A	Mound B	Mound C	n
Type				
Weeden Island Red	1	1	6	8
Weeden Island Zoned Red	—	8	1	9
Weeden Island Incised	1	1	2	4
Weeden Island Plain	5	1	1	7
Indian Pass Incised	—	—	1	1
Carrabelle Incised	4	—	—	4
Carrabelle Punctated	4	—	—	4
Keith Incised	1	—	—	1
Tucker Ridge-pinched	1	—	1	2
check stamped	—	1	—	1
complicated stamped	5	—	—	5
Papys Bayou Punctated	—	1	1	2
Papys Bayou Plain	—	1	2	3
Papys Bayou Incised	1	—	—	1
undecorated	2	—	4	6
undecorated (residual) red	2	—	—	2
Form				
effigy	—	1	8	9
plate	—	6	—	6
dish	1	2	1	4
outslanting large bowl	5	2	—	7
vertical large bowl	2	—	1	3
vertical small bowl	—	—	1	1
globular incurving bowl	3	1	8	12
bowl–vase	4	1	—	5
large pot	6	—	—	6
collared bowl–jar	4	—	—	4
Origin				
local	20	5	10	35
nonlocal	5	8	7	20
unknown	2	1	2	5

orative and formal differences between the Mound B and C assemblages. Mound B pottery is characterized by Weeden Island Zoned Red decorations, while Weeden Island Red is the modal decoration in the Mound C collection. Plate forms characterize the Mound B vessels and are associated with zoned red decorations. Effigy forms characterize the Mound C collections and are associated with red slipped decorations. Both vessel forms were only very rarely observed in the McKeithen village ceramic col-lections. These forms were not present in the Mound A assemblage; that group consisted largely of bowl–jars, large and medium pot–beaker–bowl forms, and outslanting bowls, all forms also characteristic of the midden. Differences between Mound B and Mound C pottery collections are not surprising given the headman–residential functions attributed to Mound B versus the burial function attributed to Mound C.

Beyond decorative and formal differences,

there are also differences among the mound collections in terms of the clays used in the manufacture of the vessels and in the manufacturing technologies employed. Table 7.4 lists the pottery from the three mounds according to local versus nonlocal paste types. The table shows that a significant portion of the pottery from Mounds B and C was nonlocally acquired, while most of the Mound A vessels were locally made.

In terms of manufacturing technology, once again there is a dichotomy between pottery from Mounds B and C and that from Mound A. While coiling was the predominant construction method in all contexts, pottery from the former two mounds exhibits the only consistent evidence of more complex techniques, such as combinations of coiling and slab-building (e.g., Vessel 1 from Mound C), two-part construction (e.g., Vessel 12 from Mound C), and coiling and modeling (e.g., the effigy vessels). Pottery from these contexts also has the highest proportion of appliquéd or modeled features (effigy adornos, relief decorations, etc.) and lustrous burnished surfaces. In contrast, surface finish of the Mound A vessels is more variable, with a higher proportion finished in the plastic state; most Mound A vessel surfaces also do not exhibit any luster.

Pottery from Mounds B and C exhibits the highest proportion of well-oxidized surface and core colors. The Mound A collection is characterized by poorly oxidized surfaces and cores. Although pieces of the Mound A vessels were not refired to observe color changes for inferring original firing conditions, the relation between original color and color change with increasing temperature of refiring observed for other McKeithen collections indicates that conditions of firing for most of the Mound A vessels were less oxidizing, of shorter duration, or of lower temperature than those for the other mounds.

In terms of decoration, vessel forms, clays used in manufacture, and manufacturing technology, the Mound A assemblage closely resembles the McKeithen village midden collection analyzed by Cordell. In short, the Mound A pottery assemblage is a utilitarian assemblage. Utilitarian functions for the Mound A vessels are supported by the presence of extensive fireclouding and surface carbon deposits, indicative of use over a fire. If utilitarian functions can be inferred from the utilitarian character of this assemblage, then we can only conclude that this particular configuration of materials and methods of manufacturing is one appropriate to the intended functions of the vessels on Mound A.

Explaining the presence of this utilitarian ceramic assemblage at Mound A is difficult. Perhaps the best explanation is the most obvious one: The Mound A vessels, including many large complicated stamped pots 26–34 cm in diameter at the mouth, were used in charnel (bone-cleaning) activities. Such unclean vessels were left on the Mound A charnel mound floor (and in the trash dumps) when the mound was capped. The sacred vessels that might have been present, such as pedestaled and derived effigies, were removed for deposition in Mound C along with the cleaned human bones. Another explanation for the Mound A utilitarian vessels is that they were associated with feasting that took place on the mound.

The detailed technological analysis of the pottery associated with the McKeithen site, especially the three mounds, has provided quantified and replicable conclusions regarding Weeden Island behavior and technology. The results are intriguing. Chapter 8, Knight examines the McKeithen Mound C pottery cache vessels with a different methodology, also producing provocative conclusions about Weeden Island behavior.

8

Symbolism: Interpreting the Mound C Pottery Cache and Related Weeden Island Ceramics

In this book thus far we have discussed the historic, the economic, the social and ritual, and some technological aspects of Weeden Island society. All have contributed something different to our understanding of what happened at the McKeithen site and why. In this chapter we turn to a cognitive framework for interpreting the expressive phenomena that have helped make the Weeden Island archaeological culture famous.

Animals, remarks Lévi-Strauss (1962:128), are not only good to eat, they are "good to think with" as well. In this chapter we try to reconstruct the way Weeden Island peoples viewed the animals depicted in their ceramic art. Why were certain animals portrayed? What did they symbolize in Weeden Island culture? Such a venture, though not entirely new in Southeast archaeology, is rare and a marked change from the approaches used to analyze ceramic data elsewhere in this book. We believe, however, that the use of different theoretical approaches to achieve different types of conclusions will allow greater understanding of Weeden Island culture.

The objects of analysis are the animal effigy (zoomorphic) ceramic vessels deposited as a cache on and beside the Mound C platform mound (see Chapter 5). Other similar Weeden Island vessels from Northwest Florida and the Kolomoki site in Georgia are also included in this analysis.

Our task is to unravel some of the complex animal symbolism embodied in these vessels; to determine why certain animals were "good to think with." In this discussion it is taken as a premise that aboriginal systems of animal classification and the specific classes of animals singled out for ritual attention were used as means of thinking about social categories and issues (e.g., behavior toward dead relatives). Our intention is to demonstrate how it is possible to apply sociological theories of zoological folk classification to archaeological data.

We base the analysis on theory from symbolic anthropology concerning the social uses of environmental classification. Our goal is to relate symbolically the animal species depicted on the ceramic vessels to the social contexts inferred from the archaeological remains. Because the application of such theory and method to archaeological problems is relatively new, an overview is presented.

Theoretical and Methodological Bases for the Analysis

Studies of symbolism in human societies have demonstrated intricate logical interrelations between social and natural systems of classifications. The way in which a natural classification system mirrors social status differences is seen by symbolic anthropologists as a method for understanding the specific group rules crucial to maintaining the group solidarity and avoiding disruptive behavior. Interrelations between cultural and natural classifications also are thought to explain ritual attitudes toward animals, evidence of which emerges archaeologically in the context of rites of passage in which there is a change in an individual's status, such as in a marriage (single to married) or funeral (living to dead or ancestral status) ritual.

Interest in animal taxonomies and their relation to human social structure has a long and distinguished history in anthropology. Durkheim, in *Primitive Classification* (Durkheim and Mauss 1903/1963), was first to demonstrate how, for a number of societies, systems of classification of the natural environment almost exactly mirrored social classifications. He showed how different societies divide up the observable world differently for their particular social purposes and employ the resulting categories as justifications and models for social distinctions and behaviors.

Durkheim's heirs in this enterprise have carried these insights a great deal further, and much of the relevant literature has been published since 1960. These efforts have gone in a number of different intellectual directions.

Lévi-Strauss (1966) is largely responsible for an intellectual view of primitive categorizing and thinking. This is in contrast to ideas relating interest in animal species solely to economic or utilitarian concerns, the so-called primitive "rumblings of the stomach" (Tambiah 1969: 457). Lévi-Strauss has forcefully argued Durkheim's position that the distinctions among natural species provide the bases for expressing differences in social statuses.

A somewhat different approach to the problem has been developed by Douglas, and it is her work, *Purity and Danger* (1966), that provides much of the conceptual background for the present study. Based on her research among the Lele, she has proposed a theory of "anomalous animals" (1957, 1966). The essence of this theory is that in any system of simple classification, criteria are developed for category membership that invariably leave a residue of peripheral species, animals that by these criteria are seen to be anomalous (i.e., different from all other classes). It is these animals that provide suitable material for ritual symbolism and behavior, including food prohibitions among other things. Leach's (1976:33–36) similar theory of taboo proposes that taboo is generated in any process of defining the boundaries within classification systems.

Two obvious difficulties in applying Douglas' theory are, first, that it fails to account for wide variation in the treatment of the anomalous creatures because they may be viewed either positively, negatively, or ambiguously by the culture; and, second, that it does not provide for ritual attitudes toward animals that are not seen as anomalous in indigenous systems of classification. These deficiencies have been partially addressed in the subsequent work of Bulmer (1967) and Tambiah (1969), as well as in Douglas' own more recent work (1975, especially Chapter 17).

Bulmer's research among the Karam of New Guinea (1967) and Tambiah's among northeastern Thai villagers (1969) both support the idea that natural categories and ritual attitudes toward animals are modeled after rules regulating proper marriage and relations of kinship and social distance. Bulmer proposes an additional term, *special taxonomic status,* to describe particular anomalous animal species that serve as symbols of particular social relations. Tambiah makes use of the concepts of *metonymy* (contiguity or being in contact) and *metaphor* (sameness or likeness) to clarify the particular relations he finds in the Thai data between culture and nature. Many of these concepts are used here in interpreting the Weeden Island effigy vessels.

The ideas that follow from these assertions can be used to an advantage in the archaeological analysis of symbols, even when the analytical use of ethnographic examples of, say, mythology are made difficult because of the great depth of time between ethnographic and archaeological cultures. That is not to say that any archaeological analysis can fully reconstruct a folk classification system. This is probably impossible for obvious reasons. At best the identification of some ritual animals may provide progress in understanding "the system which defines the system" (cf. Dolgin *et al.* 1977:3).

By taking archaeological animal forms that are not obvious fabrications or monsters and attributing to them "special taxonomic status" as the objects of ritual attention, it is possible to invent a method appropriate to the archaeological problem. The procedure is roughly to

1. specify, to whatever degree is possible from the depositional (archaeological) context, the social (systemic) context in which the animal effigies were the objects of ritual behavior;
2. identify, in biological taxonomy, the animals depicted to the finest possible level;
3. seek characteristics of appearance, habitat, or behavior (the bases of all folk zoological classifications) by which these animals might have been judged anomalous or out of place, accounting for the attention attracted to them, and specify roughly classes of which these might have been borderline cases;
4. search zooarchaeological remains for independent evidence of dietary restrictions for the species identified as having been objects of ritual attitudes (where possible);

5. metaphorically relate the resulting symbols to the social categories inferred from the archaeological context.

THE MOUND C EFFIGY VESSELS AND THEIR CULTURAL CONTEXTS

The deposition of the ceramic cache and human burials on and beside the Mound C platform mound appears to have been a part of a single ceremony that took place in a relatively short period of time (see Chapter 5). Sears (1958:277–278) has called such mounds "pottery deposit type" patterned burial mounds. Patterned pottery deposit burial mounds are relatively common throughout the Weeden Island heartland region.

Table 5.3 lists the 18 vessels that were recovered from the Mound C cache. A detailed ceramic technological analysis on these materials is reported in Chapter 7. Ten of the vessels are *zoomorphs,* (i.e., depict animals). Seven of those (2 undecorated bowls, 4 Weeden Island Red effigies, and 1 Weeden Island Zoned Red effigy) are either derived bird effigies (5) or pedestaled bird effigies (2). These bird effigies are characterized by modeled heads and tails, incised stylized wing designs, and geometric cutouts (small holes cut through the vessel wall before firing). The two Weeden Island Incised vessels both bear paired appliquéd bird heads near the rim area. One of these appliqué pairs represents the wood ibis; the other the roseate spoonbill. The incised designs on the vessel bodies in each case very abstractly reproduce wing and tail motifs.

Completing the inventory of zoomorphic vessels is the Weeden Island Plain bowl bearing the four adornos spaced equidistantly around the rim. Two of the adornos represent dogs, a third depicts a vulture, and the fourth is a functional spout. It is conceptually similar to a vessel illustrated by Moore from the Hare Hammock site (Moore 1902:Figure 135). Together,

the Mound C cache along with the single bird
head adorno found in Mound B at the foot of the
human burial within the structure yield the animal species listed in Table 8.1. We have not
included here the five, very fragmentary
Weeden Island Zoned Red plates/dishes from
the Mound B platform believed to have stylized
bird motifs on them.

It might be clarified at this point that although each of the vessels in the Mound C cache
might have been utilized together in a burial
ritual(s), it is misleading to think of them as a
functional group vis-à-vis village ceramics in
terms of a simple sacred–secular dichotomy, as
has been done in similar cases in the past. It is
clear that some of the more unusual or elaborate ceramic styles (e.g., Weeden Island Incised
or Weeden Island Red bowls and plates, are
found in both mound-related deposits and in
certain village contexts (see Chapters 3 and 4).
These elite ceramic styles undoubtedly functioned in sacred activities to the extent that
they are associated with social segments allowed special religious or cult privileges. There
probably is, however, a sharp distinction to be
made between these prestige ceramics and the
true mortuary styles represented by the derived
and pedestaled effigy vessels with cutouts. As
far as we know, the latter never occur in nonmortuary contexts. They are true special-use
cult objects. In this respect they are quite excep-
tional in the gamut of prehistoric Southeastern
mortuary customs. It has often been assumed,
erroneously, that certain well-made or fancy ceramic vessels buried with the dead are by that
fact mortuary pottery made for disposal. It
seems clear, especially for the great number of
Mississippian period cases in which this has
been claimed, that the difference from ordinary
ceramics is attributable solely to their former
use as prestige vessels in largely secular contexts.

The Mound C cache at the McKeithen site is
thus composed of vessels that fall into two

Table 8.1

Identification of Animal Species on Ceramic Effigies[a]

Effigy	Frequency
Birds	
roseate spoonbill *Ajaia ajaia*	1
wood ibis *Mycteria americana*	1
turkey vulture *Cathartes aura*	4
unidentified crested birds	4
Mammals	
dog *Canis familiaris*	1

[a]In this and the expanded list that follows as Table
8.2, vessel occurrences are counted rather than individual occurrences, avoiding duplication in cases of
paired adornos, and the like. In the identification of
the avian species we have had the help of William L.
Hardy, Florida State Museum ornithologist, but we
take full responsibility for any misclassifications.
Some are certainly tenuous, as is elaborated in the
discussion.

groups with radically different prior functions.
For the site as a whole, the gross functional
breakdown of ceramics might best be considered not bipartite but tripartite: utility ware,
prestige ware (perhaps not a discrete class but
differentiated from utility ware on a continuum), and cult pottery. These correspond
well to Binford's (1962) descriptive terms tech-
nomic, sociotechnic, and ideotechnic.

In Chapter 5 it was suggested that the special
class of Kolomoki-style effigy vessels with cutouts functioned prior to their deposition in
Mound C as charnel guardians at Mound A, a
function similar to the arrangement of wooden
effigies recovered by Sears (1982:38–55, 162–
169) from an almost contemporaneous context
at the Fort Center site in the Lake Okeechobee
Basin. This is an intriguing possibility, and
there is some evidence that lends it support. The
vessels were certainly made for use prior to
their single-ceremony interment in Mound C,
and they show battered or eroded bases that
suggest a long use-life.

The charnel area for processing bodies in Mound A was, to place it within Van Gennep's (1909) framework for the rites of passage, an institutional liminal (transitional) facility. *Liminality,* an anthropological concept referring to social status transitions or changes, has been greatly developed by Turner (1969), drawing partly on Van Gennep's assertion that it is funeral rites that show the greatest elaboration of transitional, or liminal, symbolism. Turner (1969:94–130) suggests that liminality in general, as an aspect of all rites of passage, refers back to a core of shared moral ideas in a given community. It is during the liminal phase in ritual when the core values of a society are brought forth and the symbolism is revealed through material sacred items that are publically paraded or demonstrated. But liminal symbols do not tend to obey universal rules. They are highly variable, and in the case of mortuary ritual perhaps more deliberately mysterious than usual (Huntington and Metcalf 1979: 58). Liminal mortuary symbols are not restricted to negative metaphors of decomposition or destruction. It is just as common to find among them symbols of life, vitality, and fertility, and the related but opposed notions of death and rebirth juxtaposed. This is of course true for many nonmortuary rites of passage that utilize the symbolism of death and rebirth as a metaphor for change in social status.

Consequently, we might expect the animal effigy cult vessels at the McKeithen site to be liminal symbols of an intermediate stage in the process of death. As the body decomposes between first burial and reburial, analogously the soul is not yet fully incorporated into the world of the dead (Hertz 1907). And we must keep in mind that these symbols, since they are liminal in nature, may be multivocal in reference to a wide spectrum of nonmortuary values in Weeden Island society; that is, the symbols may be reflective of other aspects of behavior (cf. Turner 1969:42).

A topic concerning the Kolomoki-syle pedestaled and derived effigy forms that deserves comment is the significance of the cutouts referred to in the preceding. In addition to the geometric cutouts placed on the body walls of the vessel either randomly or to accentuate an incised or modeled design, there is commonly a round hole in the center of the vessel base. In some instances this hole encompasses the entire bottom and the base is cylindrical. As mentioned earlier in this volume, a number of investigators have called these prefered kill holes, assuming that the vessels were made for mortuary sacrifice thus requiring that they be "killed." It has already been suggested that this may not have been the case. Such a supposition requires that each of the vessels be attributed a soul, or metaphysical essence, to be conveyed to the spirit world (cf. Leach 1976:83), but there is no particular basis for assuming this for the Weeden Island vessels. Instead a much simpler explanation for the various cutouts and kill holes so conspicuously present on them can be offered.

The blatant holes may very well flag the vessels as imperfect (marginal) nonpots. The people responsible for constructing these objects wanted to make their clients well aware that these were not ordinary pots and could never be used for mundane culinary purposes even if the user so desired. This idea fits rather well with the thesis that the animals depicted on such vessels were judged to be anomalous, symbolizing the liminality of the vessels (i.e., that their role is "betwixt and between" that normally applied to similar vessels that lack kill holes or cutouts).

There is probably a further symbolic value to be attached to both the color of the vessels, red, and to their material consitution, clay (earth). Very simply put, in the great tradition of Southeastern cosmology, red is the color symbol for earth and all its associations. Earth is opposed to the other cosmic category, sky, for which the

Table 8.2

Combined Identifications for Weeden Island Animal Effigy Vessels from McKeithen, Kolomoki, and Sites Explored by Moore

Effigy	n	Percentage of class	Percentage of total
Birds			
roseate spoonbill *Ajaia ajaia*	10	13.9	10.0
wood ibis *Mycteria americana*	5	6.9	5.0
great horned owl *Bubo virginianus*	14	19.4	14.0
turkey vulture *Cathartes aura*	7	9.7	7.0
unidentified crested bird	22	30.6	22.0
unidentified other bird	14	19.4	14.0
Mammals			
domestic dog *Canis familiaris*	4	18.2	4.0
white-tailed deer *Odocoileus virginianus*	3	13.6	3.0
opossum *Didelphis marsupialis*	1	4.5	1.0
mountain lion *Felis concolor*	2	9.1	2.0
bobcat *Lynx rufus*	1	4.5	1.0
human *Homo sapiens*	11	50.0	11.0
Reptiles			
rattlesnake *Crotalus* sp.	4	100.0	4.0
Bony fish			
unidentified fish	2	100.0	2.0

color symbol is white. Earth is the source—the birthplace—of humanity, and sky represents the purity to which humanity aspires. Both sustain the independent living world, and life is played out in the tension created by this most basic of oppositions. At death, the human body and soul are separated. The fate of the corpse is burial, a return to its earthly origin. The fate of the soul is ascension to the sky, or purification. If there is reason to believe that this fundamental Southeastern cosmological model had a time depth encompassing the Weeden Island period, then there is much to be gained by considering the obvious Weeden Island red–white symbolism in this light. For the present issue, perhaps the red color, and the clay itself, represent the ultimate fate of the corpse—"the medium is the message". Granting these ideas, part of the symbolism of the cutout vessels has the redundant flavor of a pun, analogous to the visual punning that is characteristic of Maya religious iconography.

Having generated a species list corresponding to McKeithen animal iconography, it must now be admitted that the brief list is inadequate. To remedy this, two other sources for stylistically and chronologically equivalent specimens from sites displaying Weeden Island ceremonialism were searched. These sources are the voluminous works of Moore on the mounds of the Florida Gulf Coast and the Apalachicola River Valley of Florida and southwestern Georgia (1901, 1902, 1903a, 1903b, 1918) and Sears' report on the large patterned Mound D at the Kolomoki site (1953, 1956). From these, an expanded species list of zoomorphic Weeden Island vessels (combined with the McKeithen data) has been compiled (Table 8.2).

This list poses certain problems, including the fact that there was a great variety of mortuary treatments evidenced by the Weeden Island mounds yielding these vessels (Brose 1979) and that there are certain chronological and geographic distinctions among them that might be made. The justification for combining them in Table 8.2 is simply that a uniformity in cosmology, if not in particular mortuary custom, for the period and region is supposed based on obvious similarities in ritual symbolism.

RELATION TO ZOOARCHAEOLOGICAL STUDIES

The zooarchaeological data available for the sites in question are rather meager, to say the least. This is decidedly unfortunate. Analysis of the food bone from the village at the McKeithen site has been carried out (see Table 4.4), resulting in a very brief list of species, definitely curtailed by the vagaries of preservation. This is true for most reported Weeden Island sites. Despite the extensive excavations, the species list from Kolomoki (Adams 1956) also is certainly not a good reflection of the site economy.

On the other hand, Cumbaa's (1972) excellent zooarchaeological data from Site 8-A-169, the Melton site in Alachua County, Florida, is relevant to the problem of McKeithen faunal procurement and consumption. The lacustrine environment surrounding the Melton site is similar to that surrounding the contemporaneous McKeithen site farther north, and it is very likely that the same spectrum of faunal resources were available to both communities.

An unfortunate aspect of the comparison is that Melton is a Cades Pond culture site, an early Weeden Island–related manifestation outside mainstream Weeden Islandism (see Chapter 2). Cades Pond ceremonialism is not well known, but in rough terms it resembles that of some Weeden Island expressions, and it is probable that Weeden Island effigy vessels were recovered from one Cades Pond burial mound (Bell 1883:635–637; for a discussion of the Cades Pond culture, see Milanich and Fairbanks 1980:96–111). Thus, while it is probable

that systems of classification and ritual attitudes toward animals overlapped to some degree between McKeithen Weeden Island and Cades Pond, it must also be emphasized that such systems are geographically quite variable and the equivalence need by no means be exact.

For comparison, a species list from Cumbaa's (1972) analysis of approximately two thirds of the total excavated faunal sample from the Melton site was extracted (Table 8.3). Comparing this with the combined inventory of Weeden Island ritual animals (Table 8.2), it is apparent that there is a mismatch between the two lists.

Of the overlapping animals on the lists, the mountain lion (panther), opossum, and rattlesnake from Melton each represent only a few individuals of the total sample (the minimum number of individuals being 2, 8, and 3, respectively). They did not contribute any significant portion of the total meat weights represented. The deer is the important exception (the minimum number of individuals being 26) and was unquestionably the dominant animal food species present at the Melton site. Its occurrence in the list of Weeden Island ritual animals requires a special explanation.

The remainder of the species on the Weeden Island ceramic list, excluding the human and generalized bony fish, are all absent as food items at Melton. The roseate spoonbill, the wood ibis, and the bobcat are not present; but this is conceivably a function of sampling or their overall rarity. The turkey vulture and the great horned owl are more conspicuous in their absence, since these are relatively abundant in the area. The turkey vulture is a very common resident of rural towns and a simple animal to dispatch should that be desired. A food taboo is at least suggested. Cumbaa (1972:52) says that it is an interesting and somewhat puzzling fact that there are no remains of the domestic dog. Again, assuming the presence of dogs, he comes close to suggesting a food prohibition.

We hasten to add that it would be extraordi-

Table 8.3

Species List of Vertebrate Animal Remains at the Melton Site

Cartilaginous fish	Reptiles
white shark *Carcharodon carcharias*	snapping turtles *Chelydra serpentina*
mako shark *Isurus oxyrinchus*	striped mud turtle *Kinosternon bauri*
requiem shark *Carcharhinus* sp.	mud turtle *Kinosternon subrubrum*
tiger shark *Galeocerdo cuvieri*	musk turtle *Sternotherus* sp.
hammerhead shark *Sphyrna* sp.	pond turtle *Chrysemys* sp.
Bony fish	chicken turtle *Deirochelys reticularia*
gar *Lepisosteus* sp.	box turtle *Terrapene carolina*
mudfish *Amia calva*	gopher tortoise *Gopherus polyphemus*
gizzard shad *Dorosoma cepedianum*	sea turtle Chelonidae
chain pickerel *Esox niger*	Florida soft-shelled turtle *Trionyx ferox*
lake chubsucker *Erimyzon sucetta*	blacksnake *Coluber constrictor*
freshwater catfish *Ictalurus* sp.	indigo snake *Drymarchon corais*
brown bullhead *Ictalurus nebulosa*	rat snake *Elaphe* sp.
sunfish *Lepomis* sp.	mudsnake *Farancia abacura*
warmouth *Lepomis gulosus*	king snake *Lampropeltis getulus*
largemouth bass *Micropterus salmoides*	coachwhip *Masticophis flagellum*
speckled perch *Pomoxis nigromaculatus*	green water snake *Natrix cyclopion*
mullet *Mugil* sp.	banded water snake *Natrix fasciata*
Mammals	brown water snake *Natrix taxispilota*
opossum *Didelphis marsupialis*	pine snake *Pituophis melanoleucas*
eastern mole *Scalopus aquaticus*	cottonmouth moccasin *Agkistrodon piscivorus*
rabbit *Sylvilagus* sp.	eastern diamondback rattlesnake *Crotalus adamanteus*
marsh rabbit *Sylvilagus palustris*	alligator *Alligator mississipiensis*
eastern grey squirrel *Sciurus carolinensis*	Birds
fox squirrel *Sciurus niger*	heron Ardeidae
southeastern pocket gopher *Geomys pinetis*	American egret *Casmerodium albus*
round-tailed muskrat *Neofiber alleni*	Louisiana heron *Hydranassa tricolor*
rice rat *Oryzomys palustris*	night heron *Nycticorax nycticorax*
cotton rat *Sigmodon hispidus*	white ibis cf. *Eudocimus albus*
porpoise Cetacea	bald eagle *Halioeetus leucocephalus*
red wolf *Canis niger*	wild turkey *Meleagris gallopavo*
grey fox *Urocyon cineroargenteus*	sandhill crane *Grus canadensis*
black bear *Ursus americanus*	coot *Fulica americana*
raccoon *Procyon lotor*	Amphibian
striped skunk *Mephitis mephitis*	southern toad *Bufo terrestris*
river otter *Lutra canadensis*	frog *Rana* sp.
mountain lion *Felis concolor*	bullfrog *Rana catesbeiana*
white-tailed deer *Odocoileus virginianus*	southern leopard frog *Rana sphenocephala*
human *Homo sapiens*	amphiuma *Amphiuma means*
	greater siren *Siren lacertina*

nary to find a one-to-one negative correlation among the two kinds of lists, even were they complete, accurate, and from the same community. This is simply because food prohibitions do not always take the form of a simple, overall taboo for everyone and always. Bulmer's (1967), Douglas' (1966), and Tambiah's (1969) data amply illustrate that food prohibitions take many forms: A given type of food may be considered only edible by children; another might be edible only on certain ritual occasions, or by a certain social group; a third might be prohibited to menstruating women; and so forth. These kinds of restrictions obviously would be very difficult to sort out in zooarchaeological data, except on some basis of diminished frequency or restricted context, and only then with ideal data sets. Nevertheless, by considering the species of ritual animals that are identifiable, it is possible to make predictions concerning dietary attitudes toward these, as Tambiah (1969) has suggested. This is attempted in the next section.

IDENTIFICATION AND SYMBOLISM OF ANIMAL CLASSES

By suggesting that each of the ritual animals of the Weeden Island sphere was granted special taxonomic status in the classification system at hand, it will be possible to ask by what criteria each one of them should have been singled out. It would be satisfying to discover that each of them should be anomalous in one way or another, a confirmation of the thesis of *Purity and Danger* (Douglas 1966). This is not the case, but that thesis does seem to account for the presence of many of the species, and for this a general conclusion might be offered.

These species are all in some sense marginal in the classification system. Consequently, they attract the sacred, and become suitable symbols of the marginality, or liminality, of the burial process. But this explanation is too simple. We need to remember that zoological symbolic relations are extremely subtle and complex and that they are parts of entire systems of ideology and do not simply refer to isolated rituals.

To attempt to account for the bulk of the species listed in Table 8.2, we will exploit Douglas' theory of animals "out of place" as modified by Tambiah (1969:448–452). This results in the use of two broad categories:

1. Animals that, by normal criteria, fall outside of major classes to which they are then considered marginal. Tambiah predicts

that these, when they attract ritual attention, will also be classed as ambiguous food (i.e., subject to partial dietary restrictions).

2. Animals not associated with any major class that are also capable of leaving their normal habitat and invading one of significant interest to humans. Tambiah predicts that these will attract outright aversion and food taboos.

Category 1: Unaffiliated Classes

One of the more commonly identifiable species in Weeden Island iconography is the roseate spoonbill, *Ajaia ajaia*. Among the collections reviewed in this analysis there were 10 examples, making the spoonbill fourth ranked in overall frequency. Its identification is rather secure, because the unique shape of the beak is very clearly depicted in most specimens. Ceramic representations of the roseate spoonbill are usually red-painted or red-slipped. The only rival interpretation would be the shoveler duck, which, however, has a much shorter beak and lacks red coloration.

The roseate spoonbill is a wading bird, normally inhabiting coastal marshes; and its diet consists largely of small fish, which it scoops out of the water with its unique bill (Allen 1942). Thus, on the basis of habitat, it might be considered taxonomically "out of place," frequenting an aquatic rather than an aerial environment. Considering the fundamental southeastern earth– sky cosmological division already mentioned and that surface water was considered within the realm of earth, this does not seem a farfetched interpretation (see Hudson 1976: 140–141 for similar comments).

Of course, the spoonbill is not the only carnivorous wading bird. But the concept of special taxonomic status suggests that one species among a number of classificatory anomalies might be singled out for symbolic purposes. In this case, considering the southeastern color symbolism outlined earlier, the crimson plumage of the roseate spoonbill may provide one of the reasons for its selection.

The spoonbill has a much wider symbolic significance in Southeast United States archaeology. It is found in Hopewellian art of the Ohio River Valley (see Moorehead 1922:112–113), and the skeletal remains of one specimen have been recovered in a Hopewellian grave in Illinois (Parmalee and Perino 1971). Hall (1979) deserves much of the credit in attempting to track down evidence for the symbolism involved by searching North American mythological sources. He finds, briefly, that the bird is associated with an archaic Asian American mythological nexus—the "master of game animals." This is a culture–nature mediator or middleman, who must be ritually appeased by hunters. It finds historical expression in the Mexican world as Camaxtli, the Tlaxcalan god of the hunt, to which other dieties such as Xipe and Zip seem to have been assimilated.

Besides the spoonbill, another of the guises of the master of game animals is the goose (Hall 1979). It is possible that some of the long-necked, unidentified avian forms among the Weeden Island effigies may represent geese (e.g., Vessel 13 from Kolomoki Mound D; Sears 1953:Plate XIII).

Among the avian forms depicted on Weeden Island vessels are several bird heads showing long, tapering, downward-curved beaks. For one of these specimens Moore (1902:324) suggested that the bird depicted was an ibis. Based on the examination of the five such effigies listed in Table 8.2, this observation seems correct. In fact, Moore's identification can be refined: Probably the effigies depict the wood ibis, *Mycteria americana*. This identification is partially by resemblance: A bare, round head, lack of a crest, dorsally located eyes, and a relatively broad-based bill are significant characteristics. A further bit of evidence is that two of the curved-beak, noncrested birds depicted at Kolomoki are clearly associated with fish. Kolomoki Vessel 7 (Figure 8.1), a human effigy, bears curved-beaked bird adornos on each shoulder, with each bird grasping a fish in its mouth (Sears 1953:Plate XI). Ibises generally are not fish-eating birds, feeding instead on molluscs and crustaceans. On the other hand, the wood ibis (which is actually not a true ibis, but a stork), like the roseate spoonbill, is characteristically a fishing bird, occupying the same kind of habitat as the spoonbill. In fact, the two species are often seen together (Pearson 1939:72). Except of course for their color (black and white), the same reasoning in considering the spoonbill anomalous applies to the wood ibis.

Should the roseate spoonbill and the wood ibis, then, be considered unaffiliated special taxa peripheral to a class approximating birds? If so, following Tambiah and remembering both that birds are eminently edible animals and that the act of eating them is metonymizing, we may predict that consequent dietary attitudes toward the two species would be ambivalent or ambiguous; that is, they would be in some way restricted as food, though not wholly tabooed.

Although we cannot support a case for them as unaffiliated, it will be appropriate at this point to mention the large residual category of unidentified bird forms in Table 8.2. With 36 examples, this is the largest single group of effigies. Although there is a bewildering variety in form for these unidentified birds; it seems certain that in many cases, if not in all of them, particular species are intended. Certainly many of them are suggestive of ducks, quail, and the like, as other investigators have pointed out (Figures 8.2–8.4). A number of features appear commonly in several combinations—large, bulging eyes; crests in a number of forms; short, stubby beaks; short necks, hen or quail-like bodies; and squared tails. Fully 61% of the unidentified birds bear crests, and this is surely significant.

Among the possible candidates for the crested

Figure 8.1 Weeden Island Red human effigy, from Kolomoki Mound D. Figure has a hair knot with a pin, ear ornaments, and a bird head (with a long curving beak) on each shoulder facing towards the back; each beak holds an object that may be a fish. Height is 23 cm. (Sears 1953:28, Plate XI, Vessel 7.)

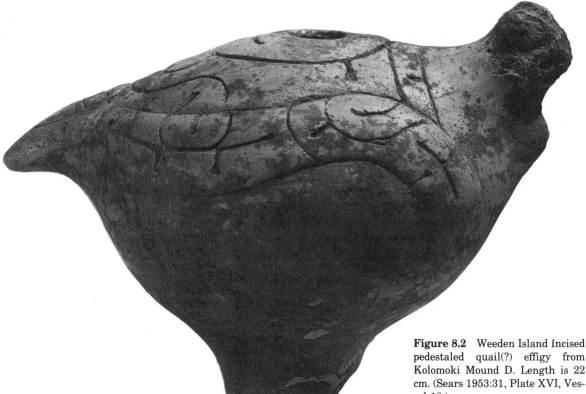

Figure 8.2 Weeden Island Incised pedestaled quail(?) effigy from Kolomoki Mound D. Length is 22 cm. (Sears 1953:31, Plate XVI, Vessel 18.)

birds, the wood duck and the kingfisher are prominent (see Hudson 1976:140–141); not only because of resemblance, but also because of the unusual habits of these species. The wood duck is of course a water bird, with all that this implies; but it is different from other ducks in that it nests not on the ground but in hollow trees. The kingfisher is another anomaly; besides its large head and fishing "occupation," it nests in an underground tunnel—surely an image fraught with earth–sky symbolism.

If the quail, or bobwhite, is among the bird forms depicted, it is perhaps relevant again to note that its habits are somewhat unusual (Figure 8.2). Humanlike families are often to be seen strolling bipedally, in line by rank, through the forest.

The only reptile to be found among the Weeden Island vessels is the rattlesnake (*Crotalus* sp.). There are only four examples, three of which are simply incised on vessel bodies (once in combination with a bird effigy) and the fourth being a series of four coiled adornos probably from the same Kolomoki vessel. Not only is it empirically dangerous, but also, as Hudson has argued, it has anomalous status. "The snake is born from an egg, like a bird, but birds hate snakes, as anyone knows who has seen a snake invade a bluejay's territory. One can encounter a snake in all realms—swimming in the water, crawling on the land, and hanging from a tree limb" (1976:144–145).

The opossum, represented by a single Kolomoki effigy (Figure 8.5), is a similarly weird

Figure 8.3 Weeden Island Incised derived duck effigy from Hall Mound, Panacea Springs, Wakulla County, Florida (Moore 1902:282–303, Figure 254). Height is 22 cm. (Photograph courtesy of Museum of the American Indian, Heye Foundation.)

creature by many conceivable folk criteria. It is, for one thing, the only North American marsupial. It has a prehensile tail, hangs upside down in trees, and is completely omnivorous. It is thus strange by standards of appearance, habitat, and diet and thus can be considered reasonable material for ritual status.

We come finally to the three nocturnal carnivores, the great horned owl, the mountain lion or panther, and the bobcat. The owl is the most frequently depicted of all the animal species, with 14 examples. These include adornos, pedestaled red-painted effigies with cutouts, and derived effigies (Figures 8.6 and 8.7). In every case the owls are shown with "ears." A rival interpretation for these specimens would identify them as screech owls, *Otus asio*. These are smaller, and much less aggressive than the great horned owl, the latter having been de-

scribed as "fearless" and "savage" (Wetmore 1939:8).

The vessels depicting the mountain lion (2 examples) and the bobcat (1 example) are all from Kolomoki (Figure 8.8). Except for one very abstract piece, these mammals and the owls show a stylistic unity in treatment that sug-

Figure 8.4 Weeden Island Red pedestaled duck effigy from Kolomoki Mound D. Height is 34 cm. (Sears 1953:29, Plate XIII, Vessel 12.)

Figure 8.5 Weeden Island Red pedestaled opossum effigy (pedestal is not reconstructed in this photograph) from Kolomoki Mound D. Length is about 15 cm. (Sears 1953:31, Plate XVI, Vessel 17.)

gests some classificatory connection among the species. Again, we refer to Hudson for a discussion of their possible anomalous status:

> A different kind of anomaly may be seen in living things which defied categories of time. We recall that in the Cherokee oral tradition about the creation, the animals who remained awake for seven nights were the owl and the cougar, both of whom are anomalous in that they can see at night and are nocturnal in their habits. Appropriately the Cherokees had a particular regard for owls. (1976:141)

Granting their special taxonomic status, it may be seen that the great horned owl, the mountain lion, the bobcat, and the opossum are all peripheral to eminently edible classes. Again we predict dietary restrictions, but not wholesale taboos, for these creatures in Weeden Island societies.

The fish effigies are not mentioned further. There is one, possibly two examples at Kolomo-

ki, and these are fragmentary and cannot be more specifically identified taxonomically; hence they defy further comment in this framework.

Category 2:
Taboo-Violating Creatures

Our second major class consists of animals that draw attention to themselves by conspicuously violating the attempts of humanity to distinguish itself radically from nature. Such a creature is the turkey vulture, *Cathartes aura* (Figure 8.9). This was the most common avian form at the McKeithen site, where the naturalistic red and buff bird head adorno from Mound B makes the identification certain. The bird motif on the Weeden Island Zoned Red plates from Mound B may represent a turkey vulture. In other cases, a bare head and hooked beak serve to identify the effigies as generic vul-

Figure 8.6 Weeden Island Incised derived owl effigy from mound near Shoemake Landing, Early County, Georgia (Moore 1907:437–438, Figures 14–16). The beak is broken off; height is 29 cm. (Photograph courtesy of Museum of the American Indian, Heye Foundation.)

carrion, and they can often be seen perching conspicuously on rooftops. In their indiscriminant dietary habits and utter disregard for most human boundaries, they are attractive as symbols of disorder in human relations. For example, in some South American mythology they are often associated with rottenness and filth. It is, of course, wholly ethnocentric to suggest some universal revulsion for the vulture. However, the only prehistoric food bone remains of *Cathartes aura* in the Southeast consist of a few bones associated with Glades culture context in southern Florida (Wing 1965:Table 1). Only rarely do they appear as good or helping creatures, and their associations for the most part seem to be strongly hedged by taboo.

On this basis it is suspected that turkey vultures were not classed in Weeden Island thought among ordinary birds. Following Tambiah's (1969:450) suggestions, we may predict that they were "the focus of strong attitudes expressed in the forms of (1) a food taboo and (2) a bad omen or inauspicious sign."

The dog, *Canis familiaris,* as a domestic animal is a different but related case. There are four instances of dog effigies, occurring as rim adornos, among the Weeden Island vessels examined. Suggestively, dogs are opposed to a vulture on the rim of the bowl from McKeithen Mound C. We have seen that, like the vulture, dog remains are absent as food bone from the Melton site, suggesting dietary taboo. Like the vulture, the dog tends to violate indiscriminantly the various behavioral prohibitions and boundary markers of great value to humans (e.g., incest taboos). Tambiah's comments on attitudes toward dogs in northeast Thailand are undoubtedly relevant. In his analysis, he employs the concepts of metonym and metaphor:

> The dog, by virtue of the fact that it lives in the house and has a close association with man, has a metonymical relation to human society. The taboo on eating dog has a metonymizing role; it cannot be physically eaten and incorporated because it is in a sense incor-

tures. Overall, these total seven specimens, two of which are questionable. It has already been mentioned that the species is conspicuously absent as food bone in the Melton site midden, despite the great abundance and the ease of capture of this meaty bird.

Urban dwellers are likely to miss the significance of the behavior of the turkey vulture. In rural areas they frequent small towns and country houses, eating garbage and filth as well as

Figure 8.7 Weeden Island Incised pedestaled owl effigy from Mound Field, Wakulla County, Florida (Moore 1902:315, Figure 299). Height is 21 cm. (Photograph courtesy of Museum of the American Indian, Heye Foundation.)

porated into human society. But at the same time the dog is considered degraded and incestuous and thus stands for the antithesis of correct human conduct. This degradation to a subhuman status is used by the villager to perform a metaphorical transfer on the basis of an analogy. Man imposes on the behavior of the dog the concept of incestuous behavior, thereby attributing a human significance to the sexual behavior of dogs. (Tambiah 1969:455)

Consequently, for the Thai villagers, the dog's behavior becomes a ritual vehicle for the correction of human taboo violations tending in the direction of incest. We might suppose that the ritual place of the dog in Weeden Island societies was as a similar negative symbol of boundary maintenance in human affairs, with a corresponding dietary taboo.

Deer and Humans

Among the identifiable animals, the white-tailed deer, *Odocoileus virginianus,* has been kept in reserve until now because the explanation for its presence is something of a special

case. There are only three examples of deer effigies, two from Kolomoki Mound D (Sears 1953:Vessels 5 and 8) and the third from Mound Field in Northwest Florida (Moore 1902:Figure 297). Of these, Sears has noted that one of the Kolomoki specimens is stylistically very close to the example from Mound Field (1956:Figure 17).

It was puzzling that the deer should make the list of Weeden Island ritual animals for two reasons. First, the white-tailed deer was a source of animal protein par excellence among prehistoric southeastern economies not focused directly on fishing (Wing 1977:87). Faunal bone from Weeden Island and Weeden Island–related sites testifies to the economic importance of deer as a game animal. Similarly for the historic Southeast Native Americans, Swanton (1946:249) states unequivocally that deer was the most important single-food animal. One must inevitably conclude that hunting and consumption of deer carried a high positive value and that its dietary importance makes it unusual among other animals that attracted attention as symbols.

Further, it cannot be accounted for by any criterion by which it might be judged an animal out of place, and therefore suitable as a symbol for marginal or ambiguous social status. Neither by appearance, nor by habitat, nor by behavior—the common bases of folk classifications—does the deer seem in any way anomalous accounting for its presumed special taxonomic status. It is presumably present by a different logic than that explaining the animals discussed thus far. In a sense, its special status as a ritual animal is relatively more arbitrary, as opposed to the others, in that it is not at some plain level based on an emperical observation.

There is a possible solution, but to understand it requires that it be prefaced by a review of Douglas' most general theory of systems of animal taxonomy (1975), in which she attempts to incorporate the data on the Karam, the Lele,

Figure 8.8 Weeden Island Incised pedestaled bobcat effigy from Kolomoki Mound D. Face is 14 cm long. (Sears 1953:30, Plate XIV, Vessel 15.)

the ancient Hebrew, and the Thai villagers into a single statement on the relation of zoological classifications to social differentiations.

Classification systems imposed on nature invariably take the imprint of social categories and so become part of the underlying shared social beliefs of a group or culture. Animal classes, relations, and behaviors are made into metaphors of social classes, relations, and processes. This line of thinking parallels and generally supports Lèvi-Strauss' (1966) important remarks, particularly those regarding totemic systems of thought as transposable codes reflecting social rules. Douglas (1975:285) asserts

that such taxonomic systems tend to address a specific class of social rules, those regarding marriage and residence. The reason is that these are the most crucial, the most sensitive rules that hold a society together and insure its survival. Related categories of social distance are reflected in rules regarding behavior toward classes of animals.

Thus, for the ancient Hebrews, an endogamous society that strictly defined and ritually protected the boundary between community members and outsiders, such boundary-crossing zoological anomalies as the pig were considered abominations and were tabooed. In

Figure 8.9 Weeden Island Red derived turkey vulture effigy—interior is also red-slipped—from mound at Bristol, Apalachicola River, Liberty County, Florida (Moore 1903a:474–480, Figure 140). Height is 22 cm. (Photograph courtesy of Museum of the American Indian, Heye Foundation.)

contrast the Lele, whose kinship system grants positive value to the incorporation of outsiders into the intimate circle of kinsmen, have a corresponding "theology of mediation" in which an anomalous animal, for example, the scaly ant-eater or pangolin, is the supreme cult animal. In sum, "it is argued that the greater the social distance between ego (a given individual) and marriageable persons, the stronger the sense of exchange between known and unknown" (Douglas 1975:303). Douglas has even forseen the archaeological application of the theory:

> Can we reverse the argument to consider the paintings of paleolithic man who left no other records of his thought? I risk the idea that if he painted animals at

all it signifies something positive about his openness to commerce with his fellows. (1975:312)

Douglas' theory of the social uses of the natural environment is compelling not only because of its comprehension, but also because it has been operationally tested in several thoroughly worked out analyses of ethnographic data. While undoubtedly imperfect as a universal explanation for all folk zoological taxonomies, it at least seems to fit with ethnographic data drawn from societies of different levels of complexity and occupying different environments.

Returning to the Weeden Island deer, there is one other fact that needs to be added. This is that each of the three deer figures represents a male of the species. They are all depicted with short knobs or points as antlers (Figure 8.10). This can mean one of two things. Either they may represent young "button" or "spike" bucks, which range in age from about 6 to 18 months; or they depict adult deer in midspring when their antlers are just beginning to regenerate. The first interpretation is favored here because the antlers shown on Vessel 5 at Kolomoki are clearly pointed spikes instead of rounded, regenerating antlers and because of its implications for the sexual maturity of the young deer. Bucks normally become sexually mature early in their second year of life. (This is variable; apparently some are much more precocious.) Thus the spike buck may portray the epitome of a recently sexually active male deer.

By taking these bits of information into consideration, and granting for our purposes the maximum amount of credence to Douglas' theory, a solution to the puzzle of the white-tailed deer finally suggests itself. The killing and consumption of the deer symbolically represents the proper marriage. It represents the positively valued act of bringing to the matrilineage the young, male outsider, who will add to the alliance network. (Exogamous matrilineages were present throughout the Southeast in early

Figure 8.10 Weeden Island Incised derived deer effigy from Kolomoki Mound E. Size is uncertain. (Sears 1951b:Plate VII, Vessel 27.)

historic times; see Driver and Massey 1957:Map 156). The spike deer symbolizes the proper husband choice, an adult from a different matrilineage.

The sister's husband–wife's brother relationship is the major source of tension in most exogamous matrilineal societies, due to competing claims on the sister–wife and her children. Balancing this tension is the need for social order, the need for the lineage structure not to be disrupted, and the need for the potentially exploitable social networks that the marriage brings. As a ritual animal in Weeden Island societies, dictated by its supreme economic value, the white-tailed deer may fill a very similar symbolic niche to that of the buffalo in northeastern Thai society described by Tambiah (1969). There the buffalo is the supremely val-

ued domestic animal; its consumption at a marriage feast symbolizes proper sex and marriage regulations as part of an intricate system of symbolic oppositions and relations among animal, human, and social distance categories.

It remains to be said that the deer–affine metaphorical transfer is realized through the metonymizing act of consuming deer. The concept of human statuses is thereby applicable to the animal, since there is no inherent link between the natural deer and the cultural human. They cannot be confused, and the positive valuation of the respective metonyms is allowed to emerge as the pertinent link.

The final class to be discussed are the human effigies (Figure 8.1). These figurines rank third in overall frequency, with 11 examples. Most are fully modeled or pedestaled free effigies and display a plain stylistic coherence that distinguishes them from the later class of Mississippian hooded human effigy bottles. Only a few seem to be simple adornos. The Weeden Island effigies are generally squat with arms folded, the faces bearing almond-shaped (perhaps closed) eyes and a pouting expression. Frequently there is a stylized crested arrangement or headdress. They are commonly red-slipped or red-painted. There are other known examples of vessels belonging in this class that are not reflected in Table 8.2. Notable among these is the very elaborate human effigy from the Buck Mound at Fort Walton Beach, Florida (Lazarus 1979). In addition, examples have surfaced outside the range of Weeden Island cultures, associated with a contemporaneous archaeological manifestation in the Lower Mississippi Valley (Belmont and Williams 1981:30–32).

The symbolism of this class of vessels, since they do not directly contribute to our emerging picture of the ritual uses of animals in Weeden Island societies, remains rather obscure. Nevertheless the mortuary context is suggestive, and there is a further animal link that is undoubtedly important to their interpretation. Namely, some of the human effigy vessels bear iconographic elements connecting them with the two wading birds, the roseate spoonbill and the wood ibis, which have been shown to be important symbols of liminality or mediation. Both of the examples from Kolomoki bear such elements. Vessel 1 (Sears 1953:Plate VIII) seems to have the head of a spoonbill incorporated as a forelock on top of the head. Vessel 7 (Sears 1953:Plate XI), an intriguing kneeling figurine, has the heads and shoulders of two birds emerging from either side of the vessel. Each bird has a long, curved, beak (perhaps that of a wood ibis) with which it is grasping a proportionately large fish. One of the human effigies from Moore's Burnt Mill Creek site (Moore 1902:Figure 33) clearly bears a spoonbill motif on the back of its head. Similarly the crest fore-

lock on the specimen from Aspalaga (Moore 1903a:Figure 150), considering its similarity with Kolomoki Vessel 1, may represent the beak of a bird.

We are not prepared to say what this might mean. In any case, there are plausible grounds to suggest that the class of human effigies as a whole may be related to the wading bird–master of game animals–death symbolic nexus. Given the facial expressions on some of the vessels, it may be that they are direct representations of the charnel house dead, the spoonbill–wood ibis motifs further expressing this condition.

INTEGRATING THE SYMBOLS

The final and most difficult task is to attempt a symbolic integration of the various structured sets. One thing that is immediately apparent, even granting a rather wide margin for error in our speculations about Weeden Island ritual ceramic symbolism, is that the ideas conveyed by these objects do not constitute the homogenous set we might have supposed. If they are all to be considered statements about the process of death for these societies, then they are certainly saying a number of different things.

Another way of looking at this problem is to suggest that the various symbols, while they do not convey precisely the same meanings in a redundant sense, are otherwise to some degree complementary. As individual terms, only simple messages are conveyed. Considered as a coherent set, it becomes possible to construct more elaborate messages (in the sense of Lèvi-Strauss 1966:54–55).

Let us consider how this might work. It has been suggested that the deer defines the proper marriageable male for the matrilineage. As such, it is a symbol of propriety—of structure. The turkey vulture and the dog are just the opposite; they suggest impropriety—antistructure. And the roseate spoonbill, the wood ibis, the nocturnal carnivores, and the opossum form an intermediate ambiguous group. These are mediators, as implied by the potential role of the roseate spoonbill as master of game animals. The group as a whole, then, seems to have a tripartite, complementary structure indicated by features selected to provide maximum contrast. This structure is illustrated in Table 8.4.

To summarize the features of this hypothetical model, it will first be recalled that we began by assuming that there should be a discoverable correlation between social and natural systems of classification in the Weeden Island world. The identification of a finite series of Weeden Island ritual animals allowed us to consider potentially relevant characteristics of appearance, behavior, and habitat that might have led to a classification of these animals as taxonomic anomalies. This procedure resulted in a preliminary sorting of the identified animals into three groups.

The largest group consists of simple anomalies. It includes the wading and fishing birds, the nocturnal carnivores, the opossum, and the rattlesnake. In the biological dimension, these are assigned a value of zero in Table 8.4, reflecting marginality, ambiguity, or mediation. A second group, consisting of the turkey vulture and the dog, is given a minus sign because its anomalous status is considered wholly negative in relation to society. The third category, consisting solely of the white-tailed deer, is not judged anomalous in any biological sense and is consequently assigned a plus sign.

When we make the metaphorical transfer from natural classification to the dimension of social classification, we must first consider edibility. Our predictions regarding the food value of the three classes, following Tambiah, are straightforward: We predict wholesale inedibility for the dog–vulture class (−); a lack of dietary restrictions for the supremely edible deer (+); and an ambiguous valuation (0) for the

Table 8.4

Hypothetical Model of Weeden Island Animal Symbolism

Object of perception	Dog and vulture	Simple anomalous creatures	Deer
Appearance, behavior, and habitat	—	0	+
Value as food	−	0	+
Social distance, marriage, and residence	−	0	+
Cosmology	−	0	+
Charnel process	0	0	0

marginal class, which might translate as partial dietary restrictions. We have seen that the zooarchaeological data, while less than adequate for a proper demonstration, nevertheless seem to be consistent with this proposition.

We would expect to see this code replicated in rules concerning social distance, marriage, and residence if Douglas is correct in asserting that these particular aspects of social life tend to be universally addressed by natural systems of classification. Hypothetically, our three animal classes would come to represent: a negatively valued partnership (−), in which partner is considered socially too near (incest) or too far removed; the ambiguous or marginal partnership (0); and a partnership of the right distance (+). The corresponding cosmological values would similarly translate as pollution (−), an intermediate category representing mediation (0), and purification (+).

Finally, with the symbolic values of the charnel process itself, we detect a shift in the code. Here, representations of all three animal classes are found together, apparently undifferentiated, in a single archaeological (and by inference, sociological) context. This perhaps can best be interpreted as an assimilation of the three classes as symbols of the mediation of life and death, the liminality of the charnel ritual.

(Death, of course, is a natural equalizer, affecting young bucks and old buzzards alike.) In Table 8.4, each of the previously distinct classes is consequently assigned the same value (0). This assimilation may be related to the anti-structure, for example, the dissolution of kinship ties and obligations, that is characteristic of liminal status (Turner 1969:16).

This is certainly a simplification of a complex symbolic reality. We have not taken into account at all further sets of meaning that crosscut the three classes, for example the red-paint-clay-imperfection (i.e., earth) symbolism found in each class. These probably have further implications, as suggested earlier, that are too difficult to interpret fully at this point. We only wish to have suggested an outline of some parameters of Weeden Island funeral symbolism.

As a postscript, in view of the rather contrived methodology as a whole, it seems imperative to expound its main deficiency. Investigators who have dealt with symbolic data have commonly reiterated that it is by means of minute ethnographic detail, of consideration of whole systems of classification, that elements of symbolism finally make sense. There are few "universals" to symbolic logic. Opossums are not everywhere considered anomalous. Dogs are not everywhere considered metonymical human beings and are not everywhere tabooed as food.

The archaeologist is thus hugely handicapped in not being capable of interviewing the objects of his or her interest. The iconographic data are limited and incomplete; data elucidating the social contexts of the icons are seldom very rich. A persistent problem is the degree to which theory dictates its own result. The archaeologist interested in symbolism must search everywhere for the stronger methodological foothold, and to this end we are just beginning.

9

Interpreting Weeden Island

In this concluding chapter we summarize the interpretations presented in the preceding seven chapters. We also examine the concept of Weeden Island in light of those interpretations and place Weeden Island within the greater context of Southeast prehistory, paying particular attention to its role and significance in understanding the cultural evolution of that region. As we proceed, some goals for future Weeden Island research are outlined, what is an archaeology report if it does not contain at least a few statements on where we should go from here?

Chronology

The radiocarbon dates obtained from the McKeithen site, all from samples of charred wood, are internally consistent and unquestionable. They leave no doubt that the early Weeden Island period, represented by sites such as McKeithen and Kolomoki, is pre-Mississippian in time.

The activities that took place on the mounds at the McKeithen site probably occurred within the period A.D. 350–500, when the ceramic vessels in Mounds B and C were manufactured and used and when the mounds themselves were constructed, used, and then capped. Occupation of the site by Weeden Island villagers began prior to mound construction and continued after the cessation of the mortuary and other mound-related activities. The radiocarbon dates from the village suggest a range for the village occupation of A.D. 200–750. Comparisons with the tristate and Northwest Florida regions indicate that the initial Weeden Island occupation in North Florida is earlier than in those two regions.

The temporal data from North Florida provide no grounds for altering the generally accepted chronological relations of the Weeden Island I and II periods (early and late) within generally accepted Southeast culture sequences. Kohler's (Chapter 4) village chronology does provide quantified data dividing the Weeden Island I period into three phases. In the ensuing years this scheme will no doubt be tested in other Weeden Island regions.

The ceramic fluorescence of the early Weeden Island culture, best known from numerous mounds excavated by Moore and from the Kolomoki site, certainly dates from within the first millennium A.D. prior to the appearance of Mississippian cultural developments. Distinctive Weeden Island pedestaled and derived effigies and other vessels, some red-slipped or red-painted, spanned at least the interval A.D. 300–500. Evidence from McKeithen indicates that the Kolomoki-style pedestaled effigy vessels, derived effigies, zoned red plates, and classic Weeden Island Incised and Punctated vessels all were manufactured in at least a portion of the period A.D. 350–500; although the total temporal range of these ceramic styles may have been somewhat broader, say from A.D. 300–700. That 400-year period is partially contemporaneous with the Quafalorma and Woodville painted pottery horizons elucidated by Belmont and Williams (1981) for the southern Mississippi River valley. (In fact, some of the Woodville Zoned Red sherds from the Woodville horizon, A.D. 400–500, are stylistically identical to Weeden Island Zoned Red sherds from the McKeithen site). Early Weeden Island is also coeval with the early Cades Pond period in North-Central Florida and the St. Johns Ia and early St. Johns Ib periods in East and Central Florida.

At the McKeithen site no complex of artifacts (other than one piece of galena; hardly a complex) was found that could in any way be construed as Hopewellian in nature. This is not surprising since early Weeden Island follows Hopewellian phenomena in the Southeast. As Sears (1962b) has pointed out, Hopewellian traits and artifacts are associated with the pre-Weeden Island Yent and Green Point ceremonial complexes. These complexes are themselves mainly associated with late Deptford and Swift Creek village traditions, respectively; both are pre–Weeden Island. Any similarities between Weeden Island mound building and burial ritual within Hopewellian cultures should be recognized as a result of evolution, not comtemporaneity. The basic culture sequence set forth by Willey (1945, 1949) stands. Today the tool of radiocarbon dating allows us to affix absolute dates to that culture chronology.

If Hopewell is Middle Woodland and Weeden Island cultures follow Hopewell, should early Weeden Island cultures be designated Late Woodland, or late Middle Woodland, or early Late Woodland? Should they be classified as meso-Indian, or neo-Indian, or quasi–neo-Indian? We choose to eschew any of these taxonomic designations; they tend to obfuscate, rather than illuminate, processes of evolution. It is sufficient to recognize that Weeden Island, as a whole, develops out of some Hopewellian-related cultures and into Mississippian cultures (generally).

An important result of Kohler's research in the McKeithen site village is the village chronology. For the first time we have a Weeden Island village ceramic sequence tied to radiocarbon dates. The specific three-phase sequence for the early Weeden Island period ceramic complex at McKeithen will in the future need to be compared with village ceramic sequences from other Weeden Island cultures. Are the same ceramic attributes present in the same sequence? Can a master seriation be established, perhaps with regional variations?

On the other hand, we have no radiocarbon dates from late Weeden Island (Weeden Island II) contexts in North Florida. However, the presumed late Weeden Island ceramic assemblage in that region—consisting primarily of check stamped, cord marked, punctated, and undecorated pottery types—has been encountered at a number of sites. This assemblage must follow early Weeden Island since such an assemblage was not present at the McKeithen site. The village excavations demonstrated an increase in check stamped pottery late in the early period. The Weeden Island II period must commence after A.D. 700, approximately the time of the abandonment of the McKeithen site. Consequently, there seems to be no reason to question the generally accepted date of A.D. 800 for the beginning of the Weeden Island II period.

The check stamped pottery from late Weeden Island contexts in North Florida is a part of a check stamped pottery horizon that apparently spans the Gulf coastal plain, from the Lower Mississippi River Valley eastward through the greater Weeden Island region into East Florida (Brown 1982:19–23; Bullen and Sleight 1959, 1960). Cord marked pottery is also a significant part of the Weeden Island II ceramic complex in North Florida, unlike other Weeden Island cultures to the west and northwest. Cord marking also is prevalent after A.D. 800 immediately to the south in the Alachua tradition of North-Central Florida (Milanich 1971) and occurs through a much longer span of time in the Georgia coastal plain to the north (Snow 1977).

During the Weeden Island II period, the classic types of Weeden Island effigies and other vessels are no longer found in either mounds or villages. The overall late ceramic assemblage in North Florida thus contrasts with the early assemblage and serves as a useful relative dating tool.

In areas other than North Florida, the late Weeden Island cultures and some Weeden Island–related cultures evolved into Mississippian manifestations such as Safety Harbor, Fort Walton, and Roods. In the McKeithen region, Weeden Island peoples, like most other peninsular Florida peoples, did not become Mississippianized in an archaeological sense: They did not regularly make ceramic water bottles or build truncated pyramidal temple mounds, and their chiefs or other officials apparently did not wear Southern Cult (Southeastern Ceremonial Complex) regalia. Possible reasons for this oversight on the part of the aborigines are discussed later in this chapter.

In summary, any of us who once might have espoused the view that classic or early Weeden Island was contemporary with Mississippian period cultures and events has been proven wrong. The absolute and relative dates for Weeden Island I and Weeden Island II place those cultures very comfortably between Hopewellian and Mississippian cultures. And, as we shall see in the remainder of this chapter, interpretations of Weeden Island cultural processes, both synchronic and diachronic, fit just as comfortably into the same slot.

VILLAGE LIFE, SETTLEMENTS, AND SOCIAL ORGANIZATION

Prior to the McKeithen project, no direct archaeological evidence for the presence of cultigens in Weeden Island I contexts had been recovered. The only cultigen documented for any Weeden Island site, early or late, is maize found at the late Weeden Island Sycamore site in Northwest Florida radiocarbon dated at A.D. 860 (Milanich 1974). Our North Florida work offered nothing to contradict this pattern, despite Kohler's best efforts to recover maize remains from the McKeithen village midden. It seems likely that maize cultivation was known to early Weeden Island peoples since maize has been documented for an earlier period in the Lake Okeechobee Basin (Sears 1982; Sears and Sears 1976). If maize was cultivated by the early Weeden Island peoples at the McKeithen site, it must not have been as important a part of the diet as it was in the more recent Mississippian period when evidence of corn cultivation is found at a number of Fort Walton sites (as well as at many other Mississippian sites).

Although we have little direct evidence for items in the Weeden Island diet in North Florida, we can surmise, until proven wrong, that their menu was similar to that of the Weeden Island–related Cades Pond peoples located to the south in North-Central Florida. At the Melton site in Alachua County, Cumbaa (1972) identified the faunal remains of more than 1500 individual animals whose bones were found in village midden. More than 90% of the species inhabited lake or marsh environments. A wide spectrum of animals, a veritable harvest, was collected, including deer, black bear, panther, muskrat, opossum, mole, rabbit (2 species), squirrel (2 species), skunk, rat (2 species), grey fox, red wolf, pocket gopher, water birds (6 species), bald eagle, turkey, reptiles and amphibians (26 species), freshwater fish (11 species), freshwater clams, and freshwater snails. All of these animals could have been, and probably were, eaten by the McKeithen Weeden Island peoples.

Small triangular chert points recovered from the McKeithen village and from the floor of the structure on Mound B (as well as the point in the left ilium of the man buried in that structure) offer convincing evidence for the use of bows and arrows. Similar small triangular arrow points have also been found in Weeden Island I period, late Cades Pond sites (Milanich 1978c:165).

The different kinds or types of Weeden Island sites in North Florida, as demonstrated from the surveys and testing program, include villages with sand mounds, villages without sand mounds, sand mounds, and task-specific camps. Clay and chert quarries also were probably used, but none have been positively identified (other than the clay sources discussed in Chapter 6 and the Appendix). No differences in settlement types between the Weeden Island I and II periods were observed; however, the total sample of sites available to study was relatively small.

All of the village sites exhibited similar locational signatures: They are found in mesic hammocks with access to permanent water sources within 0.8 km of aquatic habitats and within 1.6 km of the total array of vegetative resources. All village locales are generally well drained, being located between 30 and 40 m AMSL and all are either immediately adjacent to a sand mound or are within 3–5 km of one. This pattern of settlement apparently persisted into the historic period. After this time, villages, some associated with Spanish missions, are found at

much lower elevations in the southern portion of North Florida. Presumably, the villages were located there as a result of direct actions of the Spanish who wished the aborigines to be accessible to the missionaries who must have traveled along the east–west aboriginal path that later became the St. Augustine–San Luis (Tallahassee)–Pensacola road. The effect of the de Soto entrada (which passed through North Florida) on the sixteenth-century descendants of the Weeden Island peoples is uncertain.

Sigler-Lavelle's model of Weeden Island cultural processes (summarized at the end of Chapter 3) is supported by the excavations at the McKeithen site and by the technological analysis of the ceramics from that site, but total confirmation awaits more excavation in North Florida. Our own work was hindered by the acid soils of middens in that region that do not preserve bones of animals eaten for food or bones made into tools. That model envisions McKeithen Weeden Island as a culture lacking centralized political control; society was organized into villages made up of lineages or segments of lineages.

The model predicts that each village or lineage would have a religious practitioner who provided villagers with a link to the supernatural. It is expected that such a person would be awarded special social status, as would his or her religious paraphernalia and place of business. Within lineages, individuals were essentially equal, with differences in status based mainly on age and gender. Lineage membership and egalitarian status in life are reflected in mound burial where lineage members are physically interred together and in the same fashion (except, perhaps, for achieved or gender-based differences).

The model also notes the relations among lineages, environment, and production; that is, lineage segments living within specific locales containing greater than normal densities of resources, and a decrease in the distance between those resources relative to other locales, would have a production advantage in their ability to host village or intervillage feasts and rituals. Such an advantage would be influential in the development of social differentiation between lineages and within lineage segments. Religious specialists of such villages would have high status.

The model further predicts that villages with mounds are the focus of intralineage social interaction and would have the highest probability historically of becoming centers of interlineage exchange. The relative importance (and size) of any such village center would decrease over time as a result of the budding off of new villages and population loss, a process related to production, optimal population density, and the stage of settlement expansion in the locale. For example, on the basis of observing only the McKeithen site plan (three sand mounds, a well-defined horseshoe-shaped midden, a presumed central plaza, and a great density of artifacts on the ground surface in the midden areas), we might have been able to state that the village would have had a high probability of having been a focus of both intra- and interlineage exchange and of having a higher-than-normal status religious specialist (or headman). And we might also have predicted greater densities of artifacts, greater variety of ceramic types, and evidence of more mortuary activities than would be present at other, non-center villages—hypotheses that were certainly supported by the village and mound excavations and program of surveys and tests.

Relative to other Weeden Island sites in North Florida, the McKeithen site is an anomaly and certainly seems to fulfill Sigler-Lavelle's (Chapter 3) criteria for a short-term center. It is the only village with three mounds (one village site has two mounds and some villages have none), and it has the only dense, well-defined horseshoe-shaped village midden. Other village middens are more scattered and have fewer ar-

tifacts (quantities calculated on the basis of surface collections and excavations are much less). Some middens are quite ephemeral and consist only of scattered artifact "hot spots," presumably the location of individual households (and their structures) that were occupied for brief period. Carter Mound 1 complex and other of the villages tested by Sigler-Lavelle (see Appendix) are excellent examples of typical sites or villages that never achieved the status of McKeithen.

Is the model applicable to other Weeden Island cultures? Can we distinguish villages that were centers of interaction between and within lineages from other villages? The answer is an emphatic yes, and several sites and situations comparable to the McKeithen site come immediately to mind, all in different Weeden Island regions. Most notable is the Kolomoki site in southwestern Georgia within the Chattahoochee River Valley. Sears' excavations at that site (1951a, 1951b, 1953, 1956) show, according to our interpretation, that it was first occupied during the Swift Creek period, when a horseshoe-shaped village midden was present. That midden encompassed what was probably a central plaza. A later Weeden Island I midden overlaps at least the southern and southwestern portions of the Swift Creek midden; however, most of the later midden extends outside (south) the Kolomoki State Park boundaries and was not investigated. Nor were extensive excavations carried out in portions of the northwestern horseshoe-shaped midden. Consequently, the exact configuration of the Weeden Island midden is uncertain (see Figure 9.1, redrawn from Sears 1956:Map I).

Enclosed within the arc of the horseshoe-shaped midden are four mounds, A, B, C, and D. Mounds B, C, and D are located inside or at the inside edge of the midden. Outside of the midden arc are four and possibly five other mounds (E, F, G, H, and a mound located outside the park boundaries to the south). Sears (1956:10)

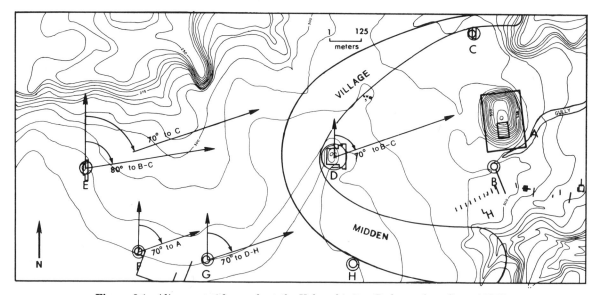

Figure 9.1   Alignments of mounds at the Kolomoki site. (Redrawn from Sears 1956.)

notes that Mound G may not be a mound (it was not excavated since it had been used in the late nineteenth and early twentieth centuries as a cemetery by a local family). Although it is always dangerous to begin to play dot-to-dot on archaeological site maps—drawing lines to determine the direction of layouts—it may be interesting to note that triangles are formed by Mounds B, C, and D and B, C, and E. (We realize that any three mounds not in a straight line form a triangle.)

The line between Mounds B and C forms the short side of the BCD triangle and is 190 m long (all measurements are based on the end map in Sears' 1956 final report on Kolomoki); Mound D is at the apex. Lengths of the other two sides (Mounds B to D and Mounds C to D) are 224 m and 260 m, respectively (compared to the McKeithen site measurements of 270 m, 270 m, and 290 m). A line drawn from Mound D to the center of the baseline between Mounds B and C is approximately 70° east of north (Figure 9.1).

The BCE triangle is an isosceles triangle with Mound E at the apex and equal sides of approx-imately 590 m. Whether such a layout is intentional is conjectural; the perpendicular bisector of the triangle (Mound E to the baseline between Mounds B and C) is oriented approximately 80° east of north (Figure 9.1).

Drawing such lines becomes downright seductive, especially when the same angles and directions begin to repeat. For example (see Figure 9.1), a line from Mound E to Mound C forms an angle 70° east of north, the same as the perpendicular bisector of the Mounds BCD triangle. This same heading is repeated by the perpendicular bisector of a third triangle, one formed by Mounds D, G, and H, with Mound D as the apex (suggesting that unexcavated Mound G might have indeed been an aboriginal construction). The 70°-east-of-north angle is also formed by the line drawn from Mound F across the center of Mound A. Are these four 70° headings simply figments of the archaeologists' imaginations? Possibly, since the heading of the rising sun at the summer solstice relative to Kolomoki is 61° 35'. But the study of mound alignments and natural phenomena at other pre-Mississippian sites might prove instructive when solar or astral sightings are considered (as opposed to schemes that simply connect lines and try to form figures; for instance, by playing dot-to-dot with various combinations of the Kolomoki mounds, we can form anything from a hightop moccasin to a cubist quadruped).

Kolomoki is the largest Swift Creek–Weeden Island site known, both in midden extent and in the number of mounds present. Ceramics from the mounds and village(s) reflect the transition from Swift Creek into Weeden Island. That some of the Weeden Island ceramic vessels from Mounds D and E are very similar to some of the McKeithen Mound C vessels suggests temporal overlap in the fifth century. If the Kolomoki village is associated with those mounds, and if the dating is correct; then we must conclude that the Swift Creek–Weeden Island transition at that site is much later (by several centuries) than we have stated in Chapter 2. This dilemma may, however, simply be one of the archaeologists' own doing, a result of a taxonomic system that relegates Swift Creek pottery to the Swift Creek period and Weeden Island I ceramics to the Weeden Island I period. Many excavators working in the Chattahoochee River Valley have noted the considerable overlap of complicated stamped ceramics with early Weeden Island ceramics. If we accept that such pottery types both occur during the Weeden Island I period in the region of the Kolomoki Weeden Island culture (as opposed to the McKeithen early Weeden Island culture where complicated stamped ceramics are very rare), then the main village occupation and the majority of the mounds at the Kolomoki site probably occurred during the interval A.D. 200–500. And, just as happened at McKeithen, social and economic factors—including, perhaps, a favored trading position between the piedmont and the cultures to the south—led to the Kolomoki site's development as a center for interlineage activities.

The center at Kolomoki may have lasted longer than that at McKeithen, accounting for the larger and more numerous mounds and the elaborate burial tombs erected for the honored individuals interred in Mounds D and E. If these individuals kept track of the rising (and setting) sun throughout the year and charted its location at the summer solstice by peering eastward along the mounds that were to become their tombs, we can offer no suggestions as to (1) why they were peering along lines of sight 70 and 80° east of north and not along the correct azimuth, and (2) why there was a 10° difference between lines of sight toward the rising sun at the summer solstice; perhaps it was simply the "new astronomy." Eventually, as at McKeithen, the importance of Kolomoki as a center declined as the village population apparently rose to a level from which new villages budded off.

The blip in the imaginary graph of evolution of cultural complexity in the Kolomoki region certainly was much higher than the blip that resulted from the activities that took place at McKeithen. But developments in the region after the decline of the site as a center were probably the same: a return to individual village–mound settlements composed of lineages or segments of lineages and a nonpolitically centralized social system. Permanent encorporation of many of the Weeden Island behavioral elements that might have been present for several generations or more at Kolomoki and other such centers did not occur until later economic changes also took place. The result of the proper economic conditions and the acceptance on a permanent basis of social ranking is the Mississippian style of life.

Another candidate for an interlineage center, one probably dating earlier than the events at either Kolomoki or McKeithen, is the Aspalaga site in Gadsden County, Florida, located in the Apalachicola River drainage just east of the river proper. This site consists of three mounds that form a very lopsided triangle and a curving midden that encompasses the long side of the triangle. All three mounds were excavated by Moore (1918) early in the twentieth century; the midden has not been excavated.

One mound contained both burials and a cache of Swift Creek (including Crystal River Incised) and Weeden Island ceramic vessels. An estimated date for the construction of use of the mounds is A.D. 100–300; the presence of Swift Creek and Weeden Island pottery indicates a period of transition from Swift Creek to Weeden Island ceremonialism. Sears (1962b) places the artifacts from the mound with the Green Point complex, a position temporally and culturally akin to our assessment. The two other mounds contained nothing of note (domiciliary, in Moore's terminology) and may have been capped platform mounds.

Aspalaga, like Kolomoki and McKeithen, probably functioned for a time as a center. By the time a Weeden Island II household was set up close by (at the Sycamore site 500 m to the northwest), the Aspalaga center had long since ceased to function. Later peoples may have recognized that something special had taken place at such centers (as evidenced by the mounds they could observe) since in the cases of Aspalaga, McKeithen, and Kolomoki, later settlements were placed immediately adjacent to or adjoining these large sites.

Other candidates for Weeden Island period centers are the Horseshoe Beach site in Dixie County, Florida (with three mounds) and the Mitchell site in Covington County, Alabama (with at least two large mounds; Sears n.d.). Although the midden deposits at Horseshoe Beach have been sampled (Kohler 1975), the mounds have been largely destroyed by pothunting activities; the Mitchell site remains unexcavated. That such multiple-mound centers are anomalies within the Weeden Island settlement system is shown in North Florida and is readily apparent for Northwest Florida

and western Florida from Moore's work (1901, 1902, 1903a, 1903b, 1907, 1918).

Village excavations to determine the presence or absence of Weeden Island social stratification have been carried out only at the McKeithen site. As recounted in Chapter 4, Kohler's investigations demonstrated that during the period of mound construction and use (the middle phase) the distribution of elite Weeden Island ceramics (Weeden Island Incised, Punctated, Red, and Zoned Red) among villagers was quite different than it was either before or after that period at the McKeithen site. It is proposed that the comparisons between the middle (mound-use) period distributions and those of the earlier and later phases reflect comparisons between a complex village center and noncenters; that is, during the mound-use period, the McKeithen site functioned as an interlineage center and did not do so during the earlier and later Weeden Island I period occupations. Kohler's data indicate that during the middle period, the overall popularity of the elite Weeden Island ceramics reached a maximum.

Also during the middle period, the distribution of the elite ceramics was more homogenous across the village than it was either earlier or later. The distribution of nonlocal ceramics (other than Weeden Island types) did not follow this pattern; their distributions were still uneven across the site. These distributions suggest that different social factors were at work during the middle period than either earlier or later; that is, contact between McKeithen Weeden Island peoples and non–McKeithen Weeden Island peoples continued throughout all three phases at about the same level. However, contact among Weeden Island peoples increased sharply during the middle period, as we might expect if during that time the site indeed functioned as an interlineage center with relatively higher status than other villages.

The findings concerning the distributions of elite ceramics, nonlocal (non–Weeden Island) ceramics, and nonlocal lithic artifacts and the determination of a population increase during the early and middle occupation phases followed by a subsequent decrease in the late phase all fit well with the model of the village as an interlineage center during the ca. A.D. 300–500 period. Unfortunately, comparable data do not exist from other Weeden Island villages. Our ideas would certainly benefit from research in other villages intended to produce similar categories of data.

When taken together with the data from the mounds, there is even stronger support for the McKeithen's site functioning as a special village entity sometime during the A.D. 300–500 period. Comparisons between the mounds at centers—such as McKeithen, Kolomoki and Aspalaga—and mounds at presumed noncenters would produce interpretations that support our contentions. And would not it be nice if we could talk Kohler or someone else into carrying out artifact distributional studies in the villages at Aspalaga and Kolomoki or other such centers, as well as in villages with single or no mounds? Although there are no absolute dates from the mounds at Aspalaga (excavated before the days of radiocarbon dating) and the dates from the Kolomoki village do not date the mounds proper, we feel that the ceramic evidence is sufficient to assume that these two sites are roughly contemporaneous with McKeithen. The mound centers at all three probably functioned sometime during the several centuries between A.D. 100 and 500 (ignoring the Mound A temple mound at Kolomoki, which may not be Weeden Island). Consequently, in the discussion that follows we assume that the kinds of social processes associated with each mound complex are of the same general order of magnitude or scale.

In Chapter 5 we described the three mounds at McKeithen; in Moore's taxonomy, they might be described as a burial mound with a cache of pottery (Mound C) and two domiciliary mounds

(Mounds A and B; B of course contained one extended burial). The three mounds at Aspalaga also consisted of one burial mound with a pottery cache and two domiciliary mounds with no ceramic cache or burials. Moore's report (1918:481–488) indicates that the burial mound measured about 30 by 33 m and contained 55 burials. We are left wondering if the oval shape was due to the outward extension of a mound cap over the ceramic cache as with Mound C at McKeithen. Moore describes the Aspalaga burials as "the lone skull, the bunch, the flexed burial, and bones scattered here and there" (1918:481). Calcined fragments of bone were also present.

The six excavated Kolomoki mounds (B, C, D, E, F, and H) would probably have been described by Moore as two burial mounds with caches of pottery (Mounds D and E) and four domiciliary mounds (B, C, F, and H). Mound D was an extraordinary structure, 6 m high and 30 m in diameter with four immediately successive construction strata, including a vertical log tomb or other structure that extended through the lower two strata (mounds) and into the third. A detailed report has been presented by Sears (1953) who has interpreted the construction–use sequence as very similar to the burial ceremony of a Natchez chief of the eighteenth century (Sears 1952).

Clearly, Mound D is much more elaborate than anything from the McKeithen site (or any other reported Weeden Island heartland region mound, although no other mounds, besides the McKeithen mounds, have been excavated systematically since Sears' work at Kolomoki). Much more effort went into Mound D's construction, and cremation was an important part of the burial ritual. Also, the log tomb burials of six adult males (five in one tomb and one in another) and the stone slab and log tomb burials of two females indicate different (higher) status for these individuals as opposed to peoples who were cremated or buried as single skulls. Sears suggested that these latter burials represent retainers and trophies; but they could just as well have been cleaned villagers' bones previously stored in a charnel house. At any rate, higher status is indicated for the six males and two females on the basis of burial differences. The Mound D male who was buried in his own log tomb may have been well on his way up the taxonomic ladder to chieftainship when he died.

Several features of Mound D are reminiscent of both Mound B and Mound C at McKeithen. Such comparisons, however, may be akin to comparing a recipe for cornbread with one for raisin bread: Both use some of the same ingredients and are baked in pans in the oven; the end result may be similar, but the exact recipes and the emic intent of the cook (and family background) are different. Similarities in burial recipes among many Southeast cultures probably can be listed: primary mounds, cremation, secondary burial, log tombs, mound caps, etc. Thus, too much emphasis should not be placed on similarities between McKeithen and Kolomoki. In fact, such trait recounting may be useless. However, several ingredients might be pointed out so that future excavators may be on the lookout for them.

These Kolomoki and McKeithen Weeden Island traits include: burial of important individual(s) near or in structures of vertical logs, with both the bodies and portions of the structures being covered by an earthen mound; the use of fire on interior mound surfaces prior to adding new mound strata; the use of large rocks on mound surfaces; circular interior and primary mounds associated with burials; caches of pottery laid on the east side of interior mounds (human bones are included in these caches); and the use of mound caps to ritually bury interior mounds, bones, cremations, tombs, and caches of bones and pottery. This brief list, except for the eastside cache, might, however, refer equally well to any number of pre-Mississippian mounds in the eastern United States, detract-

ing from their utility for defining Weeden Island burial ceremonialism.

Mound E at Kolomoki (reported in detail by Sears 1951b) is also unlike any of the McKeithen mounds. That burial mound had a submound pit that contained a cremated individual and a layer of rocks and sand fill, both of which also covered two human burials placed on the sloping upper edge of the grave pit and formed a circular primary mound. A large pottery cache (54 vessels) was placed on the east side of the primary mound, which was also capped with rocks. This entire structure was then capped with a final layer of red clay.

Mound B at Kolomoki, according to Sears (1956:10–11), "consisted of a collection of postholes." Like Mound A at McKeithen, these postholes sloped (but were much shorter) and served to anchor large posts measuring 60–75 cm diameter. Often the postholes overlapped. Mound B at Kolomoki may have had a similar function to that of Mound A at McKeithen.

Mound C at Kolomoki was simply that—a mound. Apparently built in one episode, it did not contain any interior mounds, postholes, or burials. Mounds F and H, however, both were composed of interior rectangular platform mounds that were later capped. No structures were evident on these primary mounds. Both resemble Mound B at McKeithen, however, and if any structures had been present, perhaps they were removed and the primary mound cleaned before capping. Kolomoki, then, like McKeithen, contained mounds used for burial, one of which was perhaps used for burial preparation and cleaning, and mounds possibly used as platforms for structures. Nowhere at the site do we have successive structures erected on truncated pyramidal mounds (again ignoring Mound A), a hallmark of Mississippian mound complex sites (e.g., at nearby Cemochechobee; Schnell *et al.* 1981). Kolomoki can be interpreted as supporting our contention that at some pre-Mississippian sites, anomalous complexity of social organization may develop for a short time, resulting in construction of platform mounds, burial of elite individuals, and other elaborated mortuary activities. However, such traits remained anomalies until the Mississippian cultures, when they were internalized and became the norm, albeit in altered form.

CERAMICS: TECHNOLOGICAL AND SYMBOLIC APPROACHES

Several years ago at a session of the Southeastern Archaeological Conference, James B. Griffin opined that archaeologists should spend about the same time worrying about potsherds and pots as did the prehistoric peoples who made them. It is all too easy for potsherds to become an archaeological end: Excavate them, wash them, classify and count them, quantify them, and print the results along with glossy illustrations. Fortunately for science (but somewhat disconcerting to those of us who have written some not too useful descriptions of pottery types—e.g., Sycamore Cob Marked; Milanich 1974), potsherds and pots are being made to "talk," therein providing a great deal of information beyond space–time parameters (two types of data the varieties of which can be argued over ad nauseum). Cordell's analysis, stimulated by the work of Rice at the University of Florida (1976, 1981), illustrates the kinds of new questions that can be answered by ceramic technological analysis; and Knight's (Chapter 8) daring venture into symbolism breaks ground that will certainly produce results when applied to studies of other specific Southeastern cultures. Indeed, to this list we can add Kohler's (Chapter 4) attempt to estimate village population size extrapolating from quantities of potsherds. It is fun to try to use potsherds for something besides reconstructing pots or speculating on the diffusion of sherds from, say, the southeastern piedmont to

the Georgia coast (How did they travel—in armies overland or in small groups on river rafts?).

Some archaeologists have felt that if Kolomoki was the major center of an established Weeden Island chiefdom or state, one with the continuity of a Mississippian cultural system, then many of the ornate (i.e., elite) ceramic vessels found at Weeden Island sites may have been originally manufactured at Kolomoki and traded outward. Perhaps the vessels were symbols of highly ranked individuals, the vessels being associated with a stratified layer of society and distributed from the leaders at Kolomoki to lesser chiefs at villages of lesser importance. Such elite ceramics, spilling downward through the social and settlement hierarchy, were not available to the average villager; consequently, the elite ceramics are found only in sacred contexts (mound associated with elite individuals) and not in secular (village middens) ones. Such a view likens the elite Weeden Island vessels to the paraphernalia associated with the Mississippian period Southern Cult.

The analyses of Cordell and Knight contained here offer a different picture, one that is compatible with our model of Weeden Island social and settlement systems. Technological analysis proves that not all Kolomoki-style effigy vessels were made at Kolomoki. In addition, Kohler's village excavations demonstrate beyond a doubt that some Weeden Island elite ceramics (excepting the pedestaled effigies that have cutouts) are found in village middens (broken where they were apparently used) as well as in mounds.

What do the potsherds and pots and their contents tell us? How do those data and interpretations relate to our model of McKeithen Weeden Island culture and to Weeden Island studies in general?

The pottery from the McKeithen village area (of all three periods) and the pottery found on the living floor of the Mound B structure and in the cache in Mound C greatly resemble pottery of the Weeden Island I period found at other sites in Florida, Georgia, and southeastern Alabama. The basic assumption that people who made, used, and broke Weeden Island pottery can be called Weeden Island people seems safe. We can talk about a Weeden Island culture, a Weeden Island heartland region, and a Weeden Island period entirely on the basis of a ceramic complex. This Weeden Island mound and village ceramic complex is definable and discrete, distinct from other southeastern aboriginal ceramic complexes, both those associated with Weeden Island–related cultures (a term on which we have not improved in these nine chapters) and others. On the basis of any 200 sherds randomly selected from a Weeden Island I site, we can state ummodestly that we would have no trouble identifying that site as Weeden Island and distinguishing the collection from collections taken from a St. Johns site in East Florida, a late Deptford site on the Georgia coast, or a Coles Creek site in the Lower Mississippi River Valley. Nor would most other Southeast archaeologists have any problem distinguishing such a Weeden Island collection.

During the Weeden Island II period this uniformity within the Weeden Island heartland region is not as great. Although check stamped pottery is the most popular form of surface treatment throughout the region, other forms of surface treatment differ among individual Weeden Island cultures. In the McKeithen Weeden Island region, various types of punctating, brushing, and roughening occur along with check stamping, while at the Sycamore site in the Apalachicola River Valley corn cob roughening is present. Neither of these forms is very popular at coastal Weeden Island II sites in the Florida panhandle. If potsherds *were* cultures, we might venture that these variations on a ceramic theme correlate with changes in the importance of agriculture and changes in other

aspects of culture, changes the cumulative effect of which is the appearance in some areas of Mississippian cultures. Potsherds, however, are neither people nor the whole of culture, and we have no data at this time to support this speculation; a great deal of research at Weeden Island sites is needed.

Although the sacred–secular dichotomy of Weeden Island ceramics espoused by Sears (1973) does not hold as an absolute (Sears never said it did), it is a useful concept. The pottery assemblage found in the McKeithen village during the period of mound use is different from the collective assemblage of pottery from Mounds B and C; however, the assemblages from Mounds B and C also differ from one another. The fact that some elite ceramics— Weeden Island Incised, Punctated, Red, and Zoned Red—are found in small quantities in the village, suggests that at least some of the activities associated with those vessels also took place in the village as well as the mounds. One example might be the brewing and drinking of sacred medicines.

On the other hand, pedestaled effigy vessels with cutouts, well known from Sears' (1956) excavation of the pottery caches in Mounds D and E at Kolomoki as well as from Moore's (1901, 1902, 1903a, 1907, 1918) excavations in the Weeden Island heartland and now from McKeithen Mound C, are never found in villages. They are found only in mounds associated with burials (one sherd, possibly from the McKeithen Mound C squared dish, was recovered from Mound A). Our supposition is that the effigies were associated with body cleaning ritual on Mound A and were deposited in Mound C along with cleaned bones. Such activities never occured in the villages.

Knight's work provides an anthropological paradigm in which to interpret the animals and forms associated with these pedestaled effigies as well as with other elite ceramics. The symbols represented are associated with Weeden

Island ideology and are not solely symbols associated with the activities of a chiefly class. Perhaps similar beliefs were held by other pre-Mississippian Southeastern peoples who carved wood or wove fabrics or feather cloaks with similar symbols. Pre-Mississippian ideology evolved into Mississippian ideology, which in turn evolved into the ideology of the aborigines observed by Europeans in the sixteenth through the nineteenth centuries. It is gratifying to see that ethnographic theory can be applied to a specific prehistoric culture and, apparently, be useful.

The plate forms of ceramic vessels found in Mound B, many of which are of the type Weeden Island Zoned Red and are decorated with what may be a stylized bird of prey or carrion eater, are rare elsewhere at the site. Presumably, the plates were associated with activities of the presumed religious specialist who lived in the Mound B structure. That this activity might have been carried out infrequently by others at the site is suggested by the distribution of a few sherds from plates in the village. The reader should note that this is one place where we are not going to take a guess; despite a review of Moore's many publications we simply do not have any hard data on the functions of the plates.

Cordell's (Chapter 6) application of the methods of ceramic technology to both village and mound ceramics from the McKeithen site and to samples of clay collected from North Florida provides excellent descriptive data on the Weeden Island ceramic assemblage. Just as important are her conclusions regarding origins of manufacture, the nature of the sacred—secular dichotomy, and the beginnings of craft specialization. All of these findings are not discordant with our other interpretations and help support the model.

The similarity of some of the McKeithen Mound C ceramic vessels with those from Kolomoki and from some of the sites excavated by Moore is striking, especially in view of the data that leave little doubt local McKeithen clays were used. Artisan classes or itinerant ceramists are two frivolous explanations. A more realistic one, supported by Knight's study, is great uniformity of beliefs and manufacturing techniques and skills within the Weeden Island culture. If a Carrabelle Punctated bowl from Fairchilds Landing looks identical to one from the Weeden Island site on Tampa Bay, then why cannot a bird effigy vessel from Kolomoki resemble one from McKeithen. The widespread distribution of depicted animals such as birds—either in stylized or realistic form—through time and space in the eastern United States (from Adena tablets to the wooden figures at the Fort Center site in southern Florida) suggests that many aspects of ideology may have been pan-Southeast or pan-East well before the Weeden Island period.

THE BIG PICTURE: WEEDEN ISLAND AND THE GREATER SOUTHEAST

Since the 1970s, students in Milanich's archaeology classes at the University of Florida have come up against the concept of *The Big Picture,* an interconnected macroview of the greater Southeast United States from Paleoindian to historic times. Quite honestly, many have not been thrilled by it, and nearly all have pointed to the great empty spaces in it, which reflect Milanich's own lack of knowledge about many areas and cultures. Simply stated, The Big Picture is a three dimensional spider web of old-fashioned culture history with a few sparkling dew drops of process. It's what used to be called archaeology in the days when the end result of a research project was increased understanding of peoples and cultures of the past, not simply another methodological tool.

The Big Picture, an emic grid, encompasses

time–space information as well as many other types of data. Most prehistorians probably have their own big picture, which grows and is revised with increased knowledge and understanding. At each intersection in the grid, there is a little red warning light that goes off when bits of data come together and are incompatible. An example of something that would set off such an alarm is Milanich's original contention that the McKeithen site overlapped temporally with the Mississippian period. That unsubstantiated view must have set off all sorts of lights in the minds of people who read the original grant proposals for the North Florida project. Another less dramatic example might be a Mesoamerican-looking clay figurine that someone brings into the Florida State Museum, swearing they found it at an Archaic site in Central Florida. However, after noting that the figurine does not fit with the region or the time period, it becomes likely that it was probably lost by a tourist.

In The Big Picture that encompasses Alabama, Georgia, and Florida, the Weeden Island culture occupies a very comfortable space, one compatible with its neighbors. It follows and develops out of Swift Creek in most of its heartland region; in North Florida, where the Swift Creek culture is not present, it follows Deptford. Weeden Island's origins in the lower Chattahoochee River Valley and Northwest Florida are a little hazy, however. Sites such as Bird Hammock, Kolomoki, and Fairchilds Landing all seem to indicate a period of considerable overlap of Swift Creek and Weeden Island pottery in village middens.

The basic Weeden Island I and II schema, documented first by Willey (1949), holds throughout the Weeden Island region. Weeden Island II cultures precede the early Mississippian period in Northwest Florida and the lower Chattahoochee River Valley. In North Florida a variant of the McKeithen Weeden Island II ceramic complex apparently is present up to the

time that it is replaced by the Spanish-mission-associated Leon–Jefferson ceramic complex.

Just as Weeden Island fits temporally in the big picture, so is it geographically compatible with its surroundings. Weeden Island in its several variants occupies a major chunk of coastal plain in southern and southeastern Alabama, southwestern Georgia, and northern Florida. It is a culture associated primarily with interior deciduous and mixed pine–deciduous forests with their associated lakes, ponds, and wet prairies. Some Weeden Island sites are found along the Gulf of Mexico Coast from the Big Bend area of Florida around to the Mobile Bay locale.

South of the Weeden Island heartland in North-Central Florida, the contemporary Cades Pond culture, a Weeden Island–related culture, was present from ca. A.D. 150–700. During the Weeden Island II period North-Central Florida was occupied by the Alachua tradition, ancestors of the historic period Potano.

Southeast of the Weeden Island region is the St. Johns culture. We can trace the development of the St. Johns culture tradition from Middle Archaic times; great continuity existed. The historic period descendants associated with the St. Johns IIc archaeological culture were the various eastern Timucuan tribes encountered by the French and Spanish.

Southwest from the Weeden Island cultures along the Florida peninsular Gulf Coast were Weeden Island–related cultures. Those in the Tampa Bay–central coast region developed into the Mississippian period Safety Harbor culture. Westward in the lower Gulf coastal plain of Mississippi and Louisiana were the post-Hopewellian cultures given the generic names Troyville and Coles Creek. To the northwest in Alabama were cultures such as Flint River and McKelvey. In the Georgia coastal plain, adjacent to the Weeden Island region, lived populations who manufactured cord marked pottery. Sites of this Ocmulgee ceramic complex have been located and documented but little studied. East of the Weeden Island region along the Georgia coast proper and extending inland for perhaps a maximum of 80 km were the late Deptford and Wilmington cultures.

The boundaries of the Weeden Island region were certainly not so inviolate to the Weeden Island populations, and Weeden Island sites sometime extend outside of their normal distributions as into the Okeefenokee Swamp or the Georgia central coastal plain. Just as we would expect, the definitive archaeological traits of the Weeden Island culture also become diluted along its boundaries, as evidenced by the presence of the Weeden Island–related cultures to the south and southwest in Florida and the northwest in Alabama.

We can only wonder about the ethnic affiliations of the various Weeden Island peoples. Did the people living in North Florida in A.D. 450 realize that they shared many similarities in ideology and material culture (ceramics) with the people in Northwest Florida and Southwest Georgia? How did they view the archaeologically different St. Johns people to the southeast? Such intriguing questions cannot be answered through archaeology, at least not at this time.

In The Big Picture, Weeden Island in its archaeologically defined variants represents a part of a long evolutionary continuum, a process of change through time that we can trace unbroken from the earliest well-documented inhabitants of the Southeast into the historic period. Over several thousand years, small populations of hunter–gatherers increased in size and began to domesticate certain local wild plants. Maize, first domesticated and cultivated outside of the eastern United States, was added to the diet. That dietary change was probably at first much less important than social and settlement changes that were also occurring as populations increased and true village life began.

People are always making more people, and larger populations require more complex ways to organize society. By the time of the first appearance of Weeden Island, A.D. 200–300, such anthropologically recognizable constructs as achieved statuses and lineages must have been present among all Southeast peoples. As suggested by the McKeithen study and other Weeden Island sites such as Kolomoki, more complex forms of social organization appeared for brief periods of time. Many of the pre–Weeden Island Hopewellian sites extending from the upper Midwest to the Gulf Coast and even earlier sites such as Poverty Point might be interpreted as evidence for a similar process occurring throughout the greater Southeast at earlier times. (The greater Southeast can be operationally defined as the geographic area on which members of the Southeastern Archaeological Conference give papers. This includes Missouri and Arkansas and most of the eastern United States, excepting those states from Pennsylvania and Maryland to the northeast; no one ever talks about them at the meetings.)

The thousands of years of culture change and continual population increases ultimately culminate during the period A.D. 700–1000. By the end of that time, Mississippian cultures in their variations appear throughout the greater Southeast. The economic, social, and ideological changes that took place were dependent on all that had taken place before. And the same kinds of developments—the appearance of chiefdoms and settled farming life—have taken place in many geographic areas in the world.

As we stated at the end of Chapter 5, Weeden Island offers few surprises. A good anthropologist could probably look at Late Archaic cultures and those of the Mississippian period and predict the nature of the intervening cultures such as Weeden Island. Although pottery types or other aspects of material culture may differ, many of these same processes were occurring throughout the greater Southeast during the period 100 B.C.–A.D. 700 and can probably be traced back for a millennium or more. We predict that when other Southeast cultures are examined in this light, such uniformity will become apparent.

Predictability and no-surprise archaeology are excellent signs that Southeast archaeologists are developing a firm grasp of their discipline, the prehistory and anthropology of the prehistoric peoples of the Southeast. Perhaps Weeden Island studies, like archaeology, have grown up.

Appendix

Other North Florida Weeden Island Sites

During the course of investigations in North Florida, sites other than McKeithen were located and tested. In this section we briefly present information on three presumed Weeden Island II sites (one of which is actually a complex of sites) to allow comparison of the ceramic collections from these sites with the McKeithen site village ceramics.

The first site, Johns Pond, is a small village located 1.5 km northeast from the McKeithen site. Possibly it was occupied late in the Weeden Island II period. Johns Pond site is typical of many Weeden Island village sites that do not have mounds immediately adjacent. The closest documented Weeden Island II mound is at the Leslie Mound and village site about 3 km north-northwest of John's Pond. Another, smaller Weeden Island II village, Sam's site, is found 1.6 km to the south. Johns Pond was located by Sigler-Lavelle during her survey.

The Leslie Mound and Village site is located about 5 km north of the McKeithen site. Our investigations focused on the burial mound, although the village midden was present and was tested by Sigler-Lavelle. The mound was formed out of soil scraped up in the village area; consequently the mound fill contains a collection of village ceramics.

The third example, the Carter Mound 1 complex, consists of a mound with a village immediately adjacent and three outlying villages (without mounds) located about 0.75, 2.8, and 3.0 km southward. The exact temporal relations among these four villages are uncertain.

Taken together, all of these sites suggest that Weeden Island II village ceramic assemblages are characterized by large amounts of undecorated pottery with varying amounts of check stamped, cord marked, incised, and Lochloosa Punctated–like pottery among the decorated types. Some potsherds have a simple stamped–like motif that occasionally resembles brushing or incising (and may be). At times, the eroded surfaces of some sherds makes distinguishing simple stamping, brushing, and incising almost impossible. The Lochloosa Punctated–like pottery, referred to as punctated in the tables in this appendix, encompasses potsherds displaying an array of badly executed punctated motifs. Since the percentage of decorated pottery in any one assemblage is so low, it is very difficult to compare sites based on potsherd collections of less than about 75 sherds.

The presence of check stamped and simple stamped (or simple stamped–like) sherds at Weeden Island II sites in North Florida leads to confusion, since similar potsherds are characteristics of the Deptford culture. Also, the cord marked and Lochloosa Punctated–like sherds (as well as an occasional cob marked sherd) in the Weeden Island II collections from the McKeithen region are similar to individual pot-sherds found in the North-Central Florida Ala-chua tradition ceramic complex. However, when sufficiently large collections are com-pared, the differences between a post–A.D. 750 North Florida Weeden Island II village ceramic collection and a pre–A.D. 200 Deptford ceramic collection or a post–A.D. 750 North-Central Florida Alachua tradition collection are appar-ent.

Johns Pond Village Site

The site is located on the western end of the pond from which its name is taken and is adja-cent both to multiple aquatic habitats and to a small spring. Orange Creek, which flows past the McKeithen site, flows into Johns Pond and then into Orange Pond. The spring and its run flow into the creek between the two ponds east of the site.

Table A.1 lists the potsherds recovered from a test placed in the village. In addition, 187 pieces of chert debitage, 2 broken (flat) bases from bi-facially flaked points or tools (probably Kohler's Group 7; see Chapter 4); 1 flake showing use, and 1 small Pinellas-like triangular projectile point (Kohler's lithic Group 10) were recovered from the test.

Leslie Mound and Village

This sand burial mound and village are near the 30-m contour line of the west bank of an unnamed creek that flows into Turkey Prairie. The source of the creek is a swamp, Tiger Bay, located to the south.

The mound is almost perfectly circular, mea-suring 26 m in diameter with a height of 2.1 m

Table A.1

Potsherd Counts and Frequencies from Johns Pond

Type	n^a	(%)
Undecorated[b]	33/3	47.8
Check stamped	2	2.8
Cob marked	1	1.4
Complicated stamped	5	7.2
Cord marked	9/1	13.0
Punctated	1	1.4
Simple stamped, brushed, or incised	16/1	23.1
Weeden Island Red	1	1.4
Weeden Island Plain	1/1	1.4

[a]Number of rim sherds included in the count follows the slash mark.

[b]This type includes 13 sherds with smoothed surfaces.

above the present ground surface. Other than a small pothole in the top and a cache of patent medicine bottles on the east side dating to ca. 1900, the mound was undisturbed at the time of our testing in early February, 1979. The landowner, Mrs. Leslie who resides beside the site, graciously gave her permission to test the mound.

Our excavation into the mound consisted of four 3- by 3-m excavation units forming a 6- by 6-m square on the east side of the mound and a 1.5- by 3-m unit placed on the east side of that composite unit just beyond the edge of the mound. The latter unit intersected a feature containing 12 patent medicine bottles, all dat-ing from about the turn of the century. Several still had their stoppers in place and contained liquid. Apparently they had all been placed in a paper or cloth sack (upright) and were buried in the mound. Whether or not this was done to get rid of someone's "medicines" (with their respec-tably high alcohol content) or it was some sort of modern offering to the mound is unknown. This collection of glass bottles—the molded labels of which indicate that the contents included "Her-bine" from St. Louis, an unidentified liquid from G. W. Price's "Old Reliable Drug Store" in Lake City, "Ramon's Pepsin Chill Tonic" made in Greeneville, Tennessee, a "24 Hour Fever Cure, Guaranteed," and "Chamberlain's Cough Remedy" from Des Moines—is one of the most peculiar pottery caches we have encountered in a burial mound.

The test excavation in the mound provided sufficient information to reconstruct the sequence of mound construction and use (and reuse). First, a 10-cm-thick layer of clean, clayey sand was laid down on the cleaned ground surface. A low platform mound about 30 cm high and about 9 m on at least one side (we did not determine if the platform was round, square, or rectangular) was erected. A stratum of humic soil accumulated on this original platform in at least some places. Burials were placed on this surface and covered with mound fill (a cap). The burials were bundles and consisted of skulls and long bones, all of which were in very poor condition due to the acidity of the soil.

The mound fill or cap over the first platform mound formed a second flat-topped platform mound 0.8 m high (above the first platform surface). Like the first, a humic stratum accumulated on it in places; and, like the first, bundle burials were placed on it and covered with more mound fill. This latter cap, with a plowed zone formed in modern times, forms the present surface of the rounded mound. Quite likely this two-stage burial mound was used in conjunction with two charnel houses, each of which might have been built on the respective surfaces of the two platforms and later removed when each platform and set of burials was capped.

Table A.2 presents the counts and frequencies of pottery recovered from the mound as a whole. Examples are shown in Figure A.1. None of the pottery could be determined to have been associated with activities on either of the platforms.

Table A.2
Potsherd Counts and Frequencies from Leslie Mound

Type	n^a	(%)
Undecorated[b]	464/32	69.7
Check stamped	30	4.5
Cob marked	11	1.6
Complicated stamped	2	0.3
Cord marked	23	3.4
Punctated[c]	87/2	13.1
Simple stamped, brushed, or incised	24	3.6
Weeden Island Incised[d]	7	1.0
Tucker Ridge-pinched	1	0.1
St. Petersburg Incised	1	0.1
St. Johns Check Stamped	13	1.9
St. Johns Plain	2	0.3

[a]Number of rim sherds included in the count follows the slash mark.
[b]Seven of these have a red slip.
[c]Six of these have a dentate-like stamp.
[d]Three of these have a red-slipped interior and appear to be from the same vessel.

CARTER MOUND 1 COMPLEX

Based on information provided by the Carter family, Sigler-Lavelle located three burial mounds in northern Columbia County, each with an adjacent village and other nearby villages. Surveys were undertaken around each of the sites (see Chapter 3) to locate additional sites. One of these complexes, Carter Mound 1, was arbitrarily chosen for description here as typical of such collections of Weeden Island sites in North Florida.

Carter Mound 1 Complex, Village 1

The sand burial mound itself is located in an oak hammock just south of a 5-ha pond. About 60 m east of the mound is the village, presently in a planted pine field. The village measures about 100 by 125 m and lies south of a small

Figure A.1 Weeden Island II period sherds from Leslie Mound: top row, check stamped; middle row, punctated; and bottom row, brushed or stamped. Top left specimen is 6.5 cm high.

Table A.3
Potsherd Counts and Frequencies from Carter Mound 1 Village

Type	n^a	(%)
Undecorated[b]	34	54.8
Check stamped	3	4.8
Simple stamped, brushed, or incised	8	12.9
Fiber tempered	1	1.6
Unidentifiable (eroded surfaces)	16/1	25.8

[a]Number of rim sherds included in the count follows the slash mark.

[b]This type includes 16 sherds with smoothed surfaces.

creek that flows into the pond. Immediately east of the village and mound is an extension of Sanderlin Bay, an area of poorly drained lowlands and swamps. This and the other sites in the complex lie on a north–south sand ridge that varies in elevation from about 30 to 40 m.

Table A.3 gives the counts and frequencies of potsherds recovered from the village tests. The distribution of material, like at village sites other than McKeithen, was not dense. One problem inherent in describing small ceramic collections from North Florida Weeden Island sites is evident in the table: If we call the check stamped and some of the simple stamped pottery Deptford, we might well call the site Deptford. However, when the entire collection is treated as an assemblage (which it may not be, since one fiber-tempered sherd is present), the similarity with other Weeden Island sites in the McKeithen region is apparent (including the presence of plain sherds that have the smoothed surfaces typical of some Weeden Island ceramics). The village collection also included 35 pieces of chert debitage, 4 chert flakes showing use-chipping and 5 tools.

In the mid-1960s years prior to Sigler-Lavelle's investigation of the site, the Carter 1 burial mound had been almost entirely bulldozed during land-clearing activities. Only a small portion of the eastern side remained in-

tact (about one quarter). A 2- by 8-m trench excavated through the remaining section provided information on the mound's construction and use, verified that it was a burial mound, and revealed a two-pot pottery cache. Aboriginal construction of the mound was preceded by clearing the old ground surface and depositing a layer of fine, very white sand averaging about 30 cm in thickness. This sand may have come from the banks of the Suwannee River about 1.8 km to the west. A 60-cm-thick platform mound was then built on top. Like Leslie Mound and Mound C at McKeithen, this platform may have served as the base for a charnel house. Later, bundled burials (remains of possibly seven individuals, all of whose bones were badly deteriorated due to the acid soil) were placed either on this platform or in the cap. Possibly as the 70-cm-thick cap was deposited, burials were laid down on the fresh sand and then covered. Evidence of fire was found in the cap stratum and in the primary mound.

Also in the mound cap were two ceramic vessels (Figures A.2 and A.3) and two celts. The latter, shaped like greenstone celts common at Weeden Island period sites in Florida, were instead manufactured out of a fine-grained granite possibly mined in the Appalachian Mountains. They measured 8 and 11 cm in length, respectively.

The two ceramic vessels are Carrabelle Punctated bowls; both are coiled and are made from a sand–grit clay that is probably local in origin. Vessel A is decorated with hollow reed punctations within an 3.5-cm-wide incised band that begins 1 cm below the rim. The incurving and inslanting bowl has a diameter of 11.5 cm at the mouth; a postfiring kill hole is present in the rounded bottom. Contained within the bowl were several sherds from another vessel; these were burnished on both the interior and exterior surfaces and had a fugitive red slip on both surfaces. Could these have been the last remaining pieces of an heirloomed Weeden Island

Figure A.2 Vessel A, Carrabelle Punctated bowl, Carter Mound 1; diameter at mouth is 11.5 cm.

Red vessel from an earlier period?

Vessel B, a collared bowl–jar, is decorated with a 7-cm-wide band of round to rectangular punctations. Vessel wall orientation is compound, independent restricted. The lower edge of the band is marked with an incised line; just above this band of punctations is a double row of Tucker Ridge-pinched pinchings that encircle the vessel around the collar. At this collar, the vessel is 12.5 cm in diameter. The entire rim of the bowl is broken off along with many of the pinchings, and it is not apparent if another incised line was placed above the pinched and punctated designs and below the rim. A fugitive red slip was present on both the interior and exterior vessel surfaces.

Like Vessel A, a postfiring kill hole was present in the bottom; and, like Vessel A, this bowl contained sherds of another vessel with fugitive red slips on exterior and interior surfaces. It also contained shell and charcoal fragments and the pharyngeal grinder from a black drumfish (*Pogonias cromis*).

Carter Mound 1 Complex, Village 2

The second village is on the edge of a mesic hammock some 130 m from a small spring-fed creek that empties into a floodplain swamp of the Suwannee River. Located 0.75 km south of the mound–village site, the village is about 100- by 130-m and has been extensively disturbed by clearing with a bulldozer. A small sample of ceramics was collected (see Table A.4). In addition there were 36 pieces of debitage, 2 utilized flakes, and 4 tools (all chert).

Carter Mound 1 Complex, Village 3

Located about 2.8 km southward from the mound–village complex, Village 3 is immedi-

Figure A.3 Vessel B, Carrabelle Punctated bowl with pinching, Carter Mound 1; diameter at collar is 12.5 cm.

ately adjacent to the Suwannee River (some of the site may have eroded into the river). The village is in a mesic hammock about 215 m from a spring-fed creek that empties into the river. Tests showed that the size of the village midden is about 75 by 125 m. Recovered from the midden were 21 undecorated sherds (including 1 smoothed surface sherd), 1 simple stamped sherd, and 2 unidentifiable sherds with eroded surfaces. In addition, the village collection contains 86 pieces of chert debitage and 7 tools, including one Group 10 triangular projectile point.

Carter Mound 1 Complex, Village 4

This fourth Carter village, 3 km south of the mound–village complex, is also located in a

mesic hammock area and is about 90 m from a spring-fed creek that ultimately empties into the Suwannee River. The exact portion of the hammock, which includes the village, has been cleared and planted in corn. Size of the midden is about 90 by 150 m. Only 10 sherds were re-

Table A.4

Potsherd Counts and Frequencies from Carter Mound 1 Complex, Village 2

Type	n^a	(%)
undecorated[b]	26/5	92.8
unidentifiable (eroded surfaces)	2	7.1

[a] Number of rim sherds included in the count follows the slash mark.

[b] This type includes nine sherds with smoothed surfaces, two of which are rim sherds.

covered: 9 undecorated (including one rim) and 1 cord marked. Thirteen pieces of chert debitage and 6 tools, also chert, also were recovered from the midden.

In addition to the mound–village complex and the three other villages, Sigler-Lavelle's survey within the locale of the Carter Mound 1 complex located two chert quarries, both exposures within the channel of the Suwannee River. A possible clay quarry was also located in the channel; clays from this quarry were included in Cordell's (Chapter 6) ceramic–paste analysis.

References

Adams, W. R.
    1956   Archaeozoology at Kolomoki. In Excavations at Kolomoki, final report, edited by William H. Sears. *University of Georgia Series in Anthropology* 5:104–105.

Allen, R. P.
    1942   The roseate spoonbill. *National Audubon Society Research Report* 2.

Arnold, D. E.
    1975   Ceramic ecology of the Ayacucho Basin, Peru. *Current Anthropology* 16(2):183–194.

Bell, James
    1883   Mounds in Alachua County, Florida. *Annual Report of the Smithsonian Institution, 1881,* pp. 635–637.

Bell, O. G.
    1924   A preliminary report of the clays of Florida. *Florida State Geological Survey,* 15th Annual Report.

Belmont, Johns S., and Stephen Williams
    1981   Painted pottery horizons in the southern Mississippi Valley. *Geoscience and Man* 22:19–42.

Bense, Judith A.
    1969   *Excavations at the Bird Hammock site (8 Wa 30), Wakulla County, Florida.* Unpublished M.A. thesis, Department of Anthropology, Florida State University.

Berner, Lewis
    1950   *The mayflies of Florida.* University of Florida Press, Gainesville.

Binford, Lewis R.
    1962   Archaeology as anthropology. *American Antiquity* 28:217–225.

Birdsell, Joseph B.
    1968   Some predictions for the Pleistocene based on equilibrium systems among recent hunter–gatherers. In *Man the hunter,* edited by Richard B. Lee and Irven Devore, pp. 229–240. Aldine, Chicago.

Blau, Peter M.
    1977   *Inequality and heterogeneity: a primitive theory of social structure.* Free Press, New York.

Boyd, Mark F., Hale G. Smith, and John W. Griffin
    1951   *Here they once stood.* University of Florida Press, Gainesville.

Brain, Jeffrey
    1976   The question of corn agriculture in the Lower Mississippi Valley. *Southeastern Archaeological Conference Bulletin* 19:57–60.

Brose, David
    1979   An interpretation of the Hopewellian traits in Florida. In *Hopewell archaeology, the Chillicothe conference,* edited by David S. Brose and N'omi Greber, pp. 141–149. Kent State University Press, Kent, Ohio.

Brothwell, Don R.
    1972   *Digging up bones.* Trustees of the British Museum, London.

Brown, Ian W.
    1982   The Southeastern check stamped pottery tradition: a view from Louisiana. *Mid-Continental Journal of Archaeology Special Paper* 4.

Bullen, Ripley P.
    1958   Six sites near the Chattahoochee River in the Jim Woodruff Reservoir area, Florida. In River Basin survey papers, edited by Frank H. H. Roberts, Jr. pp. 315–357. *Bureau of American Ethnology Bulletin* 169. Smithsonian Institution, Washington, D.C.

    1971   The Sarasota county mound, Englewood, Florida. *Florida Anthropologist* 24:1–30.

    1975   *A guide to the identification of Florida projectile points.* Kendall Books, Gainesville.

Bullen, Ripley P., and Adelaide K. Bullen
1976   The Palmer site. *Florida Anthropological Society Publications* 8. Gainesville.

Bullen, Ripley P., and Frederick W. Sleight
1959   Archeological investigations of the Castle Windy Midden, Florida. *The William L. Bryant Foundation, American Studies Report* 1.
1960   Archeological investigations of Green Mound, Florida. *The William L. Bryant Foundation, American Studies Report* 2.

Bulmer, Ralph
1967   Why is the cassowary not a bird? A problem of zoological taxonomy among the Karam of the New Guinea highlands. *Man* (NS) 2:5–25.

Caldwell, Joseph R.
1978   *Report of excavations at Fairchild's Landing and Harel's Landing, Seminole County, Georgia*, edited by Betty A. Smith. Report submitted to the National Park Service, Tallahassee.

Calver, James L.
1949   Florida kaolins and clays. *Florida Geological Survey Information Circular* 2.
1957   Mining and mineral resources. *Florida Geological Survey, Geological Bulletin* 39.

Cambron, James W., and David C. Hulse
1975   *Handbook of Alabama archaeology, Part 1*. Archaeological Research Association of Alabama, Inc.,

Chase, David W.
1967   Weeden Island sites. *Journal of Alabama Archaeology* 13:61–63.

Cook, S. F., and R. Heizer
1965   The quantitative approach to the relation between population and settlement size. *University of California Archaeological Survey* 64. University of California Archaeological Research Facility, Berkeley.

Cordell, Ann S.
1980   Preliminary report on technological investigations of McKeithen Site Weeden Island pottery. *Southeastern Archaeological Conference Bulletin* 22:19–21.
1984   *Ceramic technology at a Weeden Island period archaeological site in North Florida*. Ceramic Notes, 2. Occasional Publications of the Ceramic Technology Laboratory, Florida State Museum.

Cordell, Ann S., B. J. Lavelle, and J. T. Milanich
1979   Progress report on the Florida State Museum North Florida Weeden Island project. Manuscript on file, Florida State Museum.

Crandall, Keith C., and Robert W. Seabloom
1970   *Engineering fundamentals in measurements, probability, statistics, and dimensions*. McGraw-Hill, New York.

Cumbaa, Stephen L.
1972   *An intensive harvest economy in North-Central Florida*. Unpublished M.A. thesis, Department of Anthropology, University of Florida.

Dalton, George
1977   Aboriginal economies in stateless societies. In *Exchange systems in prehistory*, edited by T. K. Earle and J. E. Erickson, pp. 191–212. Academic Press, New York.

David, Nicholas
1972   On the lifespan of pottery, type frequencies, and archaeological inference. *American Antiquity* 37:141–142.

Deagan, Kathleen
1972   Fig Springs: The mid-seventeenth century in North-Central Florida. *Historical Archaeology* 6:23–46.

DeBoer, William R.
1974   Ceramic longevity and archeological interpretation: an example from Upper Ucayali, Peru. *American Antiquity* 39:335–343.

Deetz, James
1967   *Invitation to archaeology*. American Museum Science Books, Natural History Press, Garden City, New York.

Dickens, Roy S.
1971   Archaeology in the Jones Bluff Reservoir of Central Alabama. *Journal of Alabama Archaeology* 17:1–107.

Dolgin, J. L., D. S. Kemmitzer, and D. K. Schneider (editors)
1977   *Symbolic anthropology: a reader in the study of symbols and meanings*. Columbia University Press, New York.

Douglas, Mary
1957   Animals in Lele religious symbolism. *Africa* 27:46–57.
1966   *Purity and danger: an analysis of concepts of pollution and taboo*. Routledge and Kegan Paul, London.
1975   *Implicity meanings: essays in anthropology*. Routledge and Kegan Paul, London.

Driver, H. E., and W. C. Massey
1957   Comparative studies of North American Indians. *Transactions of the American Philosophical Society* 47(2). Philadelphia.

Durkheim, Emile, and M. Mauss
1963   De quelques formes primitives de classification [*Primitive Classification*, translated by R. Needham] Cohen and West, London. (Original work published by *Annee Sociologique, 1901–1902* in 1903).

Feinman, G. H., S. Upham, and K. G. Lightfoot
1981   The production step measures: an ordinal index

of labor input in ceramic manufacture. *American Antiquity* 46:871–884.

Fewkes, J. Walter
1924   Preliminary archeological investigations at Weeden Island, Florida. *Smithsonian Miscellaneous Collections* 76(13):1–26.

Flannery, Kent V.
1972   The cultural evolution of civilization. *Annual Review of Ecology and Systematics* 3:399–426.

Foster, George M.
1960   Life-expectancy of utilitarian pottery in Tzintzuntzan, Michoacan, Mexico. *American Antiquity* 25:606–609.

Fryman, Frank B.
1971   Tallahassee's prehistoric political center. *Archives and History News* 2(3):2–4. Florida Department of State, Tallahassee.

Garcilasco de la Vega
1962   *The Florida of the Inca,* translated by John and Jeanette Varner. University of Texas Press, Austin.

Goggin, John M.
1947   A preliminary definition of archaeological areas and periods in Florida. *American Antiquity* 13:114–127.
1950   An early lithic complex from central Florida. *American Antiquity* 16:46–49.
1952   Space and time perspective in the northern St. Johns archeology, Florida. *Yale University Publications in Anthropology* 47.
1962   Weeden Island Punctated and Papys Bayou Punctated. *Southeastern Archaeological Conference Newsletter* 8:19–25.

Haag, William, and Clarence Webb
1953   Microblades at Poverty Point sites. *American Antiquity* 18:245–249.

Hall, Robert L.
1979   In search of the idealogy of the Adena–Hopewell climax. In *Hopewell archaeology: the Chilicothe conference,* edited by David S. Brose and N'omi Greber, pp. 258–265. Kent State University Press, Kent.

Hally, David
1983   *Archaeological contexts and interpretation of plant remains.* Paper presented at the 40th Southeastern Archaeological Conference, Columbia, South Carolina.

Harper, Roland M.
1914   Geography and vegetation of northern Florida. *Florida State Geological Survey, 6th Annual Report,* pp. 163–437.

Harris, Marvin
1977   *Cannibals and kings: the origins of cultures.* Random House, New York.

Helms, Mary W.
1979   *Ancient Panama: Chiefs in search of power.* University of Texas Press. Austin.

Hertz, R.
1907   Contribution a une etude sur la representation collective de la mort. *Annee Sociologique* 10:48–137.

Holmes, William H.
1903   Aboriginal pottery of the eastern United States. In *Bureau of American Ethnology, Twentieth Annual Report, 1898–99,* pp. 1–237.

Hudson, Charles
1976   *The Southeastern Indians.* The University of Tennessee Press, Knoxville.

Huntington, R., and P. Metcalf
1979   *Celebrations of death: the anthropology of mortuary ritual.* Cambridge University Press, Cambridge.

Jenks, A. E., and Mrs. H. H. Simpson
1941   Beveled bone artifacts in Florida of the same type as artifacts found near Clovis, New Mexico. *American Antiquity* 6:314–319.

Jeter, Marvin D.
1977   Late Woodland chronology and change in central Alabama. *Journal of Alabama Archaeology* 23:112–136.

Jones, Calvin
1982   Southern cult manifestations at the Lake Jackson site, Leon County, Florida: Salvage excavation of Mound 3. *Midcontinental Journal of Archaeology* 7:3–44.

Knight, Vernon J., Jr.
1981   Radiocarbon dates. In *Cemochechobee, archaeology of a Mississippian ceremonial center on the Chattahoochee River,* by Frank T. Schnell, Vernon J. Knight, Jr., and Gail S. Schnell, pp. 247–251. University Presses of Florida, Gainesville.

Kohler, Timothy
1975   *The Garden Patch site: a minor Weeden Island ceremonial center on the North Peninsular Florida Gulf Coast.* Unpublished M.A. thesis, Department of Anthropology, University of Florida.
1977a   *The McKeithen site: a preliminary report.* Paper presented at the Society for American Archaeology annual meeting, New Orleans.
1977b   Preliminary report on the summer 1976 sampling excavations at the McKeithen site, 8-Co-17. Mimeograph on file, Florida State Museum, Gainesville.
1977c   Second preliminary report: winter 1977 excavations at the McKeithen site, Columbia County, Florida. Mimeograph on File, Florida State Museum, Gainesville.
1978a   Ceramic breakage rate simulation: Population

size and the Southeastern chiefdom. *Newsletter of Computer Archaeology* 14:1–18.

1978b   *The social and chronological dimensions of village occupation at a North Florida Weeden Island period site.* Ph.D. dissertation, University of Florida. University Microfilms, Ann Arbor.

1978c   *Village excavations at the McKeithen site: a lithic chronology for Weeden Island in North Florida.* Paper presented at the annual meeting of the Florida Anthropological Society, Fort Walton Beach.

1980   The social dimensions of village occupation of the McKeithen site, North Florida. *Southeastern Archaeological Conference Bulletin* 22:5–10.

Kohler, Timothy, and Sarah H. Schlanger
1980   Surface estimation of site structure and content, Dolores Project. *Contract Abstracts and CRM Archeology* 1:29–32.

Larson, Lewis H., Jr.
1980   *Aboriginal subsistence technology on the southeastern coastal plain during the late prehistoric period.* University Presses of Florida, Gainesville.

Lazarus, Yulee W.
1979   *The Buck Burial mound: a mound of the Weeden Island culture.* Temple Mound Museum, Fort Walton Beach.

Leach, Edmond
1976   *Culture and communication: the logic by which symbols are connected.* Cambridge University Press, Cambridge.

Lévi-Strauss, Claude
1962   *Le totemisme aujourd hui.* Presses Universitaires de France, Paris.

1966   *The savage mind.* University of Chicago Press. Chicago.

Long, Austin, and Bruce Rippeteau
1974   Testing comtemporaneity and averaging radiocarbon dates. *American Antiquity* 39:205–215.

Loucks, L. Jill
1978a   Suwannee County survey report, Fall 1977: an account of sites located on property owned by Owens–Illinois, Inc. Unpublished manuscript on file, Department of Anthropology, Florida State Museum.

1978b   *Origins of the Utina Indians in North Florida: reexaminations of the Leon–Jefferson ceramic complex.* Paper presented at the Southeastern Archaeological Conference, Knoxville.

1979   *Political and economic interactions between Spanards and Indians: archaeological and ethnohistorical perspective of the mission system in Florida.* Ph.D. dissertation. Department of Anthropology, University of Florida. University Microfilms, Ann Arbor.

Luer, George M.
1977a   Excavations at the Old Oak site, Sarasota, Florida: a late Weeden Island–Safety Harbor period site. *Florida Anthropologist* 30:37–55.

1977b   The Roberts Bay site, Sarasota, Florida. *Florida Anthropologist* 30:121–133.

1980   *The Aqui Esta site at Charlotte Harbor: a Safety Harbor–influenced pre-historic aboriginal site.* Paper presented at Florida Anthropological Society Annual meeting, Winter Park.

Luer, George, and Marion H. Almy
1979   Three aboriginal shell middens on Longboat Key, Florida: Manasota period sites of barrier island exploitation. *Florida Anthropologist* 32:34–45.

1982   A definition of the Manasota culture. *Florida Anthropologist* 35:34–58.

Lussagnet, Suzanne, (editor)
1958   *Les Français en Floride: Pays de'outremer, deuxième serie: les classiques de la colonisation.* Presses Universitaires de France, Paris.

Marrinan, Rochelle
1976   Archeological and historical resources: the Little Satilla watershed, Appling and Wayne Counties, Georgia. *Miscellaneous Project Report Series* 8. The Florida State Museum, Gainesville.

Matson, Frederick R.
1965   Ceramic ecology: an approach to the study of the early cultures of the Near East. In *Ceramics and man,* edited by F. Matson, pp. 202–217. Chicago, Aldine.

Milanich, Jerald T.
1968   An archeological survey of the Ichetucknee River. Manuscript on file, Department of Anthropology, Florida State Museum.

1971   The Alachua tradition of North-Central Florida. *Contributions of the Florida State Museum* 17. Gainesville.

1972   Excavations at the Richardson site, Alachua County, Florida: an early 17th century Potano Indian village (with notes on Potano culture change). *Bureau of Historic Sites and Properties, Division of Archives, History and Records Management, Bulletin* 2:35–61. Florida Department of State, Tallahassee.

1973   A Deptford phase house structure. *Florida Anthropologist* 26:105–118.

1974   Life in a 9th century Indian household, a Weeden Island fall–winter site on the upper Apalachicola River, Florida. *Bureau of Historic Sites and Properties, Division of Archives, History and Records*

Management, Bulletin 4:1–44. Department of State, Tallahassee, Florida.

1978a   *Excavation of Mound B at the McKeithen Site: Season IV of the FSM Weeden Island Project.* Paper presented at annual meeting of the Florida Anthropological Society, Fort Walton Beach.

1978b   *The mounds at the McKeithen site: Weeden Island from ranked lineages into chiefdoms?* Paper presented at the Southeastern Archaeological Conference, Knoxville.

1978c   Two Cades Pond sites in North-Central Florida: the occupational nexus as a model of settlement. *Florida Anthropologist* 31:151–173.

1978d   The Western Timucua: patterns of acculturation and change. In *Tacachale, Essays on the Indians of Florida and Southeastern Georgia during the Historic Period,* edited by Jerald T. Milanich and Samuel Proctor, pp. 59–88. University Presses of Florida, Gainesville.

1979   *Charnel knowledge: interpretation of four Weeden Island mounds, Columbia County, Florida.* Paper presented at the annual meeting of the Florida Anthropological Society, Miami.

1980a   *Conclusions from the McKeithen site, an early Weeden Island mound–village complex in Northern Florida.* Paper presented at the annual meeting of the Society for American Anthropology, Philadelphia.

1980b   Weeden Island studies—past, present, and future. *Southeastern Archaeological Conference Bulletin* 22:11–18.

Milanich, Jerald T., and Charles Fairbanks
1980   *Florida archaeology.* Academic Press, New York.

Milanich, Jerald T., Timothy Kohler, and L. Jill Loucks
1978   Current research in Florida. Mimeograph on file, Florida State Museum, Gainesville.

Milanich, Jerald T., and W. Sturtevant
1972   *Francisco Pareja's 1613 confessionario: a documentary source for Timucuan ethnography.* Florida Department of State, Tallahassee.

Mitchem, Jeffrey, and James Welch
1983   South Prong I site (8-HI-418) results—ceramics. In *Mitigative excavations of the South Prong I site, 8-HI-418, and the Cates site, 8-HI-425, Hillsborough County, Florida* by James Welch, pp. 141–166. Department of Anthropology, University of South Florida, Tampa.

Moore, Clarence B.
1901   Certain aboriginal remains of the Northwest Florida coast (Part I). *Journal of the Academy of Natural Sciences of Philadelphia* (second series) 11:420–497, 499–514.

1902   Certain aboriginal remains of the Northwest Florida coast (Part II). *Journal of the Academy of Natural Sciences of Philadelphia* (second series) 12:127–355.

1903a   Certain aboriginal mounds of the Apalachicola River. *Journal of the Academy of Natural Sciences of Philadelphia* (second series) 12:440–492.

1903b   Certain aboriginal mounds of the Florida central west coast. *Journal of the Academy of Natural Sciences of Philadelphia* (second series) 12:361–439.

1905   Certain aboriginal remains on Mobile Bay and on Mississippi Sound. *Journal of the Academy of Natural Sciences of Philadelphia* (second series) 12:279–297.

1907   Mounds of the lower Chattahoochee and lower Flint rivers. *Journal of the Academy of Natural Sciences of Philadelphia* (second series) 13:426–456.

1918   The Northwestern Florida coast revisited. *Journal of the Academy of Natural Sciences of Philadelphia* (second series) 16:515–581.

Moorehead, Warren K.
1922   The Hopewell mound group of Ohio. *Field Museum of Natural History Anthropological series* 6:73–184.

Nance, C. Roger
1976   The archaeological sequence at Durant Bend, Dallas County, Alabama. *Special Publications of the Alabama Archaeological Society* 2. Orange Beach, Alabama.

O'Brien Patricia J.
1972   A formal analysis of Cahokia ceramics from the Powell tract. *Illinois Archaeological Survey Monograph* 3.

Odum, Eugene P.
1971   *Fundamentals of ecology.* W. B. Saunders, Philadelphia.

Otto, John S.
1975   *Status Differences and the archeological record: a comparison of planter, overseer, and slave sites from Cannon's Point Plantation (1794–1861), St. Simon's Island, Georgia.* Ph.D. dissertation, Department of Anthropology, University of Florida, Gainesville. University Microfilms, Ann Arbor.

Parmalee, P. W., and G. Perino
1971   A prehistoric archaeological record of the roseate spoonbill in Illinois. *Central States Archaeological Journal* 18:80–85.

Pearson, T. Gilbert.
1939   The large wading birds. In *The book of birds* (Vol. 1), edited by Gilbert Grosvenor and Alexander

Wetmore, pp. 59–90. National Geographic Society, Washington, D.C.

Penton, Daniel T.
1970   *Excavations in the early Swift Creek component at Bird Hammock (8-WA-30).* Unpublished M.A. thesis, Department of Anthropology, Florida State University.

Percy, George
1976   Salvage investigations at the Scholz Steam plant site (8-Ja-104), a Middle Woodland habitation site in Jackson County, Florida. *Florida Bureau of Historic Sites and Properties, Miscellaneous Project Report Series* 35. Tallahassee.

Percy, George, and David Brose
1974   *Weeden Island ecology: subsistence and village life in Northwest Florida.* Paper presented at the 39th Annual Meeting of the Society for American Archaeology, Washington, D.C.

Phelps, David S.
1969   Swift Creek and Santa Rosa in Northwest Florida. *Institute of Archeology and Anthropology, University of South Carolina, Notebook* 1(6–9):14–24.

Pirkle, E. C.
1960   Kaolinitic sediments in peninsular Florida and origin of the kaolin. *Economic Geology* 55:1382–1405.

Rice, Prudence M.
1976   *Ceramic continuity and change in the Valley of Guatemala: a study of whiteware pottery production.* Ph.D. dissertation, Department of Anthropology, Pennsylvania State University. University Microfilms, Ann Arbor.
1980   Trace elemental characterization of Weeden Island pottery: implications for specialized production. *Southeastern Archaeological Conference Bulletin* 22:29–35.
1981   Evolution of specialized pottery production: A trial model. *Current Anthropology* 22:219–240.

Rice, Prudence M., and Timothy Kohler
1977   *Weeden Island ceramics from the McKeithen site, Columbia County, Florida.* Paper presented at the Florida Academy of Sciences meeting, Gainesville.

Rouse, Irving
1960   The classification of artifacts in archaeology. *American Antiquity* 25:313–323.

Rowland, L. O., and D. P. Powell
1965   Geology, physiography, and drainage. In *Soil survey, Suwannee County, Florida,* (Series 1961 No. 21), pp. 95–99. U.S. Government Printing Office, Washington, D.C.

Ruhl, Donna
1981   *An investigation into the relationships between Midwestern Hopewell and Southeastern prehistory.* Unpublished M.A. thesis, Department of Anthropology, Florida Atlantic University.

Ruple, Stephen D.
1976   A survey of the archaeological and historical resources of the Trail Ridge Project Baker, Bradford, Clay, and Duval Counties, Florida. *Florida Bureau of Historic Sites and Properties, Miscellaneous Project Report Series* 38. Tallahassee.

Sabloff, Jeremy A.
1975   Ceramics. In Excavations at Seibal. *Memoirs of the Peabody Museum of Archaeology and Ethnology, Harvard University* 13(2).

Sanders, William T., and B. J. Price
1968   *Mesoamerica, the evolution of a civilization.* Random House, New York.

Scarry, John F.
1980   The chronology of Fort Walton development in the upper Apalachicola Valley, Florida. *Southeastern Archaeological Conference Bulletin* 22:38–45.
1981   Fort Walton culture: a redefinition. *Southeastern Archaeological Conference Bulletin* 24:18–21.

Schnell, Frank T.
1981   Late prehistoric ceramic chronologies in the lower Chattahoochee Valley. *Southeastern Archaeological Conference Bulletin* 24:21–23.

Schnell, Frank T., Vernon J. Knight, and Gail S. Schnell
1981   *Cemochechobee, archaeology of a Mississippian ceremonial center on the Chattahoochee River.* University Presses of Florida, Gainesville.

Sears, William H.
1951a   Excavations at Kolomoki, season I 1948. *University of Georgia Series in Anthropology* 2. The University of Georgia Press, Athens.
1951b   Excavations at Kolomoki, season II 1950. *University of Georgia Series in Anthropology* 3. The University of Georgia Press, Athens.
1952   An archaeological manifestation of a Natchez-type burial ceremony. *The Florida Anthropologist* 5:1–7.
1953   Excavations at Kolomoki, season III and IV, Mound D. *University of Georgia Series in Anthropology* 4. The University of Georgia Press, Athens.
1954   The sociopolitical organization of pre-Columbian cultures on the Gulf coastal plain. *American Anthropologist* 56:339–346.
1956   Excavations at Kolomoki, final report. *University of Georgia Series in Anthropology* 5. The University of Georgia Press, Athens.

1958   Burial mounds on the Gulf coastal plain. *American Antiquity* 23:274–284.

1961   The study of social and religious systems in North American archaeology. *Current Anthropology* 2:223–246.

1962a   The state in certain areas and periods of the prehistoric Southeastern United States. *Ethnohistory* 9:109–125.

1962b   The Hopewellian affiliations of certain sites on the Gulf Coast of Florida. *American Antiquity* 28:5–18.

1963   The Tucker site on Aligator Harbor, Franklin County, Florida. *Contributions of the Florida State Museum, Social Sciences* 9, Gainesville.

1971   The Weeden Island site, St. Petersburg, Florida. *Florida Anthropologist* 24:51–60.

1973   The sacred and the secular in prehistoric ceramics. In *Variations in anthropology: essays in honor of John McGregor,* edited by D. Lathrap and J. Douglas, pp. 31–42. Illinois Archaeological Survey, Urbana.

1982   *Fort Center: an archaeological site in the Lake Okeechobee Basin.* University Presses of Florida, Gainesville.

n.d.   An investigation of prehistoric processes on the Gulf coastal plain. Undated report to the National Science Foundation (NSF–G–5019). On file, Florida State Museum, Gainesville.

Sears, William H., and Elsie Sears
1976   Preliminary report on prehistoric corn pollen from Fort Center, Florida. *Southeastern Archaeological Conference Bulletin* 19:53–56.

Service, E. R.
1962   *Primitive social organization.* Random House, New York.

Shepard, Anna O.
1976   *Ceramics for the archaeologist.* Carnegie Institution of Washington, Publication 609, Washington, D.C.

Sigler-Lavelle, Brenda J.
1980a   *The political and economic implications of the distribution of Weeden Island period sites in North Florida.* Ph.D. dissertation, New School for Social Research. University Microfilms, Ann Arbor.

1980b   On the non-random distribution of Weeden Island period sites in North Florida. *Southeastern Archaeological Conference Bulletin* 22:22–29.

Simpson, J. Clarence
1948   Folsom-like points from Florida. *Florida Anthropologist* 1:11–15.

Smith, Betty A.
1979   The Hopewell connection in southwest Georgia. In *Hopewell archaeology, the Chillicothe Conference,* edited by David S. Brose and N'omi Greber, pp. 181–187. Kent State University Press, Kent, Ohio.

Smith, Bruce (editor)
1978   *Mississippian settlement patterns.* Academic Press, New York.

Smith, Buckingham
1968   *Narratives of de Soto in the conquest of Florida.* Palmetto Books, Gainesville.

Snedaker, Samuel C., A. Lugo, H. Brooks, H. Horton, and D. Pool
1972   Ecology of the Ocala National Forest. In *Final environmental statement: proposal for Oklawaha River, Appendix 7.* United States Department of Agriculture, Forest Service.

Snow, Frankie
1977   An archeological survey of the Ocmulgee Big Bend Region. *Occasional Papers from South Georgia* 3. South Georgia College, Douglas.

Steinen, Karl T.
1976   *The Weeden Island ceramic complex: an analysis of distribution.* Ph.D. dissertation, Department of Anthropology, University of Florida, Gainesville. University Microfilms, Ann Arbor.

Swanton, John R.
1911   Indian tribes on the Lower Mississippi Valley and adjacent coast of the Gulf of Mexico. *Smithsonian Institution, Bureau of American Ethnology Bulletin* 43. Johnson Reprint Corporation: New York.

1946   The Indians of the Southeastern United States. *Smithsonian Institution, Bureau of American Ethnology Bulletin* 137.

Tambiah, S. J.
1969   Animals are good to think and good to prohibit. *Ethnology* 7:423–459.

Thanz, Nina, and Graig Shaak
1977   *Significance of a sponge spicule temper in Florida chalky paste pottery.* Paper presented at Florida Anthropological Society Annual Meeting, Tampa.

Trickey, E. Bruce
1958   A chronological framework for the Mobile Bay region. *American Antiquity* 23:388–396.

Trowell, C. T.
1979   *A reconnaissance of aboriginal Okefenokee, an outline of the prehistoric geography of the Okefenokee Swamp.* Division of Social and Behavioral Sciences South Georgia College, Douglas.

1980   The Okefenokee Swamp area survey—a status report: 1978. *Southeastern Archaeological Conference Bulletin* 22:66–69.

Turner, Victor
   1969   *The ritual process: structure and anti-structure.* Cornell University Press, Ithaca.
Van Gennep, Arnold L.
   1909   *Les rites de passage.* E. Nourry, Paris.
Walthall, John A.
   1972   The chronological position of Copena in eastern states archaeology. *Journal of Alabama Archaeology* 18:137–151.
   1980   *Prehistoric Indians of the Southeast.* The University of Alabama Press. University.
Wauchope, Robert
   1966   Archaeological survey of northern Georgia. *Memoirs of the Society for American Archaeology* 21.
Wetmore, A.
   1939   Owls, shadowy birds of the night. In *The book of birds,* edited by Gilbert Grosvenor and Alexander Wetmore, pp. 5–25. National Geographic Society, Washington.
White, Nancy M.
   1981a   Archaeological survey at Lake Seminole. *Cleveland Museum of Natural History Archaeological Research Report* 29.

   1981b   The Curlee site (8Ja7) and Fort Walton development in the upper Apalachicola–lower Chattahoochee Valley, Florida, Georgia, and Alabama. *Southeastern Archaeological Conference Bulletin* 24:24–27.
Willey, Gordon R.
   1945   The Weeden Island culture: a preliminary definition. *American Antiquity* 10:225–254.
   1948   Culture sequence in the Manatee region of West Florida. *American Antiquity* 13:209–218.
   1949   Archeology of the Florida Gulf Coast. *Smithsonian Miscellaneous Collections* 113.
Willey, Gordon R., and Richard B. Woodbury
   1942   A chronological outline for the Northwest Florida Coast. *American Antiquity* 7:232–254.
Wing, Elizabeth
   1965   Animal bones associated with two Indian sites on Marco Island, Florida. *Florida Anthropologist* 18:21–28.
   1977   Subsistence systems in the Southeast. *Florida Anthropologist* 30:81–87.
Wishart, D.
   1978   *Cluster IC user manual* (third ed.). Edinburgh University, Edinburgh.

Index